Change Your Career:
Nursing as Your New Profession

Change Your Career: Nursing as Your New Profession

Barbara Arnoldussen, RN, MBA

PUBLISHING

New York • Chicago

Editorial Director: Jennifer Farthing
Editor: Monica Lugo, Caryn Yilmaz
Production Editor: Karen Goodfriend
Production Artist: Virginia Byrne
Cover Designer: Carly Schnur

Published by Kaplan Publishing, a division of Kaplan, Inc.
888 Seventh Ave.
New York, NY 10106

Printed in the United States of America

December 2006
10 9 8 7 6 5 4 3 2 1

ISBN 13: 978-1-4195-9151-8
ISBN: 10:   1-4195-9151-7

Kaplan Publishing books are available at special quantity discounts to use for sales promotions, employee premiums, or educational purposes. Please call our Special Sales Department to order or for more information at 800-621-9621, ext. 4444, e-mail kaplanpubsales@kaplan.com, or write to Kaplan Publishing, 30 South Wacker Drive, Suite 2500, Chicago, IL 60606-7481.

Dedication

My inspiration while writing this book was the second career of my mother, Barbara Rudolph, RN. You don't have to successfully raise six children as she did to have a qualifying life experience. What you have to offer is as individual as you are!

Acknowledgments

The author acknowledges research and writing assistance with Part 4 by Susan E. Ullmann, MT(ASCP) MA Ed.

Contents

Chapter 4. Nursing Specializations Inside the Hospital   67

Chapter 5. Nursing Specializations Outside the Hospital   107

KAPLAN

Introducing Myself as Your Career Change Travel Guide

I have been a both a career-switcher and a return-to-school student. First, I found an initial career path and later moved in another exciting direction. Second, I enrolled in graduate studies after a gap of twenty years from my undergraduate days.

My initial career path started after I graduated from Marquette University in Milwaukee, Wisconsin. I worked as a clinical research nurse for three years at an academic medical center, collecting data about patients' responses to pain and pre-op meds. I then became the director of a medical clinic for a crisis intervention agency for young people.

After a year I took a radical change of direction—taking a job as a newspaper reporter. I capitalized on using my skill in interviewing people that nursing develops, covering school board and village council meetings as well as writing feature stories. Then I was hired as a newsmagazine editor.

When continuing at that job was made impossible by a move three thousand miles away, I returned to researching outcome data about treatment results. Midway through those nine years, I enrolled in graduate school while working and raising two preteenagers. I set a pace of taking one evening class at a time.

Five years later, my kids were teenagers and I had my MBA. That degree resulted in my taking a newly designed Continuous Quality Improvement (CQI) managerial position. My nursing colleagues told me that I would be "perfect" for the assignment. It has been over 20 years for various employers (hospital, clinic, and university) and, ahem, I am still waiting to be "perfect."

But what I am quite adept at is sharing with you what I know and have researched about deciding to change careers and choosing nursing. So, if you are reading this book to find out whether or not nursing should be your next career, you have a seasoned travel guide. I will tell you about the advantages of docking your career ship with Nursing as your home port.

Come aboard! We are ready to set sail!

I am the daughter of a second-career nurse. My mother, Barbara Anne Whitesell Rudolph, became an RN at age 59.

Her enthusiasm for a health care career might have unconsciously directed all six of her offspring into pursuing such professions: Two nurses (Judy and I), two dental hygienists (Peg and Trish), a med tech (Susan), and an industrial hygienist (Tom).

But first she pursued a different career. At age 39, she graduated from Michigan State University in Retailing and went to work as a buyer for a department store. She left when my brother Tom needed homecare after an automobile accident. Even that taste of nursing did not spur her to take action until at age 56 she became a Certified Nursing Assistant (CNA).

She so thoroughly enjoyed working with patients and their families, nurses, and doctors as a CNA! That satisfaction led her to enter the associate degree Nursing program at St. Petersburg College in Florida. She found one key to successful learning in teaming with another nursing student, Patricia Olson, for intensive study sessions. She graduated and passed the Florida State Nursing Boards on her first try.

In this book, I call such a thoughtful pace the "Mother Teresa Approach to Career Change" (See page 20). For you, I say: however long it takes you to get it right, go for it!

Introduction

Congratulations! You have chosen a book that holds great promise for your future and will help you decide, step by step, whether nursing is the right new career for you. This book contains many valuable resources, including assessment tools, practical suggestions, links to online information, a treasury of nursing-unique specialties, and motivational stories from people who have successfully transitioned into nursing from other professions.

Before you start to use these resources, read through this overview of what the nursing profession can offer you. This will allow you to accurately compare nursing to the profession in which you currently work.

AVAILABILITY OF JOBS

Probably the most well-known characteristic of the nursing profession is the current and dramatic shortage of individuals to fill open positions. Long-term predictions show that this need will not only continue but will become more acute over time. For you, these statistics mean a happy hunting ground when it comes to finding a job. And not just any job, but a job that will make you look forward to your next workday!

The chart from the federal Bureau of Labor Statistics in Figure I.1 offers data to support the critical need for the nursing profession to increase its ranks exponentially.

Figure I.1 Annual Average Job Openings

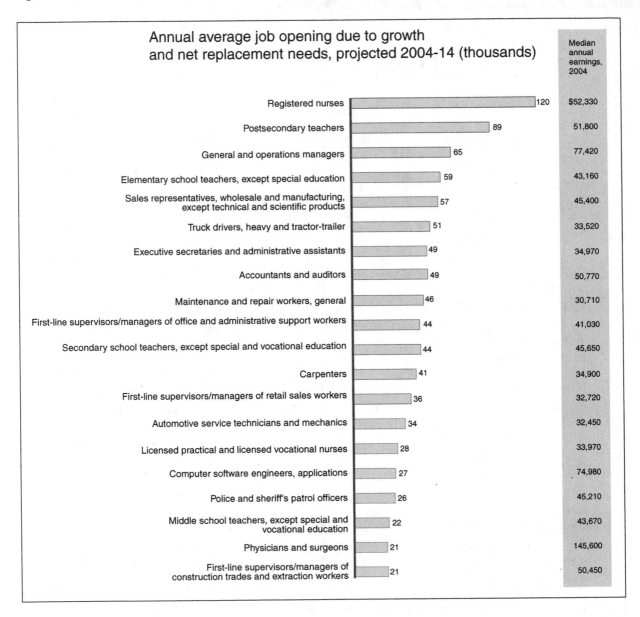

Annual average job opening due to growth and net replacement needs, projected 2004-14 (thousands)

Occupation	Openings	Median annual earnings, 2004
Registered nurses	120	$52,330
Postsecondary teachers	89	51,800
General and operations managers	65	77,420
Elementary school teachers, except special education	59	43,160
Sales representatives, wholesale and manufacturing, except technical and scientific products	57	45,400
Truck drivers, heavy and tractor-trailer	51	33,520
Executive secretaries and administrative assistants	49	34,970
Accountants and auditors	49	50,770
Maintenance and repair workers, general	46	30,710
First-line supervisors/managers of office and administrative support workers	44	41,030
Secondary school teachers, except special and vocational education	44	45,650
Carpenters	41	34,900
First-line supervisors/managers of retail sales workers	36	32,720
Automotive service technicians and mechanics	34	32,450
Licensed practical and licensed vocational nurses	28	33,970
Computer software engineers, applications	27	74,980
Police and sheriff's patrol officers	26	45,210
Middle school teachers, except special and vocational education	22	43,670
Physicians and surgeons	21	145,600
First-line supervisors/managers of construction trades and extraction workers	21	50,450

Figure I.2 National Supply and Demand Projections for Registered Nurses

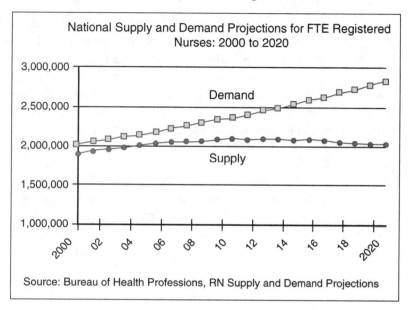

Nursing is at the top of the 20 careers listed, because it has the greatest number of annual average job openings in the ten-year period from 2004 to 2014. Their figure of 120,000 openings per year each year for the next decade is impressive. That compelling need is more than one-third higher than its nearest competitor, post-high school teachers.

The need for licensed practical nurses (LPNs) and licensed vocational nurses (LVNs) made it to number 15 on the list. While there are fewer annual average job openings than for registered nurses (RNs), you might consider trying to qualify for one of the predicted 28,000 positions per year each year for the next decade.

So that you can be assured that this predicted trend is not a short-term need, you can look at the years from 2000 to 2020 in another chart (Figure I.2).

Figure I.2 shows that the gap between the national supply and the demand for registered nurses is widening each year. So, if you're looking for a satisfying new work environment with an eager and welcoming attitude, you will find just that in the nursing profession.

COMPENSATION

If you look again at Figure I.1, you will notice that the right-hand column shows the median annual earnings for the 20 careers. The median earning for RNs is $52,330. (The median is the point at which half the people make less than that amount, and half make more.) This figure is higher for nurses than for 16 out of the other 19 careers shown. Only general and operations managers, computer software engineers, physicians, and surgeons are predicted to have larger median incomes. (If you want to join their ranks, you will have to find another career book.)

JOB SATISFACTION

A recent survey of 76,000 nurses conducted by the American Nurses Association (ANA) found that just over half of the respondents indicated that they enjoy their work (53 percent), while nearly two-thirds (63.3 percent) said they are satisfied with their jobs. Three situations prompted high levels of satisfaction:

1. Interactions with other RNs (67 percent)
2. Professional status (65 percent)
3. Career development opportunities (61 percent)

CHOICES

Nurses have a wealth of choices about where to work and in which clinical area they would like to specialize. Browse through Chapter 4 to explore what your career could be like in a hospital setting. Then go to Chapter 5 to see the huge variety of opportunities available to you outside the hospital.

The range of possible non-hospital work environments includes patients' homes, clinics, schools, industry, religious parishes, prisons, and mental health centers. The number of choices is fantastic: You can become a bedside nurse, an advanced practice nurse, a researcher, an educator, a policy maker, a community leader, or a business person. Or you could begin your own futuristic category that cares for people in a new way!

MEANINGFULNESS

Each nursing educational facility has a vision of what their curriculum offers their students. For example, the School of Nursing at Southeastern Louisiana University offers this online word picture of the profession to potential students:

> Changing lives, changing futures, improving the quality of life—this is the art of nursing today. The face of nursing has changed....

> Nursing is poised to change the face of health care as never before. Through advanced education, diversified expertise, an international network of nurse colleagues, and opportunities at every level of the health professions, nurses are now seen in bold new roles.

> Like few others, the profession of nursing offers academic education and hands-on training to men and women in a variety of specialty areas. From pediatrics to geriatrics, nursing's impact is felt across the lifespan.[1]

PROFESSIONAL STATUS

People view the nursing profession from different vantage points.

- If you are a patient, or a friend or relative of one, you might say it's a profession about caring and healing.
- If you are a nursing educator, supervisor, or colleague, you might say it's a profession about solving problems (through both standard and creative ways) and using critical thinking skills.
- If you are a hospital staffing analyst, you might say it's a profession about administering medications and other treatments to patients.

The truth is that the nursing profession is all these things and much, much more. Nursing combines the elements of caring and healing, problem solving and critical thinking, and treating patients into one exciting, dynamic career. Nurses perform a unique role in the health care world because they are skilled in all these critical functions.

---

1 "Choose Nursing." Southeastern Louisiana University. *www2.selu.edu/Academics/Nursing/recruitment.htm* (accessed August 16, 2006).

MAKING A DIFFERENCE

At the end of your workday, you might check to see if your efforts were worthwhile. Some questions to ask might be:

- Have I learned something that makes me a better professional?
- Have I contributed some activity that adds value?
- Have I made a decision that could improve the status quo, or make life better for someone?

If you can answer "yes" to one of these questions each workday, you are getting paid in a currency better than money. You are receiving a golden benefit—that of your job making a significant difference. As the author of a book published by the nursing honorary society Sigma Theta Tau International (*www.nursingsociety.org*) describes it:

> Patients of all ages recover or die in comfort because of what nurses do. At some point, including the very moment of birth, everyone has been cared for by a nurse. Business executives, political advocates, and famous movie stars all have needed the caring service of nurses. In schools, homes, hospices, and sometimes in emergency rooms, people have been touched by the healing hands and caring approach of a nurse.

> Only nurses are privileged to intimately enter a patient's life. …Nurses guide, prompt, reinforce decisions, give strength and receive strength for spur-of-the moment decisions that might save a life.[2]

So, if you want to take the empowering opportunity to join the ranks of the everyday, much appreciated hero, consider nursing!

---

2 Sharon Hudacek. *Making a Difference: Stories from the Point of Care, Vol. I.*, Indianapolis, IN. Sigma Theta Tau International, Center Nursing Press, 2005.

PART ONE

Sort Out Your Choices

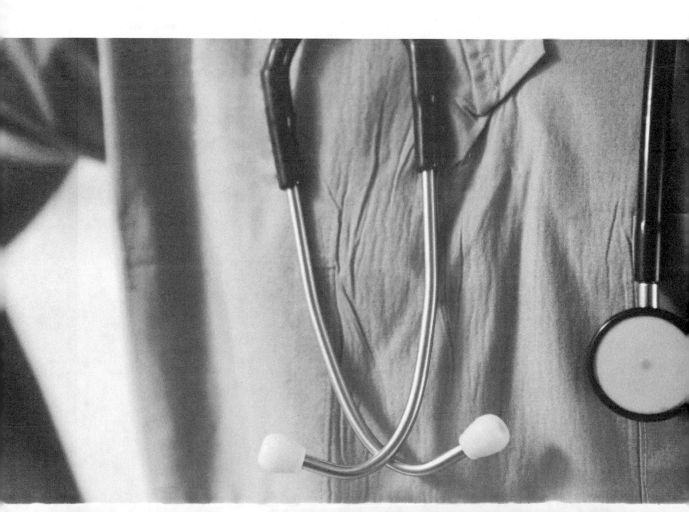

CHAPTER 1

Should You Change Your Career?

WHAT TO LOOK AT BEFORE YOU LEAP

If you are contemplating a change of career, you should know that you're not alone. It has been predicted that most people will have several different careers over their working lifetimes. So, you will have a lot of company in your search for a new and different path to job fulfillment.

Changing your career will affect almost all aspects of your life and likely will require you to make significant short-term sacrifices. Therefore you should examine the current status of your personal lifestyle characteristics before you begin. Listed below are a broad range of factors to take into account. Take a moment to consider each question in each category and jot down your thoughts. Don't worry about complete sentences. Your notes will provide enough information to assemble a global picture of your situation.

Finances

Can you afford to change your current income level?

_____

_____

Could you live on less money in the near future if you knew you were going to make a reasonably comfortable salary in the long run?

_____

_____

Do you know the cost of enrolling in an education program? If so, can you calculate how much financial assistance you would need to supplement your contribution?

_____

_____

Do you have other sources of income or sufficient savings to support yourself while going to school?

_____

_____

Health

Are you in good physical condition?

_____

_____

Are you in good mental and emotional shape?

_____

_____

Will you have acceptable and affordable medical insurance coverage if you leave your present job?

_____

_____

Time And Freedom

Have you allowed enough time and freedom from other responsibilities to thoroughly evaluate your schooling alternatives?

_____

_____

Will you have the time and money to visit your final candidates and talk to their administrators and alumni?

_____

_____

Once admitted and enrolled, will your schedule allow you sufficient hours every week to attend classes, do clinical rotations, and complete homework assignments?

_____

_____

Focus

Do you have other life situations right now that demand your attention?

_____

_____

Are you contemplating making other major changes in your life at the same time as you ready yourself for a new career (e.g. relocation, marital status change, children)?

_____

_____

Access

Is there an educational facility in your local area that offers classes you want to enroll in?

_____

_____

Do they allow part-time enrollment? Do they have a residency requirement?

_____

_____

Do you have a sense of the commute time and options for making the commute?

_____

_____

Are appropriate classes available online?

_____

_____

Are you able to relocate to attend an educational institution of your choice? How soon?

_____

_____

Stress Relief

Have you discovered methods of managing stress that work for you?

_____

_____

KAPLAN

Are there other stressors in your life in addition to looking at your career choices? Do you expect them to decrease in the near future?

_____

_____

Do you perform well with recurrent time deadlines and challenging tasks?

_____

_____

Motivation

Can you visualize yourself in a different career?

_____

_____

Do you know what you want from a new career? How does this compare to the rewards and problems you experience at your current job?

_____

_____

Have you tried "tasting" the new career, or talking to people who have experience in the field you would like to enter?

_____

_____

Support System

Do you have relationships with people who can help you when you encounter obstacles during your transition?

_____

_____

Do you have people who will encourage you and give you honest feedback?

_____

_____

Do you have someone close to you who is willing to listen to your frustrations, questions, or concerns?

_____

_____

Your Current Career Pulse

Are you unhappy in your current profession? Why?

_____

_____

Do you find yourself daydreaming about different work environments? What details do you put in your imagining?

_____

_____

Would some small modifications make it OK to continue working in your current area, putting up with a modest amount of dissatisfaction?

_____

_____

Are you sufficiently motivated to spend considerable effort, time, and money to get more education?

_____

_____

What obstacles could stand in the way of your making a successful journey down a new career path?

_____

_____

KAPLAN

Figure 1.1 Your Current Career Temperature

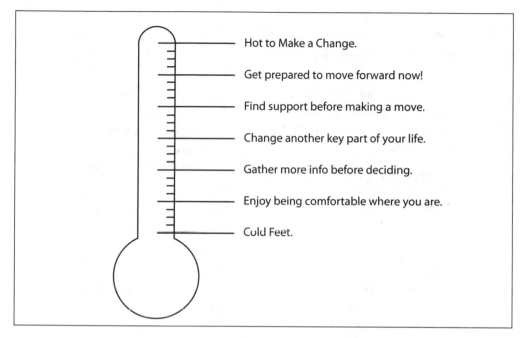

The benefit of answering these broad questions is that you can self-identify characteristics of your *current lifestyle* that will help or hinder you in changing your career. The next section helps you analyze the characteristics of your *current work situation* in a different way. Rather than having you supply details, it only asks you how much you agree with a sentence.

THE GAME OF 20 QUESTIONS ABOUT CAREER CHANGE READINESS

To confirm that changing your career has more pros than cons, you can play the game in Figure 1.2. This game is based on themes used in many vocational assessment quizzes. It is a game designed to uncover your true feelings, rather than produce test anxiety. So, for best results, don't spend time stressing about the accuracy of your answers. Just read the item, choose a response, and move to the next item. You will get a chance to look at your individual pattern right afterward.

Figure 1.2 Career Change Readiness Game

For Questions 1 through 20, rate how much you agree with each statement.

1. I can honestly say at the end of each workday that I've learned one new skill or item of practical information.

    ☐ Completely agree
    ☐ Mostly agree
    ☐ Somewhat agree
    ☐ Mostly disagree
    ☐ Completely disagree

2. When I picture myself at work five years from now, I don't have a sense that the intervening years were productive or made me happy.

    ☐ Completely agree
    ☐ Mostly agree
    ☐ Somewhat agree
    ☐ Mostly disagree
    ☐ Completely disagree

3. I'm able to make important decisions at work.

    ☐ Completely agree
    ☐ Mostly agree
    ☐ Somewhat agree
    ☐ Mostly disagree
    ☐ Completely disagree

4. If I won the lottery, I would seriously consider going back to school.

    ☐ Completely agree
    ☐ Mostly agree
    ☐ Somewhat agree
    ☐ Mostly disagree
    ☐ Completely disagree

5. I work best with people who have the same financial, educational, and cultural background that I have.

    ☐ Completely agree
    ☐ Mostly agree
    ☐ Somewhat agree
    ☐ Mostly disagree
    ☐ Completely disagree

6. I feel disappointed that my work efforts don't seem to make a significant difference.

    ☐ Completely agree
    ☐ Mostly agree
    ☐ Somewhat agree
    ☐ Mostly disagree
    ☐ Completely disagree

7. When I begin my workday, I feel energized and want to tackle my to-do list.

    ☐ Completely agree
    ☐ Mostly agree
    ☐ Somewhat agree
    ☐ Mostly disagree
    ☐ Completely disagree

KAPLAN

Figure 1.2 Career Change Readiness Game (continued)

8. I feel ready to take on new challenges.

   □ Completely agree
   □ Mostly agree
   □ Somewhat agree
   □ Mostly disagree
   □ Completely disagree

9. My last performance evaluation showed that my supervisor and I are on the same wave length.

   □ Completely agree
   □ Mostly agree
   □ Somewhat agree
   □ Mostly disagree
   □ Completely disagree

10. When I read or hear about some-one changing careers, I envy him or her.

    □ Completely agree
    □ Mostly agree
    □ Somewhat agree
    □ Mostly disagree
    □ Completely disagree

11. I am on a career path that will result in my reaching my full potential.

    □ Completely agree
    □ Mostly agree
    □ Somewhat agree
    □ Mostly disagree
    □ Completely disagree

12. I find myself taking new routes to get to work and making changes in my daily routine.

    □ Completely agree
    □ Mostly agree
    □ Somewhat agree
    □ Mostly disagree
    □ Completely disagree

13. The status quo is not great, but I can certainly hang on for an indefinite period in my current position.

    □ Completely agree
    □ Mostly agree
    □ Somewhat agree
    □ Mostly disagree
    □ Completely disagree

14. I feel I could do my job in my sleep, because I am still doing what I was trained to do many years ago.

    □ Completely agree
    □ Mostly agree
    □ Somewhat agree
    □ Mostly disagree
    □ Completely disagree

Figure 1.2 Career Change Readiness Game (continued)

15. Because I can get my work done in a timely manner, I have enough leisure time to do activities that I truly enjoy.

   □ Completely agree
   □ Mostly agree
   □ Somewhat agree
   □ Mostly disagree
   □ Completely disagree

16. Other than my salary, there's no reward or incentive for doing the work that I do.

   □ Completely agree
   □ Mostly agree
   □ Somewhat agree
   □ Mostly disagree
   □ Completely disagree

17. My colleagues and supervisors contribute to a positive work environment, since everyone helps each other succeed.

   □ Completely agree
   □ Mostly agree
   □ Somewhat agree
   □ Mostly disagree
   □ Completely disagree

18. I am finding fewer assignments at work that feel rewarding when completed.

   □ Completely agree
   □ Mostly agree
   □ Somewhat agree
   □ Mostly disagree
   □ Completely disagree

19. I often get an opportunity at work to brainstorm practical solutions to real problems, either by myself or with my colleagues.

   □ Completely agree
   □ Mostly agree
   □ Somewhat agree
   □ Mostly disagree
   □ Completely disagree

20. I don't have someone at work in whom I can confide important issues and from whom I can get honest feedback.

   □ Completely agree
   □ Mostly agree
   □ Somewhat agree
   □ Mostly disagree
   □ Completely disagree

Interpreting Your Career Change Readiness Game Responses

Statements 1 to 20 were designed to allow you to quickly measure the pros and cons of switching from your current vocation. Agreeing with the odd-numbered items is slanted toward recording good reasons to stay at your current job. Agreeing with the even-numbered ones provides a solid rationale for changing your career.

The first step is to go back to your answers to questions 1 to 20 and transfer your responses to fit the face symbols in the boxes on the next two pages. The first box has the odd-numbered questions; the second box has the even-numbered questions. Check the ☺ face if you answered "completely agree" or "mostly agree." Check the ☺ face if you said you "somewhat agree." Check the ☹ face if you responded that you "mostly disagree" or "completely disagree."

The next step is to look the faces you checked in the first box. If a majority of your responses are ☺, you might be better off continuing along the same career path. You are satisfied, for the most part. The grass you are viewing from a distance might not be greener than the turf you are standing on right now.

Then you should count the number of even-numbered items in the second box where you checked ☺. If a majority of your ratings are ☺, you have solid reasons to move forward. Begin making plans and considering arrangements to change your career now. You will not be satisfied unless you find your niche, which could well be nursing. You will learn more about that choice in later chapters of this book.

Before you leave this section, take time to do one more step—look at the themes of each question (identified in capital letters). That examination will give you an idea of what might be going right and not-so-right in your current career. Can you envision yourself working as a nurse and getting more satisfying answers?

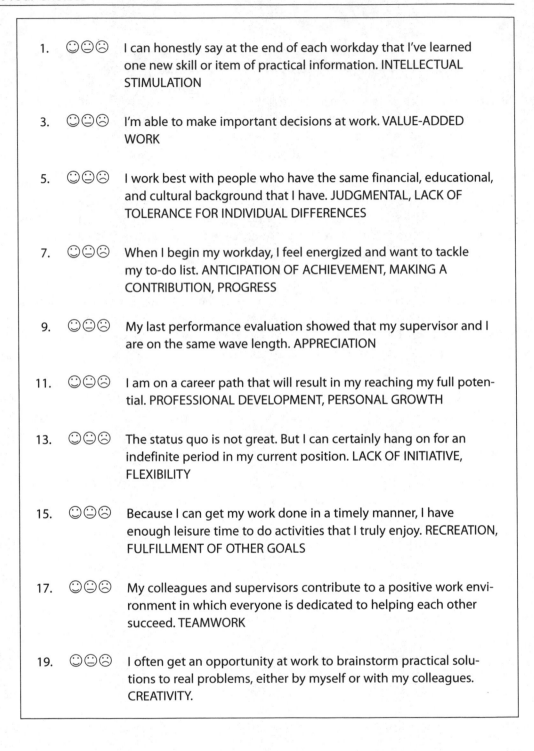

1. ☺☺☹ I can honestly say at the end of each workday that I've learned one new skill or item of practical information. INTELLECTUAL STIMULATION

3. ☺☺☹ I'm able to make important decisions at work. VALUE-ADDED WORK

5. ☺☺☹ I work best with people who have the same financial, educational, and cultural background that I have. JUDGMENTAL, LACK OF TOLERANCE FOR INDIVIDUAL DIFFERENCES

7. ☺☺☹ When I begin my workday, I feel energized and want to tackle my to-do list. ANTICIPATION OF ACHIEVEMENT, MAKING A CONTRIBUTION, PROGRESS

9. ☺☺☹ My last performance evaluation showed that my supervisor and I are on the same wave length. APPRECIATION

11. ☺☺☹ I am on a career path that will result in my reaching my full potential. PROFESSIONAL DEVELOPMENT, PERSONAL GROWTH

13. ☺☺☹ The status quo is not great. But I can certainly hang on for an indefinite period in my current position. LACK OF INITIATIVE, FLEXIBILITY

15. ☺☺☹ Because I can get my work done in a timely manner, I have enough leisure time to do activities that I truly enjoy. RECREATION, FULFILLMENT OF OTHER GOALS

17. ☺☺☹ My colleagues and supervisors contribute to a positive work environment in which everyone is dedicated to helping each other succeed. TEAMWORK

19. ☺☺☹ I often get an opportunity at work to brainstorm practical solutions to real problems, either by myself or with my colleagues. CREATIVITY.

2. ☺☺☹ When I picture myself at work five years from now, I don't have a sense that the intervening years were productive or made me happy. VISION FOR THE FUTURE

4. ☺☺☹ If I won the lottery, I would seriously consider going back to school. TAKING THE COST OF EDUCATION OUT OF THE DECISION TO PURSUE IT

6. ☺☺☹ I feel disappointed that my work efforts don't seem to make a significant difference. MEANINGFULNESS, CONTRIBUTION

8. ☺☺☹ I feel ready to take on new challenges. EXCITEMENT

10. ☺☺☹ When I read or hear about someone changing careers, I envy him or her. USE EMOTIONS TO MOTIVATE SELF

12. ☺☺☹ I find myself taking new routes to get to work and making changes in my daily routine. NEED FOR SURPRISE, SPONTANEITY

14. ☺☺☹ I feel I could do my job in my sleep, because I am still doing what I was trained to do many years ago. BOREDOM, SETTLING, BURNOUT

16. ☺☺☹ Other than my salary, there's no reward or incentive for doing the work that I do. JOB SATISFACTION

18. ☺☺☹ I am finding fewer assignments at work that feel rewarding when completed. REACHING A PLATEAU

20. ☺☺☹ I don't have someone at work in whom I can confide important issues and from whom I can get honest feedback. SOCIAL INTERACTION, CONNECTEDNESS

Question 20 refers to research on job satisfaction showing that people who have a "best friend" at work are seven times more likely to be engaged in their work. Author Tom Path in his book *Vital Friends*[1] used data from 5 million Gallup interviews. Close friendships at work boost employee satisfaction by almost 50 percent.

THE FAB FOUR

There are no right or wrong answers to the four questions on the next page. In fact, you can select multiple choices if they describe your personality. They are just designed to tease out some further thoughts about issues involved in pursuing a new career. Take time out now to choose the answer that best describes your current circumstances.

Once you finish, you should take a moment to see if a pattern emerges. You don't necessarily have to do this alone. As with all discussion topics, if you can share your thoughts you will be further ahead in your discovery process. Find someone to bounce your ideas off of, or someone with whom you can compare responses.

---

1   Tom Path, *Vital Friends: The People You Can't Afford to Live Without* (New York, Gallup Press, August 2006).

A. If you do not change your career at this time, how do you think you will feel ten years from now?

☐ I would spend time wondering what would have happened had I taken the other career path.
☐ I would feel comfortable that I did my best, considering my resources.
☐ I would think that everyone has good and bad aspects of their career choices, and they can't control their proportion.
☐ I would be glad that I waited to take advantage of surprising opportunities in my current career.
☐ I would still be a happy employee, with a steady income.

B. If you had a choice to start over again from an entry-level position in a challenging field, would you:

☐ Think about how you could handle the change.
☐ Be confident you could produce results effectively.
☐ Keep comparing it to the comfort level you now enjoy.
☐ Talk about it with someone close to you, to get further insight into what you should do.
☐ Decline the opportunity because you don't want the added stress.

C. You hear that a colleague has made the decision to change careers. At the going-away event you find yourself:

☐ Inspired to give more thought to your taking action.
☐ Thinking about the differences in luck between that person and yourself.
☐ Wanting to hear the outcome of the person's decision. Further success or a dead end?
☐ Probing to find out the details of the colleague's basis for decision.
☐ Discussing with co-workers what they feel will happen with the vacant position.

D. What is the best characteristic of your current job?

☐ The financial rewards
☐ The self-esteem-raising aspects of doing a good job
☐ The feeling of being needed by the organization
☐ The sense that everyone can find his or her own niche.
☐ The meaningfulness of your contribution to society.

MEASURING YOUR PREDISPOSITION FOR SUCCESSFUL CHANGE

Figure 1.3

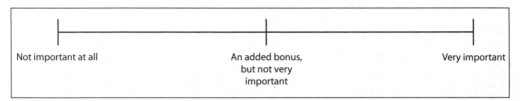

The final assessment tools are contained in Figures 1.3 and 1.4. Start by putting an "x" on the first ruler to rate how important it is that your career has these five characteristics:

1. Meaningfulness
2. Different challenges
3. Learning new skills
4. Career advancement potential
5. Having a sense of powerful influence

Figure 1.4

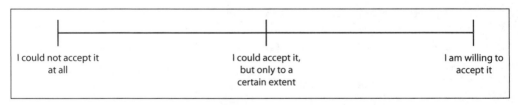

Then, put an "x" on the second ruler to indicate to what degree you would be willing to accept these five changes in order make a new career a reality:

6. More stress and deadlines than I now have
7. A completely unfamiliar school environment
8. A key assignment as a new team leader
9. Living lean and tightening my finances to afford school
10. Making important lifestyle-changing decisions

Now that you have played the Game of 20 Questions, contemplated the Fab Four discussion topics, and measured your predisposition for successful change, you are ready to leave the world of probing, measuring, and analyzing. It is time to step back and look at some differing philosophies about the best pace for implementing changes in your life. Just like Aesop's fable, the first method corresponds to the hare's way; the second one is more of a tortoise method.

MARINE CORPS APPROACH TO CAREER CHANGE

How to Shape up Your New Career Fast

Once you have decided you would benefit from pursuing a new career direction, you might sense in your behavior an "I-want-it-but I'm-afraid" hesitancy. One approach to overcoming this emotional barrier might be to take advice from an article designed for career-changing Marines. Yes, it speaks to you as though you've just entered boot camp with a tough-guy drill sergeant voice:

> If you're serious…do four things:
>
> 1. Declare to yourself and commit to paper that you want this new career and that nothing is going to stop you. This lets you move into the "What's-this-going-to-take?" phase.
> 2. Define specifically what it will take. Will you need to ask something of someone else? Will you need to cut out certain activities, have less time at home, reduce other expenses, postpone something else, or spend savings?
> 3. Ask yourself: Am I willing to do that?
> 4. If the answer is yes, figure out how to rearrange your life to support your new choice.
>
> The author acknowledges that you will have to be willing to sacrifice. It is going to be hard work to figure out all the arrangements. It will affect not only your life, but also that of those people close to you. You will need their support—especially if you move ahead at a rapid pace.[2]

---

2 Andrea Kay, "Career Change Will Affect Daily Life," *Marine Corps Times*, Gannett News Service, January 30, 2006. *www.marinetimes.com/story.php?f=1-292313-1472807.php* (accessed September 23, 2006).

MOTHER TERESA APPROACH TO CAREER CHANGE

From School Principal to Nobel Prize Winner in 35 Years

Alternatively you could choose to follow the lead of someone who slowly made thoughtful changes over time. Mother Teresa was no stranger to radical decisions: She changed her name from Gonxha Agnes Bojaxhiu to Sister Mary Teresa and moved from Macedonia to Calcutta to teach school. She taught for 19 years, rising to become a principal. After that it took her two years to receive permission from Pope Pius XII to work as an independent nun. Then it took another two years to found her Missionaries of Charity religious order.[3]

In contrast to the Marine Corps methodical march of decisions to implementing career change, the Mother Teresa approach has a slow but sure pace. Her individual circumstances did not allow her to move faster. She had to maintain her focus on the direction she wanted her life to take and allow her ultimate calling to unfold over time.

BEST OF BOTH WORLDS APPROACH

By this time, you might have figured out that your most prudent path would be a method that combines the best of the Marine Corps and the Mother Teresa approaches. It might be summarized as:

1. Get the facts
2. Make a decision
3. Commit to spending time and effort in preparation
4. Be willing to sacrifice
5. Ask for support
6. Work hard
7. Keep your focus on the final goal

---

3   Allen Butler, "The Life of Mother Teresa of Calcutta," CongressionalGoldMedal.com, March 16, 2006. *www.congressionalgoldmedal.com/the_life_of_mother_teresa_of_calcutta.htm* (accessed September 23, 2006).

Remember that although the Marine Corps and Mother Teresa approaches adopt different timelines, they both illustrate a key factor in your eventual success: perseverance. You will face challenges before you can firmly establish your new career. You will have to prevent temporary setbacks from getting the best of you.

But you can do it! And reading this book will help you at each step along the way. You will be helped to discover whether or not the nursing profession is right for your next career.

CHAPTER 2

Is Nursing the Right Career for You?

EXPANDING YOUR HORIZONS WHILE DEFINING YOUR CHOICES

After completing the assessment exercises in the first chapter, you should have a good idea of whether or not this is a good time for you to change your vocational path. Read on to explore if your best choice for a new career is found in the nursing profession. This chapter can help you confirm your choice: Nursing or Not—you be the judge!

SAMPLING THE ENVIRONMENT

Going back to school to get your nursing education is a huge commitment. If you can arrange to sample the nursing work environment before you entirely rearrange your life, you can confirm that your interest is justified. There are five ways you can get a taste of the nursing work world: Tours, Informational Interviews, Shadowing, Volunteering, and Nursing Support Jobs.

Tours

The easiest and fastest way to sample the nursing world is to take tours of your local hospitals, clinics, or nursing schools. If you know someone who works at a health care organization, ask for a guided tour. If you know someone who is going to nursing school, ask to see the classrooms, the library, and the cafeteria. This last place is a good place to informally interview other students and get some additional views of the school and its educational philosophy. Avoid going just before mid-terms or finals. You will find that students are absorbed in their last-minute studying and don't appreciate interruptions.

Another place for a tour is the Internet. In fact, online information is so easily available that Chapter 8 is dedicated to listing various ways you can obtain online nursing education. But an early warning—if you do not already have credit for clinical hands-on training, you will need to arrange for that education outside the computer world.

What Turns You On about a Nursing Career?

The National Student Nurses' Association partnered with the Bernard Hodes Group to survey over two thousand nursing students and faculty. They found the following incentives for that group (two-thirds of which were nontraditional nursing students) to become nurses: (on a scale of 1 to 5)

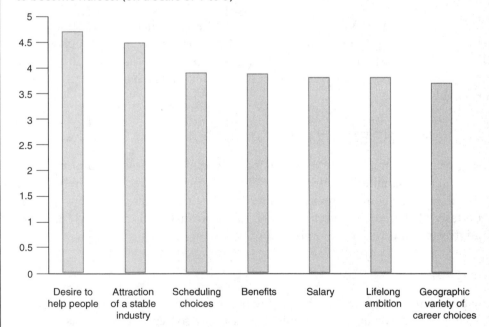

"More Nontraditional Students Pursuing Nursing Degrees," Press Release from Bernard Hodes Group; accessed March 22, 2005 at *www.hodes.com/healthcarematters/index.html.*

KAPLAN

Informational Interviews

The second method of sampling the environment is to identify people who have knowledge of nursing education and career life. Ask for a short meeting with them, typically from 30 to 45 minutes. The purpose of the discussion is to give you the benefit of their experience, tailored to your individual needs. Guidelines for making this a comfortable situation for both parties include the following:

- Be prepared to give a brief explanation of what you hope to gain from the interview.
- Schedule a time when it is most convenient for the interviewee. Make the length of time you are asking for clear from the start of your request.
- Be sure to exchange several kinds of contact information to adjust for unforeseen, last-minute changes.
- Do your homework before the interview to find out some background on the school or work environment.
- Make a written list of questions that you have in mind before the visit. Be prepared to take notes on the answers.
- Dress appropriately for the setting.
- Ask if the person knows other ways or people that could help you in your career exploration.
- Send a thank you note immediately after the interview.

Shadowing

The third approach is to shadow someone who works as a staff nurse, nurse administrator, or nurse educator. The important thing here is to make the right contacts, and to honor students' or patients' privacy and confidentiality. In contrast to the informational interview, a shadowing experience can last for an hour or two, up to a full day.

Some nursing school instructors might allow you to sit in on an introductory class so you can absorb the flavor of going back to school. Some nursing schools hold a public introductory session that you can attend without needing to make special arrangements, so you should inquire about this opportunity. You can follow up with a request to get more information by shadowing or conducting informational interviews.

Volunteering

If you want to get a firsthand look at the work that nurses do, volunteering is a wonderful option. Volunteering also has an added benefit—you can list your volunteer work on your applications for nursing school and financial aid. You can cite it at interviews as a time of thoughtful reflection, confirming your desire to become a nurse. Because health care organizations appreciate the contribution, you might find yourself the recipient of such perks as free parking, meal tickets, award luncheons, and access to information about the inside story of many situations.

Nursing Support Jobs

If you want to get a hands-on feel for the work that nurses do, taking a nursing support position is an excellent option. Listing this experience on your applications for nursing school and financial aid looks even better than listing volunteer work. The only catch is that you will need some education to get hired for the job. Depending on your training, you might be called a certified nursing assistant (CNA), home health aide (HHA), personal care aide (PCA), or patient care technician (PCT). The average pay in these positions is just over $25,000 per year.

Under the direction of a registered nurse or other health care supervisor, the nursing support person assists nursing service personnel with patient care activities. In some settings, the job is specialized, based on the population served. However, across care environments, the nursing support person usually has some standard tasks, including:

- Caring for the personal needs and comfort of patients, often initiated by answering patients' call lights
- Assisting patients with bathing, dressing, grooming, and eating
- Taking vital signs: blood pressure, pulse, respiration rate, and temperature
- Documenting intake and output, and other patient data
- Transporting patients to and from other areas within the facility
- Assisting with ambulation and a variety of established therapies
- Notifying nursing staff of changes in physical, emotional, or mental health of patients
- Changing bed linens
- Serving and collecting food trays
- Cleaning, sterilizing, storing, and preparing supplies

Each state and type of health care facility has different educational requirements. Formal training can be offered in high schools, vocational-technical centers, some nursing care facilities, and at some community colleges. Courses cover body mechanics, nutrition, anatomy and physiology, infection control, communication skills, resident rights, and personal care skills. Some online courses offer similar training.

Before you enroll in any coursework, check either in person or online to see which type of education is acceptable at the facility you would like to work. In contrast to other nursing jobs, your best route for getting a nursing support position is to contact the potential employer and then obtain the required education.

MEDIAN HOURLY EARNINGS FOR NURSING AIDES, ORDERLIES, AND ATTENDANTS IN MAY 2004[1]

Workplace	Earnings
Employment services	$11.29
Local government	11.10
Hospitals	10.44
Nursing homes	9.86
Community care facilities for elderly	9.56

The Ideal Time to Contact Nursing Organizations

Every year National Nurses Week is celebrated between May 6 and May 12. The theme for the day in 2006 was "Nurses: Strength, Commitment, Compassion." National Nurses Week is an ideal time to contact nursing organizations, because they often hold special, one-time events such as open houses or other outreach efforts to increase awareness of nurses' contributions to the local and national community. Articles in newspapers and other media often feature encouraging details about nursing opportunities, profiles of nursing leaders, and success stories of second career nurses.

In 2006, Congresswoman Eddie Bernice Johnson from Texas introduced House Resolution 245, supporting the goals and ideals of National Nurses Week. The resolution was cosponsored by 59 of her colleagues. Reading the resolution will verify the solid bipartisan political support for the "importance of nurses to the everyday lives of patients." (A copy of the Resolution can be found in Appendix D.)

---

1   *Occupational Outlook Handbook, 2006–2007 Edition*. U.S. Department of Labor, Bureau of Labor Statistics. *www.bls.gov/oco/ocos165.htm#earnings* (accessed August 6, 2006).

EDUCATION AND CREDENTIALING FOR LICENSURE

Most nursing schools require you to have a high school diploma and passing grades in English, algebra, chemistry, and biology. If you have also acquired some computer skills, you will find this a great asset. The standard nursing curriculum includes classroom instruction and supervised clinical rotations through various specialties. At the end of the nursing program, graduates must pass a state or territory board licensure examination to become licensed.

LVN/LPN

The terms *licensed vocational nurse* (LVN) and *licensed practical nurse* (LPN) refer to the same credentialing level. Only two states, California and Texas, use the LVN terminology. The rest of the United States and Canada use the LPN designation. For simplicity, this book will use the more-often-seen credential of LPN.

The training lasts from 9 to 18 months and about 1,200 vocational or technical schools offer the coursework. Other programs are available from community and junior colleges, and hospitals.

A high school diploma is usually required for enrollment, although some programs will accept candidates without it. In addition, some high schools offer the coursework as part of their curriculum.

LPN programs include both classroom study and supervised clinical practice. Lectures and textbooks cover basic science concepts, including anatomy, physiology, medical-surgical nursing, pediatrics, obstetrics, psychiatric nursing, nutrition, first aid, and administration of drugs.

The opportunity for practical nurse students to learn hands-on patient care usually is provided in a hospital, but it can take place in other health care settings. The major focus is on gaining technical skills.

After program completion, students must pass the National Council Licensure Examination for Practical Nurses (NCLEX-PN). The online test is variable in length, because the test is scored as you answer each question. New questions are added until your skill level is determined with 95 percent accuracy. The exam can range from 85 to 205 questions in length, and the limit on the testing session is five hours.

Duties of an LPN might include:

- Taking vital signs, such as temperature, blood pressure, pulse, and respiration
- Preparing and giving injections and enemas
- Monitoring catheters
- Applying dressings
- Treating pressure ulcers
- Giving alcohol rubs and massages
- Reporting adverse reactions to medications and treatments
- Collecting samples for testing
- Performing routine laboratory tests
- Feeding patients
- Recording fluid intake and output

Some duties are specific to particular environments in which on-the-job training is provided. Thus, some practical nurses can help to deliver and care for infants. In nursing homes they can help evaluate residents' needs and develop care plans. In physician offices and clinics, they can make appointments, keep records, and perform other clerical duties. If they work in private homes, they can provide individual care to the elderly and disabled.

Additionally, in some states LPN licensure allows nurses to administer prescribed medicines or start intravenous fluids. Once they become experienced, LPNs may supervise medical assistants. In the future, they might also have the opportunity to become registered nurses by completing LPN-to-RN training programs and passing the NCLEX-RN licensing examination.

In 2004, over 726,000 LPNs worked in hospitals (27 percent), nursing homes (25 percent), physician offices (12 percent), and other organizations (36 percent).

MEDIAN ANNUAL EARNINGS FOR LPNS IN MAY 2004[2]

Workplace	Earnings
Employment services	$41,550
Nursing homes	35,460
Home health care services	35,180
Hospitals	32,570
Physician offices	30,400

RN Diploma

Diploma programs are more scarcely available today than they used to be. Most of them are two- to three-year programs based in a hospital setting, often affiliated with junior or community colleges. Those colleges offer the needed basic nonnursing classes in biological, physical, and social sciences.

Only 69 programs offered this coursework in 2004. Their availability varies by state, and as of this writing these states still have diploma programs: Arkansas, Connecticut, Delaware, Illinois, Indiana, Louisiana, Massachusetts, Missouri, Nebraska, New Jersey, New York, North Carolina, Ohio, Pennsylvania, Rhode Island, Tennessee, Texas, Virginia. Many of them are affiliated with junior colleges. At that location students can take the basic nonnursing classes in biological, physical, and social sciences.[3]

Graduates of diploma nursing programs who go on to pursue a bachelor's degree in nursing may receive some college credit through placement testing. However, they should not always expect to receive full credit for taking college classes.

Associate Degree in Nursing

A two-year associate degree in nursing program (after the prerequisite classes are completed) is offered at many community and junior colleges. Some colleges, universities, and hospital schools of nursing also offer similar associate degrees. In 2004, associate degrees in nursing were granted by 846 institutions. The basic design of the

---

2 *Occupational Outlook Handbook, 2006–2007 Edition*, Bureau of Labor Statistics, U.S. Department of Labor, *www.bls.gov/oco/ocos102.htm* (accessed July 9, 2006).

3 "Directory of Nursing Diploma Programs," Minority Nurse Web site, *www.minoritynurse.com/academic/ profiles/nsgdiploma/* (accessed August 16, 2006).

curriculum is meant to balance general studies with clinical nursing education. The wide variety of clinical nursing experiences prepares graduates to deliver direct care to patients.

Some diploma or associate degree programs serve as a bridge to BSN programs or RN-to-master's degree completion programs. Before enrolling, you should ask what kind of further educational opportunities are available, regardless of whether or not you think that progression will be in your future.

Some diploma and associate degree nurses have a solid strategy: They graduate, get licensed, and then take a job that offers tuition reimbursement benefits. This allows them to pursue more advanced schooling while working, with someone else footing the bill. There are two immediate options for those with associate degrees:

1. *Getting your bachelor's degree after you become licensed as an RN.* In 2004, there were 600 RN-to-BSN programs. Some 167 of them offer a more intense, accelerated format. Program length varies from one to two years.
2. *Getting your master's degree after you become licensed as an RN.* Another option is enrolling in a RN-to-MSN program, which generally takes about three years to complete. The majority of RN-to-BSN and RN-to-MSN programs are offered in traditional classroom settings, but some are offered largely online or in a blended classroom/online format. A list of both kinds of programs may be downloaded from the Web site of the American Association of College of Nursing (*www.aacn.nche.edu*).

RN Four-Year Bachelor's Degree (BSN)

A four-year program, sometimes requiring year-round attendance, is offered at colleges and universities. BSN graduates are prepared for leadership, management, and more independent nursing roles. This preparation comes from completing courses in the theory and practice of nursing, combined with courses in the humanities and behavioral, biological, and physical sciences.

In contrast to the education of diploma and associate degree nurses, BSN students receive more training in communication, leadership, and critical thinking. In addition, they get more clinical experience in nonhospital settings. This extra education might cost more at first, but you should balance the cost against the fact that a bachelor's degree is often necessary for administrative positions and admission to graduate school. In 2004, bachelor's degrees in nursing were offered by 674 institutions.

Accelerated BSN programs offer college graduates with nonnursing degrees the opportunity to get a nursing degree. They last 12 to 18 months and provide the fastest route to a BSN for people already holding another college degree. In 2004, more than 160 of these programs were available.

Duties of an RN might include:

- Administering treatment and medications
- Educating patients and the public about medical conditions, including knowing signs, symptoms, and where to go for help
- Providing advice and emotional support to patients' family members
- Recording patients' medical histories and symptoms
- Helping perform diagnostic tests and analyze results
- Operating medical equipment
- Performing patient follow-up and rehabilitation
- Teaching patients and their families how to manage their illnesses or injuries
- Providing grief counseling to critically ill patients and their family members

MEDIAN ANNUAL EARNINGS FOR RNS IN MAY 2004[4]

Workplace	Earnings
Employment services	$63,170
Hospitals	53,450
Home health care services	48,990
Physician offices	48,250
Nursing homes	48,220

---

4   *Occupational Handbook, 2006–2007 Edition.* Bureau of Labor Statistics, U.S. Department of Labor. *www.bls. gov/oco/ocos083.htm* (accessed April 11, 2006).

Master of Science in Nursing (MSN)

A master's degree is an 18- to 24-month program that provides in-depth education in a particular area of advanced clinical training or research. A BSN was formerly required for entrance into master's degree program in nursing. Now there are many programs that accept those with a bachelor's degree in another discipline into a master's program in nursing without a BSN.

Another trend is for nurses to pursue joint degrees in related fields, such as business administration, public health, or hospital administration. A master's degree is usually the minimum requirement for teaching, clinical specialization, and administration. In 2004, there were 417 schools offering master's degrees in nursing.

Accelerated master's degree in nursing programs combine one year of an accelerated BSN program with two years of graduate study. In 2004, there were 137 RN-to-MSN programs.

Nurse Practitioner (NP, RNP)

Nurse practitioners provide basic preventive care to patients and increasingly serve as primary and specialty care providers, mainly in medically underserved areas. In all states they can prescribe medications; some states authorize this practice without requiring them to work under the supervision of a physician. The most common areas of specialty are:

- Family practice
- Adult practice
- Women's health
- Pediatrics
- Acute care
- Gerontology

In 2004, there were 329 schools that offered master's and post-master's programs for nurse practitioners. For information on nurse practitioners, including a list of accredited programs, contact the American College of Nurse Practitioners (PO Box 12846, Austin, TX 78711), or visit their Web site (*www.aanp.org*). The NP has more broadly defined functions when compared to those of the clinical nurse specialist.

Clinical Nurse Specialist (CNS)

Clinical Nurse Specialists provide direct patient care and expert consultations in a nursing specialty, including psychiatric/mental health, community health, oncology, and pediatrics. They play many roles, such as:

- Patient advocate
- Educator
- Clinical resource
- Consultant
- Role model to other nurses

In 2004, there were 218 schools offering master's and post-master's programs for clinical nurse specialists. For information on clinical nurse specialists, including a list of accredited programs, contact the National Association of Clinical Nurse Specialists (2090 Lingestown Road, Suite 107, Harrisburg, PA 17110), or visit their Web site (*www.nacns.org/cnsdirectory.shtml*).

Nurse Anesthetist (CRNA)

Nurse Anesthetists (CRNAs) administer anesthesia, monitor patient's vital signs during surgery, and provide post-anesthesia care. They have other responsibilities as well, such as performing emergency resuscitation, and managing acute and chronic pain.

In 2004, there were 92 schools offering programs for nurse anesthetists. For information on nurse anesthetists, including a list of accredited programs, contact the American Association of Nurse Anesthetists (222 Prospect Avenue, Park Ridge, IL 60068), or visit their Web site (*www.aana.org*).

Nurse Midwife (CNM)

Nurse midwives provide primary care to women, including gynecological exams, family planning advice, prenatal care, assistance in labor and delivery, and neonatal care. They have formal, collaborative relationships with obstetricians, who provide consultation and manage high-risk patients.

In 2004, there were 45 schools offering programs for nurse midwives. For information on nurse midwives, including a list of accredited programs, contact the American College of Nurse-Midwives (2403 Colesville Road, Suite 1550, Silver Spring, MD 20910), or visit their Web site (*www.midwife.org*).

Doctorate

The PhD is the preferred degree for nursing executives. In general, programs take from four to six years to complete, and the instruction includes training in research methods, the history and philosophy of nursing science, and leadership skills. In 2004, there were 93 schools offering doctoral degrees, and 46 offered BSN-to-doctoral programs.

Each doctoral degree has a different focus; some educational institutions offer a MSN/PHD dual degree.

Columbia University School of Nursing is offering a new clinical doctorate in nursing (DrNP). The program takes four years for BSN nurses, five years for other bachelor's degree holders, and two years for master's prepared nurses. Either way, the final year is a full-time clinical residency and the focus is on providing primary care.

Drexel University's DrNP program is modeled after their Doctor of Public Health degree. The focus is on nursing science, preparing for roles as research scientists, educators, or executives.

ACCREDITATION OF SCHOOLS AND PROGRAMS

Accreditation means that national standards have been met, and participation by the institutions is voluntary. You should know whether the institution you have chosen to attend is accredited. Their Web sites can confirm specific details about particular schools and programs. Some federal financial assistance and state entitlement programs required enrollment in an accredited program.

Two organizations are authorized by the U.S. Department of Education to accredit nursing schools and programs. The first one is associated with the National League for Nursing, and the second is associated with the American Association of Colleges of Nursing. Some organizations are accredited by both.

National League for Nursing (NLN)

The National League for Nursing Accrediting Commission (NLNAC) examines three major aspects of quality education: resources invested, processes followed, and results achieved. The NLNAC standards concern the institution's:

1. mission/governance
2. faculty
3. students
4. curriculum
5. instruction
6. resources
7. integrity
8. educational effectiveness

NLNAC accredits about 200 nursing programs (new and renewals) per year. In addition, they continually monitor approximately 1,700 programs. This review and monitoring function covers more than 70 percent of the nation's nursing programs. They can accredit organizations for up to eight years. Their Web site (*www.nlnac.org*) publishes a directory of their accredited organizations.

The number of NLNAC accredited programs as of December 2005 are as follows:

- Nursing doctorate: 1
- Master's: 127
- Bachelor's: 301
- Associate Degree: 606
- Diploma: 65
- Practical Nursing: 156

American Association of Colleges of Nursing (AACN)

The AACN has a Commission on Collegiate Nursing Education (CCNE) that ensures the quality and integrity of baccalaureate and graduate education programs preparing effective nurses. The CCNE standards concern an institution's:

1. mission and governance
2. institutional commitment and resources

3. curriculum and teaching learning activities
4. student performance and faculty accomplishments

The CCNE can accredit organizations for up to ten years. Their Web site (*www.aacn. nche.edu*) publishes a directory of their accredited organizations.

GATHERING STATISTICS ON EDUCATION FACILITIES

If you would like to explore a particular educational institution, a wealth of information can be found on its Web site. A thorough exploration of land-based facilities would include asking the questions below. For online nursing educational institutions, many of the questions are still pertinent. New programs also offer a blended classroom/online format, which calls for examination of both aspects.

General Characteristics

- How many years have you been in existence?
- What is your enrollment?
- What degrees do you offer?
- What accreditation do you have and for how long?
- How many degrees did you award last year?
- What is your student-teacher ratio?
- What is the average class size?
- How many units of credit must be satisfied for graduation?
- How many hours of clinical practice are required? For online education, what arrangements are in place to assure a clinical practice component?
- Is enrollment limited to full-time students?
- Are there evening or weekend classes?
- Is there a tutoring or mentoring program?
- For online learning, what are the hardware and software requirements?
- What are the required computer skills to have before taking the first online course?
- Which Web browsers are compatible with the online courses?
- What technical support is offered for online learners?

Faculty Characteristics

- What percentage of faculty are full-time educators?
- How many are RNs? Master's prepared? Holding doctorates?
- What is the percentage of tenured faculty?

Acceptance Characteristics

- How many students are accepted annually?
- What percentage of applicants is accepted?
- What is the deadline for enrollment?
- What are the statistics about incoming students last year? High school class rank? High school grade point average? Test scores?

Retention and Graduation Characteristics

- What is the retention rate for students over the time from enrollment to graduation?
- How many people graduated last year?

Student Body Characteristics

- What is the male to female ratio?
- What is the average age of entering students?
- What is the percentage of international students?
- Are there statistics about ethnicity or race?

Library Characteristics

- How many books are housed in the library?
- How many subscriptions were ordered last year?
- What are the hours for the facility or is there online access?
- Can books be checked out, or must they be used on the premises?
- Does the library offer reference librarians, computers, and printers?

Costs Estimates

- Is there an application fee?
- How much are tuition and fees?
- Are enrollment expenses expected to increase in the years before graduation?
- How much should I plan to pay for room and board?
- How much should I plan to pay for books and supplies?

Financial Aid Characteristics

- What is the percentage of students receiving aid?
- What is the average amount received?
- What is the average percentage of total expense covered?

After-Graduation Characteristics

- What percentage of students are employed within six months of graduation?
- What is the average starting salary of graduates?
- What is the student placement budget per graduate?

ADDITIONAL INFORMATION

Here are some other nursing organizations that provide information on nursing career options. Each group looks at the profession from its own viewpoint, solid proof of the many different facets nursing offers.

- *American Association of Colleges of Nursing* (AACN) (One Dupont Circle NW, Suite 530, Washington, DC 20036; 202-463-6930; *www.aacn.nche.edu*). Its president, Dr. Jeanette Lancaster, announced at the onset of her two-year term in March 2006 that she will "work to build consensus on future directions for nursing education, pursue legislative support for nursing workforce development, raise public awareness about the importance of nurses in health care delivery, and advance the goals of professional nursing education, research and practice."
- *American Nurses Association* (ANA) (8515 Georgia Avenue, Suite 400, Silver Spring, MD 20910; 301-628-5000; *nursingworld.org*). Its motto is "Caring for Those Who Care." It states that it represents the 2.9 million RNs in the United

States through its 54 member associations. Its mission is to advance the nursing profession by fostering high standards of nursing practice, promoting the economic and general welfare of nurses in the workplace, projecting a positive and realistic view of nursing, and lobbying the Congress and regulatory agencies on health care issues affecting nurses and the public. Its overarching goal is that nursing be acknowledged as the unifying force in advancing quality health for all. One goal they wish to achieve is for nursing to be among the most frequently chosen careers.

- *American Academy of Nursing* (AAN) (55 East Wells Street, Suite 1100, Milwaukee, WI 53202-3823; 414-287-0289; *www.aannet.org*). The AAN is compromised of over 1500 nursing leaders in education, management, practice and research. One of its strategic directions is strengthening the nursing and health care workforce.

- *American Association for the History of Nursing* (AAHN) (PO Box 175, Lanoka Harbor, NJ 08734; 609-693-7250; *www.aahn.org*). This organization believes that, "Nursing history is a vivid testimony, meant to incite, instruct and inspire today's nurses as they bravely trod the winding path of a reinvented health care system."

- *American Nurses Credentialing Center* (ANCC) (8515 Georgia Avenue, Suite 400, Silver Spring, MD 20910, 800-284-2378; *www.nursingworld.org/ancc*). Its motto is "Nursing Excellence: Your Journey—Our Passion." The ANA founded ANCC in 1973 and it became a subsidiary in 1991. More than 150,000 nurses in the United States and its territories hold ANCC certification in 40 specialty and advanced practice areas. It has a program, Open Door 2000, that invites all qualified RNs, regardless of their education, to become certified in five specialty areas: gerontology, medical-surgical, pediatrics, perinatal, and psychiatric and mental health nursing.

- *American Nurses Foundation* (ANF) (8515 Georgia Avenue, Suite 400, Silver Spring, MD 20910, 301-628-5227; *www.nursingworld.org/anf*). One of its goals is to serve as the national conduit for scholarships to promote entry into nursing and educational development within the profession.

- *American Organization of Nurse Executives* (AONE) (Liberty Place, 325 Seventh Street, NW, Washington, DC, 20004; 202-626-2240; *www.aone.org*). Founded in 1967 as a subsidiary of the American Hospital Association. Its members are more than 5,000 nurses who design, facilitate, and manage health care. AONE's vision is "Shaping the future of health care through innovative nursing leadership."

- *International Council of Nurses* (ICN) (3, Place Jean Marteau, 1201-Geneva, Switzerland, 41-22-908-01-00,; *www.icn.ch*). The ICN is a federation of national nurses' associations, representing nurses in 128 countries. Founded in 1899, it has three goals: to bring nursing together worldwide, to advance nurses and nursing worldwide, and to influence health policy. Its five core values are: visionary leadership, inclusiveness, flexibility, partnership, and achievement.

- *National Council of State Boards of Nursing* (NCSBN) (111 E. Wacker Drive, Suite 2900, Chicago, IL 60601; *www.ncsbn.org*). This not-for-profit organization's membership comprises the boards of nursing in the 50 states, the District of Columbia, and five U.S. territories: American Samoa, Guam, Northern Mariana Islands, Puerto Rico, and the Virgin Islands. Its purpose is to unite boards of nursing in common concerns.

- *National League for Nursing* (NLN) (61 Broadway, New York, NY 10006; 212-363-5555); *www.nln.org*). Founded in 1893 to establish and maintain a universal standard of nursing training, the American Society of Superintendents of Training Schools for Nurses became the first organization for nursing in the United States. In 1952 it combined with the Association for Collegiate Schools of Nursing to establish the NLN. The NLN's current purpose is to promote quality nursing education to prepare the workforce to meet the needs of diverse populations in an ever-changing health care environment.

- *National Organization for Associate Degree Nursing* (N-OADN) (7794 Grow Drive, Pensacola, FL 32514; 850-484-6948; *www.noadn.org*). N-OADN is an advocate for associate degree nursing education and practice, and a promoter of collaboration in charting the future of health care education and delivery.

- *Nurses for a Healthier Tomorrow* (NHT) (c/o Sigma Theta Tau International, 550 West North Street, Indianapolis, IN 46202; *www.nursesource.org*). This is a coalition of 43 nursing and health care organizations working together to wage a communications campaign to attract people to the nursing profession. The NHT's motto is "Nursing. It's Real. It's Life." Elizabeth Dole and Luci Baines Johnson are the honorary chairpersons.

- *Nursing 2000, Inc.* (9302 North Meridian, Suite 365, Indianapolis, IN 46260; 317-574-1325; *www.nursing2000inc.org*). Nursing 2000 is a collaborative that promotes registered nursing careers. It is especially active in the eleven counties in central Indiana that it serves, funded by five Indianapolis area hospitals. However, it is a model for nationwide efforts that "will result in stronger career pipelines for primary and second career opportunities, graduate education, as well as a more diverse workforce."

- *Sigma Theta Tau International Honor Society of Nursing* (550 West North Street, Indianapolis, IN 46202; 317-634-8171, or toll-free in the United States and Canada, 888-634-7575; *nursingsociety.org*). This honor society's vision is to head a global community of nurses who lead in using scholarship, knowledge, and technology to improve the health of the world's people. On their Web site, they extend a generous invitation: "Feel free to e-mail any one of us directly for career advice, post a question in our Member Community forum, or give us a call toll free."

PART TWO

Nursing Career 101

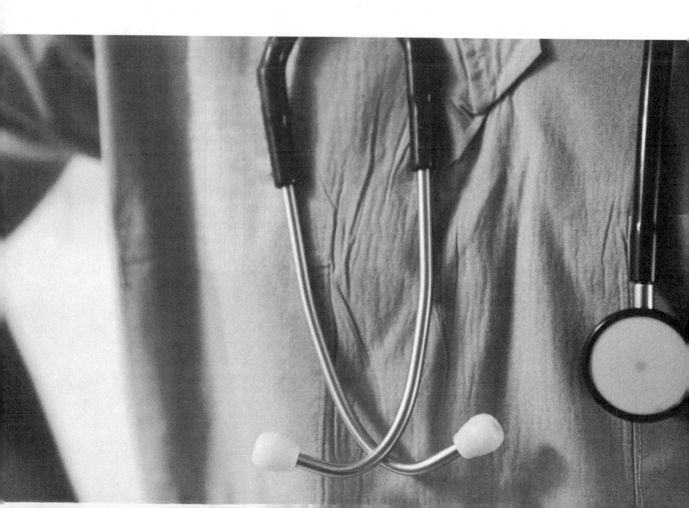

CHAPTER 3

Sorting Out Fact from Fiction

We choose our careers for a variety of reasons, some based on practical concerns and some based on emotional ones. It's not unusual, no matter what your age, to ask yourself "What do I *really* want to do?" The very idea that you can choose a second career means that you have an opportunity to make a fresh start. You have an advantage that you might not have had the first time you chose a career; this time, you can base your decision on self-knowledge and experience (see Chapters 1 and 2, if you haven't been there) and more complete knowledge of a particular career path.

So, now it's time to look at the stories you might have heard about nursing school and nursing jobs to discover what is based on factual evidence and what is a misconception. What follows are some common myths and the truths behind them so you can get a clearer picture of what being a nurse is really like.

YOU MUST WANT TO GIVE INJECTIONS AND BE ABLE TO STAND THE SIGHT OF BLOOD

It's true that giving injections is a skill you will learn in nursing school. Traditionally, nursing students practice giving injections to fruit. They also practice drawing blood and starting IVs on themselves and their colleagues. In an ever-growing number of schools, dummies are available to bypass some of these more invasive techniques.

It's also true that you will see more blood than you would in many other careers. The results of body injuries and surgical interventions are situations in which you will witness it firsthand. At times, nursing students and clinicians have frontline positions in these situations, often in active roles. Most students and clinicians become quite comfortable over time as they perform these tasks.

In nursing school, you will be required to rotate through various clinical settings that involve seeing and handling blood. You will also encounter blood in the operating room, emergency department, and surgical unit. However, rest assured that you will receive help to deal with any negative or anxious emotions due to these situations in a positive and educational manner.

Because your teachers and employers want to prevent you from suffering any illness due to contact with blood, you will receive clear instructions and training on how to protect yourself from harmful contact.

YOU WOULD MUCH RATHER BE A DOCTOR THAN A NURSE

Because this is such a common misconception about nurses, author Janet Katz includes the headline "Nurses Are Not Doctor Wannabes" in the first chapter of her book, *Majoring in Nursing*. In the following excerpt, she begins debunking this myth by pointing out the verbal triggers that expose it:

> I can guarantee you every nurse has heard the following at one time or another: "Why didn't you go on to be a doctor?" "You're so smart; you should be a doctor."

She then answers these questions with the following points:

> Can you imagine the reverse? "Doctor, why didn't you go on to be a nurse?" "You're so smart; you should become a nurse!" … or, best of all, "Doctor, you're so good with patients you should be a nurse!" The absurdity of these makes them quite laughable.[1]

---

1   Janet Katz, *Majoring in Nursing: From Prerequisites to Postgraduate Study and Beyond* (NEW YORK: Farrar, Straus, & Giroux, 1999), p. 5.

Nursing is as different from being a doctor as being a teacher is from being a guidance counselor—both of whom work in the field of education with different roles and licensing requirements.

If you are interested in diseases, their causes, and how to get rid of or cure them, then medicine might be for you. If you are more interested in working and caring for people to help them regain or maintain their health, then nursing might be for you. Perhaps the most important point to remember as you make your choice to become a nurse is this: Do not select nursing as your career with the feeling that it is second best to being a doctor. You should only choose nursing because the breadth of opportunities it provides is right for you.

YOU WILL FIND THAT NURSING SCHOOLS HAVE A VERY TRADITIONAL CURRICULUM

Quite often, this simply is not the case. For example, several nursing schools offer study-abroad programs. Michigan State University's College of Nursing, for instance, has for more than 20 years offered a five-credit program during a summer session in London.

For more than 30 years, Florida State University has also offered nursing classes in London that take place in buildings on the British National Heritage list, with a study center dating to the seventeenth century.

Loyola University Chicago School of Nursing offers opportunities for nursing students to travel to Belize, Rome, and England. In England, students can work for the British National Health Service or make home or hospice visits.

Several other colleges offer study-abroad programs as well. The University of Iowa's College of Nursing has study-abroad programs in Jamaica, Japan, and Iceland. The University of Virginia and State University of New York Brockport have programs in Australia for students. The University of Wisconsin—Eau Claire just started a six-week summer session in Costa Rica, where students live with host families in San Jose, the capital city.

Other schools provide students an opportunity to care for people with whom they might not otherwise come in contact. For example, the University of Arizona's College of Nursing gives students the opportunity to teach health education classes to the women and children sheltered in Bethany House, where residents are homeless or undergoing substance abuse rehabilitation.

Vanderbilt University's School of Nursing offers a forensic nursing focus area, an expansion of their correctional nursing program. Clinical sites may be located in prisons, jails, domestic violence services, emergency rooms, forensic psychiatry sites, police departments, courts, child sexual abuse clinics, medical examiner's offices, and other settings throughout the criminal justice system.

For over a dozen years, nursing students at Emory University have provided health care to migrant farm workers and their families. The two-week intensive health service delivery initiative provides routine care for muscle strains; back problems; foot fungus; eye, urinary tract, and parasitic infections; and diabetes. Nurse-midwives offer expanded services for women, including pap smears, sexual health education, and prenatal care.

Georgetown University in Washington, DC, and South Texas Community College are jointly developing a training program for nurses and other care providers in which they provide services in Texas and multiple locations during seasonal migration.

YOU MUST LIKE TO WORK WITH SICK PEOPLE AND PEOPLE IN PAIN

When you read Chapters 4 and 5, you will realize that, in the long run, as a nurse you have many more opportunities than dealing exclusively with illness and suffering. However, you should know that in nursing school you will be trained to deal with these "downers" on a regular basis. The fact is that three out of five nurses work in hospitals, which treat sick people and those in pain.

Patience is required to provide patient care. Don't worry if you are not naturally blessed with this virtue; your involvement in the healing process will help you adjust to the pace. You will see both ends of the spectrum—from the dramatic results that surgical interventions can make to the day-by-day changes of regular medical care.

YOU MUST LIKE TO CARRY OUT ORDERS FROM PHYSICIANS

The Nightingale Pledge, written for a nursing class graduating in 1893 from a Detroit, Michigan, nursing school, was meant to parallel the Hippocratic Oath for physicians.

The pledge included the words: "With loyalty will I endeavor to aid the physician in his work." It is among the evidence cited to prove a handmaiden concept of nursing. That is defined as:

> A person with little intelligence, knowledge, judgment, or autonomy, a person who exists only to assist the physician. The idea of the purpose of nursing being service to the medical profession instead of service to the patient was promoted by physicians in the 19th and 20th centuries.[2]

That "Yes, doctor; whatever you say, doctor" attitude has given way, in large part, to the more current philosophy of collaboration. Interdependence and respectful interaction form the basis of most current approaches to health care provision.

As Annette Vallano says in her book *Your Career in Nursing*:

> The idea that what nurses do is dictated by and supervised by physicians is inaccurate … Nursing and medicine are collaborative professions.[3]

However, two facts continue to contribute to the idea of nurses as the hands of the physician. One fact is that nurses do follow doctors' orders to meet patient needs; since prescribing certain interventions is outside the scope of regular nursing practice. Even the activities of advanced practice nurses have some limitations. Despite these restrictions, Vallano makes clear the mistake of seeing nurses as servants who blindly follow doctors' orders:

> Nurses who blindly carry out medical regimens without regard for how the status of the patient may indicate otherwise or the appropriateness of the order are failing in their responsibility to protect the patient from harm. Such lack of action regarding professional nursing judgment can result in discipline or revocation of one's license.[4]

The second fact is that, as is true in the structure of most businesses, there is a definite visible hierarchy in health care. Physicians are often found at (or near) the top of the organizational structure in hospitals and clinics. And nursing staff members are often found in the lower boxes of the organization chart.

---

2   "Nurse Stereotypes," *http://en.wikipedia.org/wiki/Nurse_stereotypes* (accessed August 16, 2006).

3   Annette Vallano, *Your Career in Nursing*, 3d Ed. (New York: Simon & Schuster, 2006), p. 115.

4   Ibid., p. 116.

However, it's becoming increasingly common for nurses to carve out their own spheres of influence. For example, to become certificated as a magnet hospital (see Chapter 4), a hospital has to demonstrate "high levels of nurse autonomy and nurse control over practice."

YOU WILL WEAR A WHITE UNIFORM AND THOSE OH-SO-PRACTICAL WHITE NURSING SHOES

If your vision of a nurse includes a white cap, smock, apron or dress, stockings, and the dreaded white, tie shoes, you will find that the nursing dress code has changed dramatically. In many settings, nurses wear lab coats, street clothes, or scrubs. And clogs and tennis shoes have replaced the tie shoes.

My Mother Is a Nurse

As a child, I would watch her put on her white uniform, white stockings, white shoes, and carry her nursing cap in her plastic carrying case as she went off to work.

I thought, "Someday I'll do that."

I loved the feeling I got when I went to work at our community hospital. I never got to wear a starched uniform or carry my hat in a plastic case, but I love my scrubs and white tennis shoes—I love being a nurse.[5]

YOU WILL BE JOINING A WOMAN'S PROFESSION

Although the number of men graduating from nursing schools has been steadily increasing, they still comprise only 5.4 percent of the nurses in the United States. New campaigns designed to attract and recruit men into the field are currently underway. By looking at the World War I era recruitment poster in Figure 3.1, you can clearly see how perceptions of nursing have changed over the years.

Today, men are being recruited into nursing. An article in *Advance for Nurses* confirmed the viability of that vocational choice for men. It quoted four men discussing their opinions about entering nursing as a positive career move for each of them:

"I researched careers to find out which could offer me the best ten-year plan, one with a lot of growth potential and diversity."

---

5   Carol Nephew, "BayCare HomeCare Nurses are Special," BayCare HomeCare home page. *www.mortonplant. com/baybody.cfm?id=472* (accessed August 16, 2006).

Figure 3.1 The Greatest Mother in the World

Courtesy of the National Museum of the U.S. Army, Army Art Collection

"[I chose nursing] based on the job stability, the pay scales, and also because I had a bunch of friends who were going to nursing school.

"I enjoy the high-tech part of nursing, but I also like being a people person… "

Today, I enjoy the hands-on care, the variety in the cases, and it's both challenging and humbling to be an ED nurse. …. Nursing is financially rewarding, employment is always there, and it's one of the best jobs ever."[6]

Not every man in the nursing profession wishes to be identified as a *male nurse*. Nurse Thomas Schwartz took exception to the Oklahoma Nurses Association's calendar project to increase recruitment of men. His editorial published in the *American Journal of Nursing* said:

While I've been an RN since 1979—and a person of the male persuasion even longer than that—I don't allow anyone to call me a "male nurse." If someone I meet uses that qualifier, I politely explain that it's unnecessary. I'm a nurse. Period. I'm no more or less a nurse because of my sex than my female colleagues are because of theirs…

Nursing's recruiting efforts shouldn't set up a false dichotomy between "real men" and some other kind that subtly reinforces what we hope to abolish.[7]

If you are a man, as you finalize your plans for nursing school you might want to find out how men in general are perceived at the schools you are considering. Recently, the American Assembly for Men in Nursing (AAMN, *www.aamn.org*) began a new tradition by annually giving a prize for the best nursing school or college for men in the United States. The first-ever AAMN's Best Nursing School or College for Men Award went to East Carolina University in 2004, and in 2005 the award went to the University of Texas at Austin.

---

6   Sandy Keefe, MSN, RN, "Happy to Be Here: Men in Nursing at Health First Chose the Profession for Practical and Personal Reasons," *Advance for Nurses* 7(2) (2006): 21.

7   Thomas Schwarz, "I Am Not a Male Nurse." *American Journal of Nursing* 106.2 (2006), page 13.

YOU HAVE TO WORK EVENINGS, NIGHTS, HOLIDAYS, AND WEEKENDS

24/7 scheduling, which means 24-hour coverage seven days a week, is needed for many clinical and some administrative hospital positions. That comes from the requirement to provide around-the-clock care. As a newcomer, you would probably be assigned to the least desirable shifts. You could be assigned rotating weekend shifts. However, you would know your weekend assignment weeks in advance so you could plan your time accordingly. With seniority you can usually request more regular daytime shifts. Because these shifts can significantly interfere with your personal schedule, hospitals have added some benefits to somewhat compensate for the disruption.

For nighttime and weekend hospital shifts, the employer often adds a *shift differential,* meaning an additional percentage to your salary. For some individuals, this financial incentive outweighs the drawbacks. In fact some nurses choose to specialize in the harder-to-fill shifts. Other people like the slower pace of the "off hours" and volunteer to work those shifts.

Although this need to provide round-the-clock coverage affects the schedules of a large number of hospital workers, those who work in other settings, such as clinics or public health facilities usually have regular daytime schedules. In these workplaces, the likelihood of weekend and evening shifts is greatly decreased.

YOU HAVE TO BE A TOTAL "PEOPLE PERSON"

Successful nurses range in personality from the most outgoing who enjoy working with many people to those who are more comfortable with one-to-one interactions. Technology is a critical part of all nursing jobs, which means that people who enjoy computers, compiling medical records, and using medical devices can find their own niches within the field.

It's also important to note that communication skills include both verbal and non-verbal communication. In an article titled "Penn and Teller 101: Could Your Nursing Practice Use Some Vegas Magic?"[8] Penn Jillette and Teller describe how both of their approaches are used to benefit patients. Penn is a constant talker, while Teller is the strong, silent type.

---

8 Diane L. Stuenkel, "Penn and Teller 101: Could Your Nursing Practice Use Some Vegas Magic?" *Advance for Nurses for Northern California and Reno, NV,* July 3, 2006, Page 10.

Here is Penn's verbal approach:

> Part of the "art" of nursing comes from being able to encourage, reassure, and assess the patient during the procedure. "How are you doing? You hanging in there? Almost done. You are doing a terrific job holding still!"

Contrast that with Teller's quiet approach:

> Body language, touch, proximity, and vocalizations are all alternative communication forms that can enhance the nurse-patient relationship. For the critically ill patient, nonverbal forms of communication may be more appropriate than a constant verbal barrage.

YOU WILL BE POORLY PAID

This is simply not true. In fact, the increase in salaries in this field has outpaced inflation. One continuing factor is that the law of supply and demand has helped raise salaries.

Money magazine and Salary.com rated careers on growth, pay, stress levels, and other factors. Registered nurses ranked 47th in the top 50. The average pay was found to be $68,872. The ten-year job growth rate was predicted to be 29.35 percent. Average annual growth, including new jobs and replacement, was 120,343.[9]

The U.S. Department of Labor reported that as of May 2004, only the lowest-paid 10 percent of registered nurses in the United States earned less than $37,000 per year. The mid-range of median annual earnings of registered nurses (middle 50 percent) earned between $43,370 and $63,360. The highest 10 percent earned more than $74,760 annually.[10]

According to U.S. Department of Labor statistics, on average RNs make $53,450 in surgical hospitals and over $48K in home health care services, in nursing care facilities and when working in the offices of private physicians.[11]

---

9   Tara Kalwarski, Daphe Mosher, Janet Paskin and Donna Rosato, "Best Jobs in America," CNNMoney.com. *www.money.cnn.com/magazines/moneymag/bestjobs*

10   Occupational Outlook Handbook, 2006–2007 Edition, Bureau of Labor Statistics, U.S. Department of Labor, *www.bls.gov/oco/ocos083.htm* (accessed July 9, 2006).

11   ibid

The American Nurses Association says that annually the average clinical nurse specialist earns $41,226 and the average nurse practitioner $71,000, and that nurse anesthetists are paid $113,000 on average.[12]

YOU WILL NOT BE ABLE TO MOVE UP THE CAREER LADDER

To the contrary, there is ample room for the exercise of ambition and the use of influence in nursing circles and health care organizations. Some factors that come into play are:

- Your basic education. If you have a bachelor's degree, you have the widely regarded minimum level of education for career advancement.
- Your final goal. Many leadership positions have a prerequisite of a master's degree in a related field, which may or may not be nursing.
- The breadth and depth of your experience. Two types of background seem to be widely prized: previous supervisory and financial experience. You could have obtained these qualifications either before or after you entered nursing.

YOU HAVE TO LIFT HEAVY PATIENTS

Because the profession has much to lose if nurses are injured on the job, many efforts are underway to make sure that lifting of heavy patients is subtracted from the usual equation of patient care. It is true that there will always be some hospitalized or home care patients that need to be moved or turned to avoid skin breakdown. However, a combination of lift-teams and equipment are available when needed. In addition, both nursing schools and employers train students how to avoid back injuries while moving patients.

---

12 RNmen homepage, *www.rnmen.com*, accessed August 16, 2006.

A recent article in *Nurse Week*[13] listed the following initiatives:

- American Nurses Association "Handle with Care" campaign
- Equipment to safely raise a 550-pound patient from the floor
- Lift team for patients who weigh over 120 pounds and are disoriented or combative
- State law requiring nurses on state Safe Patient Handling Committee
- Ceiling lifts in all hospital rooms
- Nursing course on how to use state-of-the art lift equipment

YOU HAVE TO HAVE A TOUGH SKIN TO DEAL WITH CRITICISM

In order to get your schoolwork or job done at the highest level of excellence, you will have to accept feedback, judge its relevance, and incorporate practical suggestions for improvement. This proves more true in nursing than in some other professions, because some clinical situations involve life-and-death decisions or the need to move quickly in a new direction.

If you find that you don't have a tough skin at the beginning, there are ways that you can develop some protective armor. Here are some suggestions to help you cope with difficult situations you might face as a nurse:

- Don't grade yourself according to how often patients accept your advice. Instead, rate your educational efforts according to how clear your explanation was as far as outlining expected outcomes and necessary steps.
- Don't forget that there are always ways to work around a problem. For example, you cannot convince someone to stop smoking. You can, however, set limits on an individual's ability to smoke in your area.
- Put limits on what is and what is not acceptable behavior from patients as early as you can, and hopefully you can avoid an uncomfortable situation altogether.
- Don't feel that you have to go it alone in handling difficult situations. Ask for assistance from your team members well before your need for support is crucial.

---

13 Phil McPeck "Watching Our Backs—RNS Get a Life from 'No Lift' Policies," June 19, 2006, *Nurse Week*. *www2.nurseweek.com/Articles/article.cfm?AID=22078* (accessed August 16, 2006).

- Don't think that you have been singled out for negative attention. You were in the wrong place, or presented unhappy news to a patient, or unknowingly touched a nerve. It is not your fault, so don't feel like you're to blame.
- Try to de-escalate the behavior of a patient by responding quickly and calmly to the situation. Remember to maintain a nonaggressive posture and keep a safe, nonthreatening distance between you and the patient.
- Have a list handy of how to contact other resources that handle specific non-clinical complaints, such as admission, billing, or insurance offices.

YOU WON'T GET RESPECT AS A NURSE

Actually, the public trusts nurses above most other professionals. A CNN/USA Today/Gallup annual survey on the honesty and ethical standards of various professions finds nurses at the top of the list, as they have been in all but one year since they were first added to the poll in 1999. Americans were asked to rate the honesty and ethical standards of people in 23 different professions as very high, high, average, low, or very low. Eighty-three percent of respondents said the honesty and ethical standards of nurses are very high or high. The exception came in 2001, when firefighters outscored nurses in the wake of the September 11 terrorist attacks.

YOU WILL FIND IT DIFFICULT TO GET INTO NURSING SCHOOL

It is true that most nursing schools are becoming very selective, and that more people apply to nursing school than are accepted. Many factors have contributed to this phenomenon: an insufficient number of faculty; lack of clinical sites and classroom space; and budget constraints. According to the American Association

Here is some helpful advice from nurses who have learned to handle difficult situations:

"Sometimes patients can be very difficult and order you around like a servant, when they are plenty capable of doing things themselves safely. In this case, the key is to be assertive, be polite, and professionally encourage them to do things for themselves." —

"Communicating with some patients can be difficult and can make or break your day. While it may require extra work, what these patients really need is some extra attention. The natural tendency is to spend as little time as possible in their rooms. Don't do that. If you take the time to work with them, at the end of the day, they are much more comfortable and happy."[14]

14 Barbara Arnoldussen, *Training Wheels for Nurses, What I Wish I'd Known My First 100 Days on the Job: Wisdom, Tips, and Warnings from Experienced Nurses. New York,* Kaplan Publishing, 2004.

of Colleges of Nursing (AACN), in 2004 alone, U.S. nursing schools turned away 26,340 qualified applicants to entry-level bachelor's degree nursing programs.

However, do not be discouraged by these numbers, because there are steps you can take to make your application more favorable:

- Check with the institution that you want to enroll in to see if they offer any kind of preferential treatment. For example, Evergreen Valley College in San Jose, California, gives priority for enrollment to those living in their community college districts who have successfully completed at least 12 units of coursework. They offer nursing program information workshops regularly during the school year, and a course called Nursing 100, Introduction to Nursing, for prospective applicants.
- Speak with admissions officers at the schools you're considering to learn what they look for and what you need to do to fill in any gaps in your qualifications.
- Know what your schools of choice look for and emphasize on their applications. For example, some schools look for candidates who are well-traveled, while others are more academically oriented. Some schools may require prerequisite courses that you might take at a local community college before you apply to a nursing program.
- If you do volunteer work before applying to nursing school, make a strong, positive connection with your supervisor. This can result in a glowing recommendation that carries even more weight than one from a former instructor.
- Use the Internet to make contacts and find valuable information. You can perform Google searches for contacts in various nursing specializations. For example you could type in e-mail and CRNA (for certified nurse anesthetist) to find e-mail addresses of experienced professionals who can give you helpful tips and advice on how to make your application stand out.

YOU HAVE TO WANT TO WORK IN HOSPITALS

The 57 nursing specialties listed in Chapter 5 are good evidence that this is not true for all nurses. However, it is a fact that a considerable part of your training will occur in this traditional setting. In nursing school, you will rotate through a series of roles that focus on different aspects of health care: medical-surgical, pediatric, operating room, geriatric, and home care. This scheduling gives you an overview of the variety of problems you will be asked to handle as a nurse.

YOU WILL ALWAYS BE WORKING FOR OTHER PEOPLE

While most nurses do work for an employer, the National Nurses in Business Association (NNBA) Web site posts two frequently asked questions and answers. The first one talks about the benefits of self-employment, which they list as follows:

- Rewards for hard work
- Job satisfaction
- Less stress
- Job security
- Increased income and more tax breaks
- Be your own boss
- Work with happy people
- Never be fired, laid off, called off, called down, retired, or refused employment[15]

If those characteristics sound like your vision of the ideal career, here are four categories of small business and self-employment options that NNBA identifies as opportunities with similar characteristics:

1. Nurses who review, analyze, and plan patient care (e.g., legal nurse consulting, life care planning, case management, elder care, forensic nursing)
2. Nurses who provide patient care (e.g., independent contractor, nursing agency, home health, private duty, holistic, nurse practitioner, esthetic nurses)
3. Nurses who teach (e.g., education, seminars, speaking, writing, CPR, ACLS, training program management, business-to-business and person-to-person)
4. Nurses who design, manufacture, or sell a product[16]

---

15 "Self-Employed RN" National Nurses in Business Association Web site, *www.nnba.net* (accessed August 16, 2006).

16 Ibid.

YOU WILL HAVE TO FOLLOW RULES AND REGULATIONS

It is true that there are many guidelines that serve as a structure for providing health care. A few of them are:

- *Evidence-based standards of practice.* These are methods of caring for specific illnesses and diseases according to methods that are supported by research. They have been documented to be consistent across assessment and treatment settings.
- *Joint Commission on Accreditation of Healthcare Organizations (JCAHO) standards.* These standards address the whole spectrum of functions of a health care workplace—from leadership to medications, from patient and staff education to equipment maintenance.
- *Policies and procedures that are organization specific.* They cover handling routine situations and responding to emergency events.
- *Local, state, and federal laws.* Sometimes these have to do with billing, such as Medicare. Other times you need to know how laws affect emergency room admission and discharges to other care settings.
- *Health care insurance guidelines.* The financial aspects of health care coverage (or noncoverage) affect access to care.

YOU WILL HAVE A MESSY JOB WHERE YOU CLEAN UP AFTER PEOPLE

Messy can be a relative term and is true of many nursing positions. It is not just blood, pus, mucus, feces, and dirt that provide challenges; there's also the emotional and psychological messiness of the chaos caused by injury and illness.

Often, nurses serve as lifeboats that rescue people from becoming overwhelmed. Nurses who go into home health care can also find themselves in environments that are unorganized due to the financial or physical effects of ill health.

YOU HAVE TO BE VERY STRONG, BECAUSE ONLY THE STRONGEST SURVIVE

It is true that experienced nurses can set up obstacles for nurses entering their mutual workplace, calling for extraordinary stamina for the newcomers. In fact, a recent book, *Ending Nurse-to-Nurse Hostility*,[17] takes this topic as its focus for intervention. Long hours, difficult physicians, and the emotional demands of the job can take their toll and cause nurses of all ages to act hostile toward one another.

Because this is a threat to everyone considering entering the nursing profession, nursing leaders have called for placing this type of nurse-to-nurse conflict in context of the whole environment. Here is how Donna Cardillo responds to this issue in her article, "Do Nurses Really Eat Their Young?"[18]

> The truth is that there will always be certain people in every profession who need to lash out at new members of the profession for their own reasons. It happens to a certain extent in almost every workplace, almost every profession. ….To those nurses who are caring and supportive, who teach and encourage new nurses, speak up and debunk the negative stereotype that nurses eat their young… who take phone calls at home and even in the middle of the night from novices who need guidance…join me in starting a new mantra: Nurses nurture their own.

YOU ARE TOO OLD TO ENROLL IN NURSING SCHOOL OR WORK AS A NURSE

The cover of the July 3, 2006, *NurseWeek* newsmagazine featured a smiling Milve Hamilton, RN, BSN. The 81-year-old nurse celebrated her birthday by working the night shift in the OB unit. When asked how she handles a 12-hour shift at her age, she replied: "It's a lot of walking; that's good for me. That's probably why I have no health problems, thank the Lord. Once in awhile, I have trouble opening a cap on something, and they'll help me."[19]

Not everyone has the fortune of being established in a career that brought Milve back at age 65. What is really important to the career changer concerned about the age issue are the answers to these questions:

---

17 Kathleen Bartholomew, *Ending Nurse-to-Nurse Hostility: Why Nurses Eat Their Young and Each Other*, (Marblehead MA, HCPro, Inc. 2006).

18 Donna Cardillo, "Do Nurses Really Eat Their Young?" *Nurse Week*. January 10,, 2005: *www.nurseweek.com/news/Features/05-01/DearDonna_01-10-05.asp* (accessed September 23, 2006).

19 Janet Wells, "Decades of Caring: Retaining Nurses with Years of Experience," *Nurse Week www2.nurseweek.com/Articles/article.cfm?AID=22219* (accessed August 16, 2006).

- What is the likelihood that I will be accepted into nursing school at my age? If accepted, how soon can I begin my studies? What will it be like to be in a classroom with students younger than me?
- How many years will it take me to graduate from nursing school? How much will that cost?
- After that, how many years do I have to work as a nurse? Will my income more than cover the cost of my education?
- What will it be like to be in a workplace with colleagues younger than me?

The answers to most of these questions are very subjective, depending on your age, what level of nursing you target, the acceptance rate of applications to a specific school, the cost of education, and local salaries (unless you relocate). As a final discussion on this topic, you can read how eight people answered a query put up on the Web site AllNurses.com.[20]

---

20 Allnurses.com *http://forums.nurses-forum.com/thread1840.html first posted 10/19/04* (accessed September 23, 2006).

Too Old to Go to Nursing School?

The question: I am 37 and looking to become an RN as a career change. Should I start as a CNA or LPN first? What are your thoughts on my age?

I currently work in the manufacturing sector as a tool designer. I am concerned with the outlook of my job along with the health issues. I spend 90 percent of my day sitting in front of a computer.

Your thoughts and suggestions would be of great help! Thanks!

Answer #1: I think it's great that you're considering going into nursing now. At 37, you are definitely not too old! There are a few "older" students in my class, a few in their 30s, a few in their 40s, and one in his 50s. To start with, I would recommend getting your CNA certification; it was required for us to get into nursing school anyway, so you may need it, depending on your school requirements. Once you get your CNA, you'll get a good idea if nursing is what you want to get into and if it's the right thing for you.

Answer #2: NO, you are still very young! The health care field is my second career. I started college back in 1992, when I was 32 years old. I knew from the start I wanted to be a nurse; however, the ADN waiting list was so long it would take a couple of years for me to reach the top of the list. So, I took the prereq courses for both the ADN and Surgical Technology programs. I was accepted to the surg tech program right away (completed 1995). I worked in surgery as a certified surgical technologist (CST) for a year, then received a call, while at work, I'd been accepted to the ADN program. I worked 32 hours per week as an CST, as a male single parent, while in the ADN program (completed 1998 at 38 years old).

IMHO, besides the CNA option you might want to consider an Associate of Applied Science in Surgical Technology program (CST). I had no trouble at all with the ADN clinicals, which was due to my CST experience. Nevertheless, I do suggest you seek some kind of health care work as a warm up to an RN program.

Another thought—if you can go straight to a BSN program, rather than an ADN program, go for it! I chose the ADN route because it was quicker in the short run.

However, I just recently finished my BSN (at 43 years old) with UTMB Galveston's online program, while working 40+ hrs per week. At least my sons are now in their 20s and not living at home. Now, I'm taking organic chemistry. A prereq for the Army Nurse Anesthesia Masters (CRNA) program. I'm currently a critical care nurse in the USAR, as well as a civilian OR nurse.

BTW, in my first career I was active duty USMC (avionics) for eight years, then a civilian aircraft electrician for three years.

Answer #3: I hope 37 isn't too old! I started RN school when I was 37. Of course that was a long time ago—I'm 38 now and just a couple weeks from finishing up.

If you have no health care experience, then I would suggest beginning work as a CNA as soon as you qualify. At the school I went to this was available after we completed the first semester.

Also—to give you a bit more encouragement—I am not the oldest person in my class. There are several who are my age and older. We have one guy who is 45 and just retired from a 20+ year career with Verizon as some kind of manager. There are a couple girls in the class who are in their late 30s and decided they didn't want to be waitresses anymore. In fact most of the people in my class are 30 years or older. There are a few who are in their mid 20s and one who is 22, but the median age is between 30 and 35.

You are not too old. Age is an advantage, definitely not a hindrance. Older students tend to do very well in nursing school. The few students who have had to drop out or were held back a semester were mostly younger students. You will do fine as long as you work hard and dedicate yourself to school.

As far as LPN vs. RN, if I were you I would go for RN right off the bat. RN school is only a semester longer than LPN school and you will always find yourself wishing that you did it to start with. LPNs are paid less and do basically the same job as an RN in most capacities. If you go to LPN school you may find yourself deciding to transition to an RN later on. Around here that's a three semester course of study. If you go RN to start then it's only one semester additional. Not only that, but after your third semester of RN school you can qualify to sit for the LPN boards if you want.

Answer #4: I am 31 and going back for my BSN now. It is actually nice to have "older" guys around to help the "young" guys. I think with age and experience in life you have a great deal to offer the profession. I agree with going for the RN right from the start. You may even want to look at the differences in time commitment for the BSN program.

Answer #5: Two more cents from a newbie! I'm 37 (38 in January) and I will be starting my prereq's for an LPN in January. I researched several options and because of time, money, and family constraints, I decided to get my LPN, and then I'll let my employer pay for my RN and/or whatever else I go for.

Answer #6: Am in my first semester and I am 30. My buddy is going through it too and he is 33. We were both downsized welders; there are also a couple of former (downsized) machinists in the class: 37 and 55. The oldest person in my class is 60 and he is doing fine.

Answer #7: I was 26 when I started an access-to-nursing course. Now 28, I am on my first placement of the second year and I'm loving it. The placement is at the accident-and-emergency. I didn't think I'd like it so much as I had always been drawn toward the idea of neuroscience nursing having been a career for people with neurological conditions, but after meeting the consultant nurse in A&E and the ENPs, I found there was a lot more to learn in other departments. So watch out medical world because us oldies are the short-lived leaders of the future health care, and if technology really is that good we will be able to rule with false hips and knees.

Answer #8: I am 47 and doing a RN program. Never attended college before in my life, and currently have a 4.0 GPA, so see, you are never too old if you try. I also was wondering if age was an asset or hindrance, but I do believe that experience in life will more than offset any age related shortcomings.

CHAPTER 4

Nursing Specializations Inside the Hospital

INTRODUCTION

The majority of nurses working today (57 percent) practice within a hospital organization. The good news is that this gives you a choice to work at more than 5,000 different locations in the United States. Most of these are community hospitals, which means that, as a nurse, you could literally contribute to the health of your friends and neighbors.

Hospitals offer more than just an entry into the profession; they also offer substantial experience on your résumé. They can:

- Connect you with seasoned colleagues who can share their experiences
- Offer organized mentoring and continuing education programs for professional growth
- Provide you with orientation sessions so that you can learn the ropes. Some have internships; others have temporary positions for new graduates that can become permanent
- Give you the opportunity to take care of more acutely ill patients with more complex diseases while the information you learned about their treatment from textbooks and clinical rotations is fresh in your mind
- Help you understand how hospitals operate so you can move up a clinical or administrative ladder

The bottom line is this: With hospital experience you can handle most everything that a nurse will encounter and include it on your résumé.

MAGNET STATUS HOSPITALS—AN ATTRACTION

If you envision yourself working at a particular hospital in the future, you should know that not all hospital environments are created equal. Don't just join an organization because it's either geographically convenient or you know some of the employees; consider the results of recent research on nursing job satisfaction, which considers working conditions after the establishment of the Magnet Recognition Program by the American Nurses Credentialing Center (ANCC). Hospitals are awarded magnet status after they prove to the ANCC that they meet the following standards:

> A magnet hospital is one that attracts and retains nurses who have high job satisfaction because they can give quality care. Magnet recognition goals identify excellence in providing nursing, recognize institutions that act as a "magnet" by creating a work environment that recognizes and rewards professional nursing, and provide a method to disseminate successful nursing practices and strategies.[1]

Research studying the characteristics of magnet status hospitals found that they offer:

- Higher nurse-patient ratios
- Competent coworkers and higher staff retention
- Control over practice
- Educational and promotional opportunities[2]

Research comparing magnet status hospitals with ones that do not have this status found that:

> Clinical nurses at magnet hospitals had more autonomy and control over their practice setting compared to nonmagnet nurses. This meant that nurses at magnet hospitals had *independence* to deploy needed *resources*

---

1 American Nursing Association, "Scope and Standards for Nurse Administrators," *The American Nursing Association,* 2003.

2 M.L. McClure and A.S. Hinshaw, Eds. *Magnet Hospitals Revisited: Attraction and Retention of Professional Nurses* (Washington, DC: American Nurses Publishing, 2002).

for patient care delivery, were *accountable* for patient care issues, and had relative *freedom to make patient care decisions*. Magnet hospital nurses characterized their work environment as one of support from administration more often than nurses in nonmagnet settings.[3]

For a list of more than 200 hospitals in over 40 states that have achieved magnet status, check out *www.nursingworld.org/ancc/magnet*. If you are seriously considering working at a nonmagnet hospital, keep in mind the four working environment characteristics highlighted in the above quote before making a commitment:

- independence
- resources
- accountability
- freedom of patient-care decision making

These are all important qualities in a workplace. Because you already have career experience, you have high expectations for your next career. Let's look at the 36 career choices you have in a hospital setting, if that is where your initial nursing career is headed.

3   Valda V. Upenieks, PhD, RN. "Assessing Differences in Job Satisfaction of Nurses in Nonmagnet Hospitals," *JONA: Journal of Nursing Administration* 32:11 (2002): 564-576.

BURN CARE NURSE

Definition: Nurses who work in specialized units to care for individuals recovering from injuries suffered from fires, explosions, and contact with caustic agents.

Want Ad: Burn NP needed. The burn NP acts as liaison for patients on the burn unit as they move from inpatient to outpatient services. Responsibilities include conducting history and physicals, ordering and interpreting labs tests, prescribing medications and developing and monitoring treatment plans. The NP will maintain a burn trauma registry, establish a quality improvement program, and perfrom staff education.

> **Quote from a Burn Care Nurse:** *"Burn nursing is physically and psychologically demanding and is certainly not for everybody, but it is one of the most gratifying and satisfying areas of nursing.*[4]

Professional Association

■ American Burn Association (ABA) (*www.ameriburn.org*). The ABA is dedicated to improving the lives of everyone affected by burn injury through patient care, education, research, and advocacy. Their interest spans acute care through rehabilitation, and includes prevention of burns. ABA members include burn care physicians, nurses, physical and occupational therapists, social workers, psychologists, nutritionists, rehabilitation experts, and research personnel. Firefighters, attorneys, administrators, prevention educators, and burn patients also comprise the ABA membership. Membership is open to health care professionals and others with a demonstrated interest/accomplishment in the field of burns.

Professional Journal

■ *Journal of Burn Care & Research.* Articles present the latest information on surgical procedures, acute care, rehabilitation, reconstruction, burn prevention, and research and education. Other topics include physical therapy/occupational therapy, nutrition, current events in the evolving health care debate, and reports on the newest computer software for diagnostics and treatment. The Journal serves all burn care specialists, from physicians, nurses, and physical and occupational therapists to psychologists, counselors, and researchers.

Media Coverage

Since the Consumer Product Safety Commission lowered safety standards for children's pajamas in 1996, Shriners Hospitals for Children, which treat more than 20 percent of all major pediatric burn injuries in the United States, has experienced a significant increase in sleepwear-related burn injuries. The 1996 decision overturned a 1972 requirement that all children's pajamas, nightgowns and other sleepwear be made of flame-resistant materials.

---

4   Debra Wood, "Spotlight on Burn Care Nursing," NurseZone.com, *www.nursezone.com/stories/ SpotlightOnNurses.asp?articleID=13806* (accessed September 23, 2006).

CARDIAC CARE NURSE   *Also Known As:* CARDIOVASCULAR NURSE, CARDIAC REHABILITATION NURSE, CORONARY CARE NURSE, CARDIOTHORACIC NURSE

Definition: Nurses who work with patients and the families of patients who suffer from heart disease. While cardiac care nurses are often specialized critical care nurses in the hospital, they can also work with patients in the home, assisting with cardiac drug monitoring and providing care to patients who have undergone bypass, valve replacement, heart catheterization, angioplasty, stent placement, or pacemaker surgery. They can educate patients about lifestyle changes to increase cardiac functioning, and monitor them during physical workouts to prevent overexertion and/or injury.

Want Ad: The Cardiac ICU is designed and staffed specifically for the acute medical management of pediatric cardiac diseases and post-operative cardiac surgical care, as well as critical life-saving technologies. The population and cases seen include pacemaker implantation, repair of hypoplastic left heart syndrome (Norwood, Sano, Glenn, and Fontan repair), ECMO, and intraaortic balloon pumps. This is a high-acuity environment that offers opportunities for learning and career advancement.

> **Quote from a Cardiac Care Nurse:** *"A cardiovascular nurse deals with a wide range of things—from watching a telemetry patient for just one night to assisting the surgeons during an emergency operation in a patient's room—that's what makes this job so exciting."*[5]

Professional Associations

- Council on Cardiovascular Nursing (*www.americanheart.org/presenter. jhtml?identifier=1148*)

- Preventive Cardiovascular Nurses Association (PCNA) (*www.pcna.net*)

- American Association of Cardiovascular and Pulmonary Rehabilitation (AACVPR) (*www.aacvpr.org*)

- American Association of Critical-Care Nurses (AACN) (*www.aacn.org*)

- American Association of Heart Failure Nurses (AAHFN) (*www.aahfn.org*)

- American College of Cardiovascular Nursing Practice (ACCN) (*www.accn.net*)

Professional Journal

- Journal of Cardiovascular Nursing. Articles focus on the physiologic, psychological, and social needs of cardiovascular patients and their families in a variety of environments.

Media Coverage

Emmy award-winning comedian David Letterman, who suffers from a family history of high cholesterol, underwent emergency quintuple bypass surgery in 2000 in order to clear a severely blocked artery. Upon his return to his show on February 21, 2000, Letterman brought onstage all of the doctors and nurses who had participated in the surgery and his recovery (with extra teasing of a nurse who had given him bedbaths—"This woman has seen me naked.") In an unusual show of emotion, Letterman was nearly in tears as he thanked the health care team with the words, "These are the people who *saved my life!*" The episode earned an Emmy nomination. [6]

---

5   Dawn Hunck, "A Day in the Life of A Cardiovascular Nurse," Nurse.com, *www.nurse. com/NurseContent/Community/NurseCommentary/ Cardiovascular* (accessed August 16, 2006).

6   "David Letterman, Heart Surgery, Wikipedia, *http://en.wikipedia.org/wiki/David_Letterman* (accessed September 23, 2006).

CRITICAL CARE NURSE
Also Known As: INTENSIVE CARE UNIT (ICU) NURSE, STEP-DOWN UNIT NURSE, TRANSITION UNIT NURSE, PROGRESSIVE/INTERMEDIATE ICU NURSE

Definition: Nurses who care for patients acutely ill or patients in critical condition. These nurses often must use sophisticated computerized equipment. They are responsible for the emotional welfare of patients and their families at times of life-and-death crises.

Want Ad: Demonstrated ability to calculate and manage vaso-active drugs. Demonstrated experience with managing ventilated patients. Demonstrated ability to provide a consistently high-quality of service to patients, visitors, and staff at all times. Must be able to work ICU and cross-train to Stepdown Unit. The Pediatric ICU cares for critically ill children of all ages. We see a variety of conditions, including respiratory failure, traumas, transplants (liver, kidney, renal, and BMT) and neuro problems. The Neonatal ICU treats neonates, mostly for surgical conditions. Common diagnoses seen include respiratory distress, abdominal surgeries, and hydrocephalus.

> **Quote from a Critical Care Nurse:**
> *"I am devoted to teaching ICU nurses things that will help them take better care of patients and families. No job is more challenging or exciting. I love nursing and nurses, and I try to instill in all the value of what they do."*[7]

Professional Associations

- American Association of Critical-Care Nurses (AACN) (*www.aacn.org*)

- Canadian Association of Critical Care Nurses (CACCN) (*www.caccn.ca*)

- Society of Critical Care Medicine (SCCM) (*www.sccm.org*)

Professional Journals

- *Critical-Care Nurse (www.critical-care-nurse.org)*. This journal is meant to keep all critical care nurses informed about issues that affect this realm of nursing.

- *American Journal of Critical Care (www.ajcconline.org)*. This journal's focus is clinical and evidence-based articles.

Media Coverage

The Boston Globe newspaper featured second-career nurse Julia Zelixon and her ICU preceptor M.J. Pender in a four-part, front-page series in October 2005. A four-minute video and a seven-minute audio featuring reporter Scott Allen and photographer Michele McDonald is available at *www.boston.com/news/special/nursing/top/*. Free registration at the site gives access to read the account of how the 35-year-old fared in her first seven months as an ICU nurse in Massachusetts General Hospital in Boston.

---

7   Bree LeMaire, April 30, 2003 "Maurene Harvey, on Critical Care Nursing," *Nurse Week* Web site, *www.nurseweek.com/5min/harvey.asp* (accessed August 16, 2006).

DERMATOLOGY NURSE   *Also Known As:* ASTHETIC NURSE

Definition: Nurses in this field provide education and care for patients undergoing diagnosis and treatment of wounds, rashes, and diseases of the skin.

Want Ad #1: The incumbent will take child and adult histories, and do skin examinations; understand routine, simple dermatology cases (e.g., acne, eczema, psoriasis, seborrhic dermatitis, and warts); participate in the formulation of a problem list; write prescriptions and perform simple surgical procedures, such as cryotherapy; coordinates and monitors a health maintenance program for patients; initiates the referral of patients to other departments and agencies as necessary; participates with dermatology hospital consultations; understands and can administer ultraviolet light therapy.

Want Ad #2: Provides phone advice, patient teaching, phototherapy, extensive dressing changes, and other nursing treatments. Must be willing to study and learn dermatology diagnoses, treatments, extended role protocols, etc. Must be knowledgeable about topical medications.

> **Quote from a Laser Surgery Dermatology Nurse:** *"For every patient I treat, there is time set aside for education, depending on how often they come in. All patients ask some questions. ... I identify with so many of the patients' problems because I had them. When they look at me and say my skin looks great, I tell them that 18 months ago I was where they are. That gives them hope and makes them so much more relaxed. Their embarrassment and shyness melt away."*[8]

Professional Associations

- Dermatology Nurses Association (DNA) (*www.dnanurse.org*). Celebrating 25 years of working with this specialty, it offers news to keep dermatology nurses up-to-date on new advances, methods, and practices. Nurses can post their résumés for free.

- The American Academy of Dermatology (AAD) (*www.aad.org*).

- The Degos Patients Support Network (*www.degosdisease.com*)

Professional Journal

- Dermatology Nursing Journal (*www.dermatologynursing.net*). This is the official journal of the Dermatology Nurses Association.

Media Coverage

Dermatology Online Atlas (*www.dermis.net*) is a dermatology information service. It offers image atlases complete with diagnoses, case reports, and additional information on almost all skin diseases. It includes photographic images, therapeutic measures, and skin care suggestions. The Web site is a collaboration between the Department of Clinical Social Medicine at the University of Heidelberg, Canada, and the Department of Dermatology at the University of Erlangen, Canada.[9]

---

8   Ruth Carol, "Culture is Skin Deep," *http://minoritynurse.com/features/nurse_emp/ 06-06-06-1.html* (accessed September 23, 2006).

9   DermIS home page, *http://dermis.net* (accessed August 16, 2006).

EMERGENCY DEPARTMENT NURSE COORDINATOR

Also known as: TRAUMA NURSE

Definition: Nurses who work to maintain vital signs and prevent complications and death. Nurses in this field provide care for patients in the critical or emergency phase of an illness or trauma, and must be able to recognize life-threatening problems and rapidly arrange necessary care. These nurses are not limited to only working in the emergency room of a hospital.

Want Ad: ER nurse with current Basic Cardiac Life Saving, Acute Cardiac Life Saving preferred. Radiology nursing knowledge/skills essential. Programming and functionality of power injectors for contrast studies. General knowledge of cardiac stress tests and drugs used for pharmacological stress. Pediatric venipuncture skills.

Quote from a Trauma Nurse Coordinator: *"I always think that as emergency nurses, we see patients and families on the day that they will probably describe as 'the worst day of my life because my child was hit by a car… my husband had a heart attack… I had a baby in the back of my car…or I had a reaction to a medication and almost died,' but I like knowing that maybe I can make it a little better by helping them out, possibly correcting the problem, and being there for them psychologically and emotionally."*[10]

Professional Associations

- Emergency Nurses Association (ENA) (*www.ena.org*). ENA is the specialty nursing association serving the emergency nursing profession through research, publications, professional development, and injury prevention. ENA's mission is to provide visionary leadership for emergency nursing and emergency care. ENA is an organization seeking to define the future of emergency nursing and emergency care through advocacy, expertise, innovation, and leadership.

- Society of Trauma Nurses (*www.traumanursesoc.org*).

- American Trauma Society (*www.amtrauma.org*). As the Web site of the American Trauma Society (ATS) points out, it is the premier national trauma association that serves the entire spectrum of trauma providers and trauma interests, bringing together the entire trauma team. ATS provides unique information on trauma centers across the country. Members network with peers for problem solving and a general exchange of information regarding daily problems they confront.

Professional Journal

- *Journal of Emergency Nursing* (*www.ena.org/publications/jen*). This bimonthly publication is the official journal of the Emergency Nurses Association.

---

10 Kristin Rothwell, "Careers in Nursing: Emergency Nursing—First on the Scene," Nurse Zone Web site. *www.nursezone.com/stories/ SpotlightOnNurses.asp?articleID=7861* (accessed September 23, 2006).

ENDOCRINE NURSE

Definition: Nurses who work with patients with a broad spectrum of metabolic and hormonal clinical conditions.

Want Ad #1: The endocrine nurse coordinator arranges diagnostic procedures and provides educational support to patients and families in administration of endocrine therapies and home management. Patients have disorders of puberty, hypoglycemia, genital abnormalities, bone mineral disorders, adrenal and thyroid abnormalities, and disorders of the anterior and posterior pituitary.

Want Ad #2: Assesses, plans, implements, evaluates and documents care of patients in accordance with facility and department policies, and in accordance with the standards of professional nursing practice. The educator utilizes specialized knowledge, judgment, and nursing skills necessary to provide care appropriate to the age of the patients in the department. Two years experience in diabetes education and current certification by the National Certification Board for Diabetes Educators is preferred. Candidate must demonstrate clinical knowledge and expertise in diabetes care and the ability to work with adult and geriatric populations.

Professional Associations

- Endocrine Nurses Society (*www.endo-nurses.org*)
- Pediatric Endocrinology Nurses Society (*www.pens.org*)

Professional Journals

- *Journal of Endocrinology* (*www.joe.endocrinology-journals.org*). This journal is published by the Society for Endocrinology Policy and includes articles on original molecular, biochemical, and physiological research pertaining to the structure and function of the endocrine and endocrine-related systems. Papers are considered if they supply new, substantial, and mechanistic advances in the science of endocrinology.

- *The Journal of Clinical Endocrinology and Metabolism* (*www.jcem.endojournals.org*). This is a peer-reviewed journal for endocrine clinical research and clinical practice reviews. Each issue provides coverage of new developments in order to enhance readers' ability to understand, diagnose, and treat endocrine and metabolic disorders. The journal features clinical trials, clinical reviews, clinical practice guidelines, case seminars, and controversies in clinical endocrinology, as well as original reports of significant advances in patient-oriented endocrine and metabolic research.

Media Coverage

Thirteen million Americans have a thyroid disorder, and more than half of them are not aware of it. Three people whose Graves Disease became public knowledge include former president, George H.W. Bush and his wife, Barbara, and 1992 and 1996 Olympic track champion Gail Devers.[11]

---

11 National Graves Disease Foundation home page, *www.ngdf.org* (accessed August 16, 2006).

GASTROENTEROLOGY NURSE

Also known as: ENDOSCOPY NURSE, GI LAB NURSE

Definition: Nurses who work with patients who need testing or treatment for conditions that affect the esophagus, stomach, and colon. The patients could have an acute illness, with symptoms such as severe abdominal pain or diarrhea, or chronic conditions such as ulcers.

Want Ad #1: The GI nurse specialist performs medical histories and physical examinations, and conducts basic GI consultations and colonoscopy screening sessions. Provides coverage for urgent visits. Documents assessments of patients' health and illness status. Under guidelines, determines medications to be used for identified diagnosis. Able to relate to a wide range of patient ages from infants to the elderly.

Want Ad #2: 40-hour position for RN in the Gastroenterology Procedure Unit. Seeking motivated nurse to work in fast-paced endoscopy procedure unit with pediatric/adolescent patients. Will be involved with patient assessment; sedation; IV insertion; and pre-, intra-, and post-procedural care of GI and pulmonary patients. This state of the art unit offers practice in an academic, family-centered pediatric care facility. 3 to 5 years pediatric/adolescent or endoscopy experience required.

Quote from a 48-year-old Gastroenterology Nursing Student Intern: *"I get the patients ready for the (colonoscopy) procedure and start the IVs, and work closely with the patient. Everybody is anxious when they come in for a colonoscopy, but 90 percent leave knowing the worst was the prep…Every day is new and fresh, and you get the opportunity to help people. I go home feeling pretty good about my day….My message to others is it's never too late to find a career you love."* [12]

Professional Association

■ Society of Gastroenterological Nurses and Associates (SGNA) (*www.sgna.org*)

Professional Journal

■ *Gastroenterology Nursing* (*www.gastroenterologynursing.com*). This is the only journal pertaining specifically to the gastroenterology field. It keeps readers up-to-date on GI-related procedures, developments, and techniques.

---

12 Terry Rindfleisch, "GI Joe: The Summer Nursing Internship," La Crosse Tribune as quoted on the Gundersen Lutheran Medical Center Web site *www.gundluth.org/web/misc/rsi. nsf/8a155831a7ba541b8625703600655a76/ 3faa8745c6ab3b20862571bf0050d913!OpenDocument* (accessed September 23, 2006).

GENETICS NURSE   *Also Known As:* GENETIC COUNSELORS

Definition: Genetic counselors work as members of a health care team, providing information and support to families who have members with birth defects or genetic disorders and to families who may be at risk for a variety of inherited conditions. They identify families at risk, investigate the problem present in the family, interpret information about the disorder, analyze inheritance patterns and risks of recurrence and review available options with the family.

Genetic counselors also provide supportive counseling to families, serve as patient advocates, and refer individuals and families to community or state support services. They serve as educators and resource people.[13]

Want Ad: Nurse to build strong relationships and excellent communication and collaboration with key members of the rare disease community. He/she will: (1) support patient advocacy efforts to create and manage educational materials, outreach programs, and other activities; (2) participate in educational activities designed to increase awareness of the company's presence in human genetic disease landscape of stakeholders; (3) provide support and resources for the patient community and their families; and (4) facilitate and enhance collaborative relationships with patient organizations, investigators, institutions, and other key decision makers strategic to product development (investigational and approved).

> **Quote from a Genetic Counselor:**
> *"My past experience in obstetrical nursing has been invaluable in working with teratogen exposures and running a teratogen information service. More recently, my credentials as a pediatric nurse practitioner have opened up new aspects of clinical genetics. For example, I now staff a fetal alcohol syndrome clinic without a physician—I do the history, physical exam, risk estimate, and counseling."[14]*

Professional Associations

■ Genetic Alliance (*www.geneticalliance.org*). Genetic Alliance increases the capacity of genetic advocacy groups to achieve their missions and leverages the voices of millions of individuals and families living with genetic conditions.

■ International Society of Nurses in Genetics (ISONG) (*www.isong.org*). ISONG is a nursing specialty organization dedicated to fostering the scientific and professional growth of nurses in human genetics. Its motto is: Caring for people's genetic health. The mission is: To foster the scientific, professional, and personal development of members in the management of genetic information.

---

13 "FAQs about Genetic Counselors and the NSGC," on the Web site of the National Society of Genetic Counselors, Inc. *www.nsgc.org/about/faq.cfm* (accessed September 23, 2006).

14 "Genetic Counselors with Multiple Degrees and Job Experiences," National Society of Genetic Counselors Web site, *www.nsgc.org/career/degrees_ex.cfm#nurse* (accessed September 23, 2006).

- National Society of Genetic Counselors (NSGC) (*www.nsgc.org*). Their biannual Professional Status Survey offers an inside view of the profession, from salary ranges to work environments to faculty status, and even to job satisfaction.

- The American Board of Genetic Counseling (ABGC) (*www.abgc.net*). This organization certifies genetic counselors and accredits genetic counseling training programs.

Professional Journal

- *The Journal of Genetic Counseling.* This is the official journal of the National Society of Genetic Counselors. It publishes peer-reviewed original research, essays, review articles, analysis of case material, and letters to the editor.

Media Coverage

Nurse Week Magazine has suggested that genetics nursing is becoming an increasingly influential field because of recent technological developments in the field of medicine. In "Treasure Map," Glen Fest writes that more and more nurses are pursuing education and credentials in genetics because of the field's burgeoning applicability to modern medicine. Even nurses in other areas are incorporating genetics education in their work because of a projected increase in the demand for genetic testing services and counseling.[15]

15 Glen Fest, "Treasure Map," *Nurse Week, www. nurseweek.com/news/features/03-12/genome.asp* (accessed August 16, 2006).

GYNECOLOGY/OBSTETRIC NURSE *Also Known As:* PERINATAL NURSE, LABOR AND DELIVERY NURSE, POST-PARTUM NURSE

Definition: Nurses in this field provide care, support, and education for female reproductive health, from a woman's first menstrual cycle through menopause. Nurses in this field provide care and support to women and their families before, during, and after childbirth. They also educate mothers about natural childbirth techniques and prenatal health, provide comfort during delivery, and teach mothers about mother-child bonding after the baby has been born.

Want Ad: Nurse practitioner will provide primary health care and specialized health services to an assigned caseload of neonates and their families. Diagnose medical conditions, plan and implement interventions, and evaluate patient responses under the direction of and in partnership with a collaborating physician or designated supervising physician.

> **Quote from an OB/GYN Nurse Working with High-Risk OB Patients:**
> *"They have that daily, almost hourly, fear or expectation that something is going to go terribly wrong with their baby... We spend 24 hours a day with them talking about their diagnoses and what's going on. We're very good....A lot of them (mothers) will come back and tell us how much it meant to get the treatment."*[16]

Professional Associations

- Association of Women's Health, Obstetric, and Neonatal Nurses (AWHONN) (*www.awhonn.org*).

- National Association of Neonatal Nurses (NANN) (*www.nann.org*).

- National Association of Neonatal Nursing (NANN) (*nann.org*). The NANN vision statement says that the lives of all newborns, infants, and their families will be improved through excellence in neonatal nursing practice, education, research and professional development. Its mission statement says that NANN is the professional voice that shapes neonatal nursing practice.

Professional Journal

- *The Journal of Obstetric, Gynecologic, and Neonatal Nursing* (*www.blackwellpublishing.com/journal.asp?ref=0884-2175&site=1*). This publication, which is written by nurses and for nurses, is the official journal of the Association of Women's Health, Obstetric, and Neonatal Nurses and offers comprehensive research and information relating to this field.

---

16 Phil McPeck, "Small Miracles," NurseWeek, *www.nurseweek.com/news/features/02-09/wright_web.asp* (accessed September 23, 2006).

HEAD AND NECK NURSE   *Also Known As:* OTORHINOLARYNGOLOGY NURSE

Definition: Nurses who provide care and support to patients undergoing medical and surgical procedures relating to disorders of the ears, the nose, the throat, and other structures of the head. Such diagnoses include cleft palate, ear and sinus disorders, allergy, plastic and reconstructive surgery, and head and neck cancer.

Want Ad: Head and neck surgery outpatient nursing experience preferred. Must have experience with sterile technique in procedural area. Good leadership and team building skills required. Must be willing to provide in-service and training to staff and health teaching to patients. Must be able to function independently and manage own nursing schedules. Must have good verbal and written skills. Must be willing to work under established guidelines.

Professional Association

■ Society of Otorhinolaryngology and Head-Neck Nurses (SOHN) (*www.sohnnurse.com*). SOHN fosters the professional growth of the otorhinolaryngology and head-neck nurse through education and research. SOHN is dedicated to advancing the professional growth and development of nurses dedicated to the specialty of ORL nursing. SOHN promotes innovations in practice, research, and health care policy initiatives.

Professional Journal

■ *ORL-Head and Neck Nursing* (*www.sohnnurse.com/pub_orl.html*). This quarterly journal is included in membership to SOHN or is available by subscription.

Media Coverage

About Face USA (*www.aboutfaceusa.org*) is a nonprofit organization dedicated to providing information, emotional support, and educational programs to individuals who have a facial disfigurement, and to their families. Its goal is to assist all persons with facial differences to have a positive self-image and positive self-esteem so that they can participate fully in their communities. They have information designed to educate new parents of babies born with cleft lip and palate, Crouzon or Apert Syndrome, and other craniosynostosis syndromes, Moebius Syndrome, Microtia, as well as cancer.[17]

---

17 "Making a World of Difference in a World of Facial Differences," About Face USA home page, *www.aboutfaceusa.org* (accessed September 23, 2006).

HEMATOLOGY NURSE

Definition: Nurses in this field provide care to people with hemophilia, sickle-cell, leukemia, and other diseases of the blood and blood forming organs. They also help to educate and care for the families of those with such diseases. Because these diseases are closely associated with cancer, these nurses often specialize in both hematology and oncology nursing.

Want Ad: Nurse for unit that specializes in the care of hematology/oncology patients. This includes, but is not limited to: leukemia, solid tumors, sickle cell disease, lymphomas, complications associated with chemotherapy, immunologic deficiencies, and respiratory illnesses. Opportunity to work collaboratively with a health care team dedicated to family-centered care.

Quote from a Hematology Nurse: *"I teach the parents how to stick their kids. I've taught parents of two- and three-year-olds. That's hard. It's emotionally hard; it's difficult to find a vein, difficult to get cooperation from a kid. But parents are part of a team. What's nice about working in hemophilia is the [factor] manufacturers support a lot of training programs and so does the National Hemophilia Foundation. I go to some sort of hemophilia training every month. I've had to become pretty sophisticated with the coagulation system."*[18]

Professional Associations

■ The Association of Pediatric Oncology Nurses (APON) (*www.apon.org*). APON aims to provide and promote expert practice in pediatric hematology/oncology nursing to its members and the public at large.

Professional Journals

■ *American Journal of Hematology*. This journal covers hematologic issues in both humans and in animals.

■ *Journal of Pediatric Oncology Nursing* (*jpo.sagepub.com*).

■ *Journal of Pediatric Hematology/Oncology* (*www.jpho-online.com*). This journal focuses on actual case studies to improve the diagnosis and treatment of cancer and hematological disorders in children.

Media Coverage

Hemophilia treatment has come a long way since the days when such patients were called *sufferers*, and their life expectancy was less than 30 years, according to the National Hemophilia Foundation. (NHF) (*www.hemophilia.org*). NHF is dedicated to finding better treatments and cures for bleeding and clotting disorders and to preventing their complications. They have a Nursing Working Group who offer a bibliography of print resources, a directory of their members, and downloadable slide presentations, including one on tattoos and body piercing. [19]

---

18 Janet Wells, "Blood Relations," *Nurse Week*, *www.nurseweek.com/news/features/03-07/blood.asp* (accessed August 16, 2006).

19 "Nurses Working Group," on the National Helophilia Foundation Web site, *www.hemophilia.org/NHFWeb/MainPgs/MainNHF.aspx?menuid=58&contentid=74* (accessed September 23, 2006).

INFUSION NURSE   *Also Known As:* IV TEAM MEMBER, IV THERAPY NURSE

Definition: Nurses in this field, also called intravenous nurses, provide care to patients by administering fluids, medication, or blood products through injections into patients' veins or by maintaining arterial catheters. These nurses are also responsible for monitoring patients, maintaining their tubing and bandages, and recognizing potential drug interactions and complications. Infusion nurses work in hospitals, long-term care centers, clinics, and home health agencies.

Want Ad: Clinical Liaison Nurse for a Home Infusion Department. This infusion department services patients who receive chemotherapy at home, and the liaison nurse will meet the patient/client at a local hospital, where the medication will be placed in the pump and the patient will return home. The liaison nurse will also follow up with patients at home. Treatment series can be two days to six weeks long. The CL nurse will also meet with hospital case managers, discharge planners, physicians and other clinicians, and may also be asked to present educational programs to them. The ideal candidate will be an RN with strong infusion experience, preferably chemo-certified. Home care experience would be helpful but is not required. Candidates should have a positive upbeat attitude with an ability to positively influence outcomes and create relationships.

Professional Associations

- Infusion Nurses Society (INS) (*www.ins1.org*) INS has a mission to develop and disseminate standards of practice, provide professional development opportunities and quality education, advance best practice through evidence-based research, support professional certification, and advocate for the public.

- Canadian Intravenous Nurses Association (*www.cina.ca*). The CINA's mission is to establish and promote standards of IV therapy to enhance patient care and safety, establish and promote educational programs, provide a forum for discussion, and link with other groups.

Professional Journal

- *The Journal of Infusion Nursing* (*www.journalofinfusionnursing.com*). This unique journal is the only one of its kind to exclusively deal with infusion therapy. This publication is the official journal of the Infusion Nurses Society.

Media Coverage

Established in 1993 by the Infusion Nurses Society, the Gardner Foundation provides grants and scholarships for INS members wishing to pursue careers in infusion therapy, and to promote infusion nursing research and educational programs. The foundation provides this funding in order to promote nursing excellence, patient advocacy, and advancement of the practice of infusion therapy. Through the annual scholarship awards, the foundation also seeks to recognize infusion nurses who are dedicated to advancing the quality infusion therapy, enhancing the specialty through rigorous standards of professional ethics, and promoting research and education in their specialty.[20]

---

20 "Overview of the Gardner Foundation," Infusion Nurses Society Web site, *www.ins1.org/gardner* (accessed August 16, 2006).

LACTATION CONSULTANT   *Also Known As:* BREASTFEEDING EDUCATOR

Definition: Nurses who help new mothers master breastfeeding and cope with problems that may arise. Additionally, they advocate for breastfeeding mothers in the workplace. They sponsor health policy initiatives to encourage the development of progressive breastfeeding programs and legislation.

Want Ad: To fulfill this role as a registered nurse, you'll assist in providing mother-baby services such as education, assessment, postpartum newborn care, lactation support, birth certificates, and newborn screening.

> **Quote from a Lactation Consultant:**
> *"Lactation consultants are relatively new members of the health care field. We are professional breastfeeding specialists trained to help mothers with latching difficulties, painful nursing, low milk production, or inadequate weight gain. A teacher as well as a counselor, supporting their efforts to learn how to feed their babies."*[21]

Professional Association

- International Lactation Consultant Association (ILCA) (*www.ilca.org*). The ILCA is the professional association for International Board Certified Lactation Consultants (IBCLCs) and other health care professionals who care for breastfeeding families. ILCA has more than 4,000 members from 50 nations, and includes a wide variety of health professionals, including IBCLCs, midwives, nurses, physicians and medical practitioners, childbirth educators, dietitians, and many more.

Professional Journal

- *Journal of Human Lactation* (*www.jhl.sagepub.com*). Written for professionals by professionals, the Journal of Human Lactation deals with the practical, everyday topics that nurses, lactation consultants, midwives, nutritionists/dieticians, public health and social workers, therapists, and physicians face, such as:

  - Patient counseling

  - Sociological and ethnic issues in dealing with breastfeeding

  - Practical discussions of diseases and conditions, such as mastitis, candida infections, engorgement

  - Care plans developed to help mothers and babies that require special care

  - Economics of breastfeeding

  - Educating physicians, hospital administration, and other departments

  - Practical training for lactation consultants

Media Coverage

According to *Nurse Week Magazine*, numerous studies have demonstrated a link between breastfeeding and baby health—including fewer bouts of respiratory ailments, ear infections, diarrhea, and a lower risk of SIDS. Furthermore, recent research suggests that breastfeeding is a factor in long-range health benefits in later life. Lactation consultants can play an important role in disseminating this kind of information to new mothers.[22]

---

21 Baby Center home page, *www.babycenter.com* (accessed August 16, 2006).

22 Donna Hemmila, "Got Milk?" *Nurse Week, www. nurseweek.com/news/Features/04-08/Breastfeeding. asp* (accessed August 16, 2006).

MEDICAL-SURGICAL NURSE   *Also Known As:* MED-SURG NURSE

Definition: Nurses who work in hospitals, acute care units, home care, and long-term care facilities to provide care for primarily adult patients before and after surgical procedures. They also attend to those who are being treated with pharmaceuticals (medications) to manage illness.

Want Ad: Responsible for planning, executing, and evaluating the nursing care given to Med/Surg patients. Has patient contact during the immediate pre-, intra-, and immediate postoperative periods, monitors the activities of all nursing staff during the procedure to which she or he is assigned, demonstrates clinical skills, and serves as team leader on-call emergency situations.

Professional Association

■ Academy of Medical-Surgical Nurses (*www.medsurgnurse.org*).

Professional Journal

■ *MEDSURG Nursing Journal (www.ajj.com/ services/pblshng/msnj/msnjmain.htm*). Known as the Journal of Adult Health, this peer-reviewed publication is published six times per year and is written to keep med-surg professionals informed to provide the best care possible.

Media Coverage

The annual Academy of Medical-Surgical Nurses Convention is a five-day long opportunity for nurses to network with colleagues, learn about the committees and special interest groups available to med-surg nurses, enjoy exhibits presented by leading health care companies, view poster presentations from around the country, and meet other nurses from all over the world. Convention organizers declare that, "You'll come away with a new and energized appreciation for yourself and the nursing profession."[23]

---

23 Academy of Medical-Surgical Nurses Web site, *www.medsurgnurse.org/cgi-bin/WebObjects/ AMSNMain.woa/1/wa/viewSection?s_ id=1073744075&ss_id=536873277&tName= conventionWelcome* (accessed August 16, 2006).

NEONATAL INTENSIVE CARE NURSE   *Also Known As:* NICU NURSE

Definition: Nurses who provide care for very sick or premature newborn babies and support their families during the clinical crises.

Want Ad: This unit sees babies who are born too soon, too small, or with serious illnesses or conditions. Infants are transported from within a 100-mile radius. The registered nurse provides optimal patient care, utilizing knowledge and skills within the context of evidence-based nursing practice and the theory of human caring. The registered nurse is accountable for individualized patient care and outcomes over an entire episode. When possible, the family or those significant to the family are considered as part of the assessment, planning, intervention, and evaluation efforts.

Quote from a Neonatal Intensive Care Nurse: *"I see cultural and ethnic differences in people born and raised outside this country and I'm sometimes able to perceive what they're thinking and how they may perceive their child's health in the NICU. Sometimes you question just how far we go to save a baby and think that it wouldn't survive if it was born in another country. But then you see a child leaving the NICU who you never thought would live a normal life, and it's a great feeling knowing that you played a role in saving that child."* [24]

Professional Association

■ National Association of Neonatal Nurses (*www.nann.org*)

Professional Journals

■ *Journal of Neonatal Nursing* (*www.neonatal-nursing.co.uk*).

■ *The Journal of Perinatal and Neonatal Nursing.* Each issue of this peer-reviewed journal pertains to a single topic, which is then covered comprehensively.

Media Coverage

The March of Dimes organization reports that the number of preterm and low birth-weight births is on the rise. The March of Dimes's stated mission is to improve the health of babies by preventing birth defects, premature birth, and infant mortality. The organization sponsors Walk America, an annual event that raises funds, augments awareness, and supports research efforts across the country. Since 1970, WalkAmerica participants have raised more than $1.5 billion, thereby bringing the March of Dimes closer to saving all babies from premature birth and other serious infant health problems. [25]

---

24 Ruth Carol, "Neonatal Need." MinorityNurse.com, *http://minoritynurse.com/features/nurse_emp/ 11-01-03a.html* (accessed August 16, 2006).

25 Walk America Web site, *www.walkamerica.org/ walk2005_about.asp* (accessed August 16, 2006).

NEPHROLOGY NURSE   Also Known As: DIALYSIS NURSE, RENAL NURSE

Definition: Nurses in this field care for patients of all ages who are experiencing, or are at risk for, kidney disease. Often, patients' kidneys have failed and they need to have toxic byproducts removed from their circulatory system by mechanical means. Sometimes this need is acute and short term. More likely the condition is chronic and it must be done on a regular basis, two or three times a week.

Want Ad: Demonstrated leadership competencies and skills for the position, including excellent communication, customer service, continuous quality improvement, relationship development, results orientation, team building, motivating employees, performance management, and decision making. Demonstrated management skills necessary to provide leadership in the supervision of dialysis personnel and to ensure the delivery of maximum quality care to all patients. Employees must meet the necessary requirements of Ishihara's Color Blindness test as a condition of employment.

> **Quote from a Nephrology Nurse:**
> *"Chronic renal failure affects every aspect of a patient's life—their diet, their family life, their work. If you ask me why I've been in nephrology for 25 years plus, I'd say it's because these patients are the most courageous in the world."*[26]

Professional Associations

■ American Nephrology Nurses Association (ANNA) (*www.annanurse.org*)

■ Canadian Association of Nephrology Nurses and Technologists (*www.cannt.ca*)

Professional Journal

■ *Journal of the American Nephrology Nurses Association (www.nephrologynursing.net).* The Nephrology Nursing Journal is a refereed clinical and scientific resource that provides current information on a wide variety of subjects to facilitate the practice of professional nephrology nursing. Its purpose is to disseminate information on the latest advances in research, practice, and education to nephrology nurses to positively influence the quality of care they provide. The *Nephrology Nursing* Journal is designed to meet the educational and information needs of nephrology nurses in a variety of roles at all levels of practice. Review of critical issues promoting the advancement of nephrology nursing practice.

Media Coverage

The American Nephrology Nurses Association (along with 56 other specialty nursing associations) participates in a partnership with the John A. Hartford Foundation Institute for Geriatric Nursing and the American Nurses Association, known as the Nurse Competence in Aging (NCA) initiative. This initiative focuses on improving the quality of health care for older adults by enhancing the knowledge, skills, and attitudes of over 400,000 nurses associated with NCA. The primary goals of this initiative include enhancing the geriatric activities of national specialty nursing associations, promoting gerontologic nursing certification, and providing an online geriatric nursing resource center. The NCA sponsored Web site (www.geron-urseonline.org) provides up-to-date, practical resources regarding care of the aging adult.[27]

---

26 Karen Steib, "Careers in Nephrology Nursing," MinorityNurse.com, *http://minoritynurse.com/features/nurse_emp/10-25-05d.html* (accessed August 16, 2006).

27 "Spotlight on Older Adults," American Nephrology Nurses' Association Web site, *www.annanurse.org/cgi-bin/WebObjects/ANNANurse.woa/1/wa/viewSection?wosid=obcu32dsNhtY2GG8nXx6KW70aX7&tName=agingDefault&s_id=1073744385&ss_id=1* (accessed August 16, 2006).

NEUROSCIENCE NURSE   *Also Known As:* NEUROLOGY NURSE, NEUROSURGERY NURSE

Definition: Nurses who provide care and support for patients diagnosed with dysfunctions of the nervous system, including spinal cord injuries, head trauma, and seizures. They can work in hospitals, especially in the acute phase of these conditions, or in free-standing centers dedicated to this specialty.

Want Ad #1: Position on the neuro-science unit which provides diagnostic, therapeutic and preventative care for patients, ranging in age from newborn to young adult, with nervous system disorders. Long-term EEG monitoring, seizure management, chemotherapy, and post-operative care after brain and spinal surgery also provided by this unit.

Want Ad #2: Unit cares primarily for adult neurology patients and offers seizure monitoring for children. Nurses do valuable post-ictal exams as directed by the attending physicians to ascertain focus of disease process. Unit equipped with cardiac telemetry; ten rooms equipped with hard-wired technology to provide continuous pulse oxImetry, blood-pressure measurement, and EKG.

Want Ad #3: The clinical access nurse acts as a coordinator of care for newly diagnosed neuro-surgical patients, to facilitate patient transfers to the hospital, post-surgical treatment, and to improve referral relationships. Centered within the Dept. of Neurosurgery, this nurse also helps to establish, promote, and coordinate a multidisciplinary and collaborative program with physicians (neurosurgeons, neurologists, neuro-oncologists, radiation oncologists, etc.), NPs, PAs, other patient care providers, and patient care coordinators.

Professional Associations

- American Association of Neuroscience Nurses (AANN) (*www.aann.org*)

- Neuroscience Nursing Consultant (*www.neuronurse.com*)

Professional Journal

- *Journal of Neuroscience Nursing* (*www.aann.org/journal*) This bimonthly publication is the official Journal of the American Association of Neuroscience Nurses. Although its focus is on the neuroscience field, it is intended for general use throughout any health care institution.

Media Coverage

AANN gives nurses, their colleagues, patients, and families the chance to celebrate the spirit of neuroscience nursing through the Spirit of Neuroscience Nursing Photo Contest. Judged annually, submissions that convey the spirit of neuroscience are accepted throughout the year and are later shared through AANN media.

Pictures received by March 15 of any given year are entered into that year's contest, with the photos displayed during the AANN Annual Meeting in April. During that time, attendees vote on their favorite and the individual who submitted the winning image receives a complimentary conference registration to next year's meeting.[28]

---

28 "Spirit of Neuroscience Nursing Photo Contest," American Society of Neuroscience Nurses Web site, *www.aann.org/about/SpiritContest.html* (accessed August 16, 2006).

NURSE ANESTHETIST

Also Known As: CERTIFIED REGISTERED NURSE ANESTHETIST

Definition: Nurses who administer local or general anesthesia to patients undergoing surgery or other procedures in settings ranging from operating rooms and dental offices to outpatient surgical centers.

Want Ad: Seeking a CRNA/Nurse Anesthetist to administer anesthesia to patients undergoing a surgical procedure according to the anesthesia plan defined by the attending physician. This position requires advanced experience in the administration of anesthesia to high-risk oncology patients. Complex cases include prolonged abdominal surgery, thoracotomy, hepatic resection, major vascular surgery, extensive reconstructive surgery, as well as a variety of experimental procedures and robotic surgery.

Quotes from Nurse Anesthetists:

"This career allows nurses to do what we got into the profession to do. The patients' lives are in our hands and we are there to care for them."

"As a nurse anesthetist, I can actually write orders for other people to implement. I can decide that an intervention is necessary and have that decision carried out."[29]

Professional Association

- American Association of Nurse Anesthetists (AANA) (*www.aana.com*). Founded in 1931, AANA is the professional association for more than 35,000 certified registered nurse anesthetists (CRNAs) and student nurse anesthetists. CRNAs are advanced practice nurses who are the hands-on providers of approximately 65 percent of all anesthesia given in the United States each year. They administer every type of anesthetic, work in every type of practice setting, and provide care for every type of surgery or procedure, from open heart to cataract to pain management.

Professional Journals

- *The Internet Journal of Anesthesiology* (*www.ispub.com/ostia/index.php?xml FilePath=journals/ija/front.xml*). This peer-reviewed journal is published online.

- *Canadian Journal of Anesthesia* (*www.cja-jca.org*).

Media Coverage

CRNAs are the sole anesthesia providers in approximately two-thirds of all rural hospitals in the United States, according to the AANA. Of the 24 million anesthetics given annually, about 20 percent are administered by CRNAs practicing independently and 80 percent by CRNAs in collaboration with physician anesthesiologists, says AANA. They are working in the oldest of the advanced nursing specialties. There are more than 30,000 CRNAs in practice nationwide.[30]

---

29 Marquand, Barbara. "From RN to CRNA." MinorityNurse.com, *http://minoritynurse.com/ features/nurse_emp/08-18-03.html* (accessed August 16, 2006).

30 "Your Nursing Career: A Look at the Facts," American Association of Colleges of Nursing Education Center Web site, *www.aacn.nche.edu/ Education/career.htm* (accessed September 23, 2006).

ONCOLOGY NURSE   *Also Known As:* CANCER NURSE, CHEMOTHERAPY NURSE

Definition: Nurses in this field provide care and support for patients diagnosed with cancer. These nurses are responsible for administering chemotherapy and managing symptoms related to cancer illnesses.

Want Ad: Promotes and restores patients' health by completing the nursing process; collaborating with physicians and multidisciplinary team members; providing physical and psychological support to patients, friends, and families; supervising assigned team members. Duties: identifies patient care requirements; establishes a compassionate environment; promotes patient's independence by establishing patient care goals, teaching patient, friends, and family to understand condition, medications, and self-care skills, as well as answering questions; assures quality of care; resolves patient problems and needs by utilizing multidisciplinary team strategies.

Quote from an Oncology Nurse:
"Oncology nursing is a great field to get into, especially if you want to be involved in improving the health of minority populations. People of color are at a disproportionately high risk for nearly all types of cancer." [31]

Professional Associations

- Association of Pediatric Oncology Nurses (*www.apon.org*)

- International Society of Nurses in Cancer Care (*www.isncc.org*)

- Oncology Nursing Society (*www.ons.org*)

- Canadian Association of Nurses in Oncology (*www.cos.ca/cano/index.html*)

- CancerSourceRN.com (*www.cancersourcern.com*)

- Onconurse.com (*www.onconurse.com*)

Professional Journals

- *Clinical Journal of Oncology Nursing* (*www.ons.org/publications/journals/CJON/*). As the official journal of the Oncology Nursing Society, this publication, offered six times per year, strives to improve awareness and care in the field of oncology.

- *Journal of Pediatric Oncology Nursing*

Media Coverage

For many children, spending a night out at the movie theater is fun, commonplace pastime. But for youngsters in hospital cancer wards, who are more threatened by infection in public places, it is a pleasure they are often unable to enjoy. CBS News recently featured a story about a not-for-profit organization meant to fill that gap.

Reel Angels, begun by oncology ward volunteer Jessica Angel, benefits hospital-bound children by bringing them first-run family films. Having a red carpet experience (complete with snacks, the movie screening, and occasionally a visit from the movie's stars) allows children to temporarily escape their monotonous surroundings, gray walls, ominous equipment, and tinted windows. (*www.reelangels.org/Mission.html*)[32]

---

31 "Susan Wessling, "Closing the Cancer Gap," MinorityNurse.Com *www.minoritynurse.com/features/nurse_emp/01-27-02d.html* (accessed August 16, 2006).

32 "Bringing Hollywood to Hospitals: Charity Turns Children's Hospital Rooms Into Screening Rooms, CBS News, New York, January 28, 2006, *www.cbsnews.com/stories/2006/01/27/earlyshow/saturday/main1248606.shtml* (accessed August 16, 2006).

OPERATING ROOM NURSE   *Also Known As:* OR NURSE, RECOVERY ROOM NURSE,
POST ANESTHESIA CARE UNIT (PACU) NURSE

Definition: Nurses in this field provide care and support to patients before, during, and after surgery. These nurses are responsible for maintaining a sterile environment in the operating room, monitoring the patient during surgery, and coordinating care throughout the process. They are also responsible for making sure the OR team provides the patient with the best care possible.

Want Ad #1: Responsible for the nursing care of the perioperative patient. Acts as the patient's advocate and works as a member of the surgical team, is knowledgeable in the areas of aseptic technique, infection control, emergency procedures, and general operating room procedures. Able to work with highly technical, ever-changing equipment, in an accelerated pace.

Want Ad #2: RN will observe, assess, and record symptoms, reactions, and progress in patients.

- Assist physicians during surgeries, treatments, and examinations.
- Administer medications.
- Assist in rehabilitation.
- Develop and manage nursing care plans.
- Instruct patients and their families in proper care.
- Help individuals and groups take steps to improve or maintain their health.
- Arranging patients for hospital admission and laboratory services.

Quotes from Operating Room Nurses: *"It [perioperative nursing] is an ever-changing environment. Every day is new. If you're not interested in the same old same-old, if you truly want to be a fully independent practitioner, this field is for you."*

"It's unpredictable. It's always 'let's go, let's go.' But it's exciting rather than stressful. I love the rush of it all. Even after 12 years as a perioperative nurse, I can still hear the passion in my own voice."[33]

Professional Associations

- Association of Perioperative Registered Nurses (*www.aorn.org*)
- American Society of PeriAnesthesia Nurses (*www.aspan.org*)

Professional Journal

- *Journal of PeriAnesthesia Nursing* (*www.jopan.org*). The goal of this journal is for perianesthesia nurses to share their experiences so that others may learn from them.

---

33 Sylvia Fotti, "Peri Opportunities." MinorityNurse.com, *http://minoritynurse.com/features/nurse_emp/09-17-02b.html* (accessed August 16, 2006).

OPHTHALMIC NURSE   *Also Known As:* EYE CLINIC NURSE

Definition: Nurses who provide care and support for patients diagnosed with disorders of the eyes, including blindness, visual impairment, cataracts, glaucoma, or eye trauma.

Want Ad: Experienced registered nurse needed. We are dedicated to increasing the independence and mobility of people who are blind or visually impaired through the use of specially bred and trained Seeing Eye dogs. Candidate must be a licensed RN. Experience with diabetics a real plus.

Professional Association

■ American Society of Ophthalmic Registered Nurses (*webeye.ophth.uiowa.edu/asorn/*)

Professional Journal

■ *Insight: The Journal of the American Society of Ophthalmic Registered Nurses* (*webeye.ophth. uiowa.edu/asorn/INSIGHT/Guidelines.htm*). This journal contains original articles relating to the interests of ophthalmic nursing.

Media Coverage

Marijuana has been shown to lower the intraocular pressure in some eyes in a few studies but this is generally not used clinically. Studies in the early 1970s showed that marijuana, when smoked, lowers intraocular pressure in people with normal pressure and those with glaucoma. The first patient in the U.S. federal government's Compassionate Investigational New Drug program, Robert Randall, was afflicted with glaucoma and had successfully fought charges of marijuana cultivation because it was deemed a medical necessity (*U.S. v. Randall*) in 1976.[34]

---

34 "Glaucoma: Drugs," Wikipedia, *http://en.wikipedia. org/wiki/Glaucoma* (accessed August 16, 2006).

ORTHOPAEDIC NURSE *Also Known As:* ORTHO NURSE

Definition: Nurses who provide care and support for patients with musculoskeletal diseases, educating the patients and the families about self-care and available support systems.

Want Ad #1: 40-hour/week position in the Orthopaedic Clinic, a high-volume clinic that offers comprehensive pediatric care for children and young adults with a wide range of developmental, congenital, neuromuscular, and post traumatic problems of the musculoskeletal system. Requires the ability to be flexible in a collaborative setting working with multiple orthopaedic specialists, orthopaedic surgeons, nurse practitioners, nurses, outpatient administrative staff, and inpatient staff.

Want Ad #2: Requires a licensed registered nurse. New grads are very welcome to apply. Excellent orientation program for new grads. Common procedures include total joint replacement, general surgery that includes fractures and oncological procedures with limb salvaging and spinal surgeries; telemetry monitoring available Pilot unit for many innovations in nursing, including care of patients who have had minimally invasive hip surgery and a nationwide global pain initiative.

Professional Associations

- National Association of Orthopaedic Nurses (*www.orthonurse.org*)

- Canadian Orthopaedic Nurses Association (*www.cona-nurse.org*)

Professional Journal

- *Orthopaedic Nursing Journal* (*www.orthopaedicnursing.com*). This international journal is dedicated to providing continuing education for orthopaedic nurses.

Media Coverage

The years from 2002 to 2011 have been named the Bone and Joint Decade in a new media campaign ("Good Moves for Life). This touches the more than 35 million Americans who suffer from restricted movement due to some type of musculoskeletal disorder, ranging from arthritis to osteoporosis to sports traumas. The Bone and Joint Decade, an international initiative, aims to increase awareness, augment research, and further disseminate information on bone and joint disorders. As a result, U.S. patient and physician health care organizations, government agencies, and industry representatives are all working together to help prevent future bone and joint disorders, and to improve the quality of life for those affected.[35]

---

35 "Good Moves for Life," Bone and Joint Decade Web site, *www.usbjd.org/index.cfm* (accessed August 16, 2006).

PEDIATRIC NURSE   *Also Known As:* PEDS NURSE

Definition: Nurses who specialize in the care and treatment of young patients, ranging in age from infancy to late teens. They may specialize in areas such as immunology or oncology.

Want Ad: The pediatric nurse is a registered professional nurse who develops expertise in assessing, planning, implementing, and re-evaluating the need of the pediatric patient and their families. Utilizing the nursing process, collaborates with physician in providing the delivery of safe, quality health care while recognizing physical, psychosocial and emotional needs of the patient/family. Encourages family participation in the decision-making processes surrounding the direction followed in the delivery of the service to the patient/client. Maintains skill level by utilizing current pediatric trends and practices.

Professional Associations

- American Pediatric Surgical Nurses Association (*www.apsna.com*)

- Society of Pediatric Nurses (*www.pedsnurses.org*)

- Northeast Pediatric Cardiology Nurses Association (*npcna.org*)

- National Association of Pediatric Nurse Practitioners (*www.napnap.org*)

Professional Journals

- *Pediatric Nursing* (*www.pediatricnursing.net*). Published six times per year, this journal includes regular features on research, legislation, and other information pertaining to pediatric nursing.

- *Journal for Specialists in Pediatric Nursing* (*www.blackwellpublishing.com/journal.asp?ref=1539-0136*). This popular journal makes an effort to have all feature articles be directly relevant to the field. This is accomplished with a section called "How do I apply this information to nursing practice?"

Media Coverage

A recent report published by the *International Journal of Pediatric Obesity* suggests that the rate of childhood obesity throughout the world will balloon during the current decade. Some estimates suggest that by 2010, almost half of all the children in North and South America will be overweight, compared to about one-third today.

Nurses can prevent obesity by helping children maintain appropriate body weight as they grow. Measures to decrease the threat of an overweight childhood include promoting combinations of healthy lifestyle habits—for instance, good nutrition as well as physical activity—rather than focusing on any one aspect responsible for weight gain.[36]

---

36 Christina Calamaro, "A Weighty Challenge." *Nurse Week*, www.nurseweek.com/news/Features/05-04/Clinical_Obesity.asp (accessed August 16, 2006).

PLASTIC SURGERY NURSE

Definition: Nurses who care for patients undergoing cosmetic procedures anywhere on the body. These procedures can be elective, such as dermabrasion to assure a smooth complexion, to more complicated procedures necessary for physical and psychological well-being, such as facial reconstruction after an accident or breast replacement after a mastectomy.

Want Ad: Plastic surgeon seeks top professional for skincare and cosmetic surgery practice. The best candidate is a committed, loyal, passionate, team player who will work with the physician and the management team to: deliver excellence in patient education and surgery, develop a committed team of clinicians, attain national accreditation, implement treatment protocols and operating standards, and assist with special projects. Excellent customer service, knowledge of plastic surgery, three years OR and clinical management, OR/ recovery room experience, and experience developing and training an effective team is required. Prior aesthetics and private practice is a plus.

Professional Association

- American Society of Plastic Surgical Nurses (*www.aspsn.org*)

Professional Journal

- *Plastic Surgical Nursing*. A peer-reviewed journal for nurses in plastic and reconstructive surgical nursing practice. The journal includes clinical articles covering a variety of surgical procedures, as well as patient education techniques and research findings. Additionally, continuing education contact hours are provided in every issue.

Media Coverage

Operation Smile is a private, not-for-profit volunteer medical services organization providing reconstructive surgery and related health care to children. Their motto is "Changing Lives One Smile at a Time." Their mission is to repair childhood facial deformities while building public and private partnerships that advocate for sustainable health care systems for children and families. Roma Downey of the TV show "Touched by an Angel" is their spokesperson. Videos of her supporting their cause are featured on their home page along with videos showing the success of the volunteer medical teams.[37]

---

37 Operation Smile home page, *www.operationsmile.org* (accessed August 16, 2006).

PSYCHIATRIC NURSE   *Also Known As:* MENTAL HEALTH NURSE, NURSE
PSYCHOTHERAPIST, COUNSELOR

Definition: Nurses who support the mental, emotional, and behavioral health of patients with acute or chronic needs.

Want Ad #1: Counseling service has a history of providing quality mental health services to the local community. Experienced staff serving over a thousand clients a year. Collegial atmosphere with workable, motivated client base. Psychotherapy with adults and couples. Would prefer, but it is not necessary, experience with children, adolescents, and families or with substance abusers.

Want Ad #2: Member of a multidisciplinary team in a program of assertive community treatment providing mobile treatment psychiatric and case management services. Provides individual, group, family, and dual diagnosis and case management services. Responsible for maintaining medical records and developing treatment plans. Provides nursing services on team—administers IM meds, coordinates lab services, takes vital signs; blood sugar levels using glucometer.

Professional Associations

- American Psychiatric Nurses Association (APNA) (*www.apna.org*)

- Association of Child and Adolescent Psychiatric Nursing (ACAPN) (*www.ispn-psych.org/html/acapn.html*)

- International Society of Psychiatric-Mental Health Nurses (ISPN) (*www.ispn-psych.org*) ISPN offers registered psychiatric nurses the opportunity to obtain continuing education credits via online accredited courses

- Canadian Federation of Mental Health Nurses (CFMHN) (*www.cfmhn.org*)

Professional Journal

- *Journal for Advanced Practice Psychiatric Nurses* (*www.blackwellpublishing.com/journal.asp?ref=0031-5990&site=1*). In addition to regular features on the biology of mental disorders, this journal also provides research to improve the knowledge of psychiatric nurses.

PULMONARY CARE NURSE   *Also Known As:* RESPIRATORY CARE NURSE

Definition: Nurses who work with patients with diseases that affect the lungs, including chronic obstructive pulmonary disease (COPD), tuberculosis, asthma, respiratory failure, and cystic fibrosis. They also work with patients who are being weaned off ventilators. While pulmonary care nurses are often specialized critical care nurses in the hospital, they can also work with patients in the home, assisting with pain management from diseases like lung cancer and emphysema.

Want Ad: The registered nurse opening is in our Respiratory Care Unit (RCU) of the Critical Care Department. The fully monitored RCU provides quality nursing care for adult patients with a primary respiratory diagnosis. Conditions of patients admitted to the RCU include but are not limited to: acute bacterial infections, acute viral infections, acute respiratory failure (non-ventilated) asthma, hypovolemia, pneumonia, pulmonary embolism. To fulfill this role as a registered nurse, you'll work alongside other highly experienced RCU staff including other RNs, LPNs, CNAs, and unit assistants to provide clinical monitoring of vital signs, pulse oximetry, physical assessment, multidisciplinary collaboration, education and discharge planning.

Professional Association

- American Association for Respiratory Care (*www.aarc.org*). AARC represents more than 37,000 members who provide clinical respiratory care, diagnosis, rehabilitation, neonatal and pediatric, sleep, adult critical care, and long-term care to patients in the United States and throughout the world. The AARC's mission is to advance the science, technology, ethics, and art of respiratory care through research and education for its members and to teach the general public about pulmonary health and disease prevention.

Professional Journals

- *Heart & Lung—The Journal of Acute and Critical Care.* This publication presents original, peer-reviewed articles on techniques, advances, investigations, and observations in acute and critical care. The journal's acute care articles focus on critical care provided for a short time, often outside the intensive care unit. Other sections focus on infection control, neonatal nursing, advanced practice nursing, pharmacotherapy, ethical issues, and patient education.

- *Respiratory Care Journal (www.rcjournal.com).* This is a peer-reviewed journal published by the American Association for Respiratory Care (AARC), and is available online each month.

Media Coverage

Health Day News reported that U.S. researchers have identified an overactive protein that may play an important role in causing cystic fibrosis (CF). Researchers at Johns Hopkins say the protein kills an important chloride transporter in the cells of CF patients. This leads to a dangerous buildup of mucous in several organs, which can aggravate the malnutrition, chronic lung infection, and lung damage frequently seen in CF patients.

In this test-tube study, researchers used RNA interference to successfully intercept signals sent out by the protein which prevented cell damage. These findings show promise for restoring cells to normal status in CF patients.[38]

---

38 "Rogue Protein May Be Key to Cystic Fibrosis," July 7, 2006, HealthDayNews, *www.healthday.com/view.cfm?id=533626* (accessed August 16, 2006).

RADIOLOGY NURSE   *Also Known As:* CARDIAC CATH LAB NURSE

Definition: Nurses who provide care and support to patients undergoing diagnosis in radiation imaging environments, including ultrasonography, magnetic resonance, and radiation oncology. These nurses aid in the diagnosis of heart disease and help administer interventional procedures. They are responsible for aiding doctors in the implantation of pacemakers and implantable cardioverter-defibrillators (ICDs) and must keep up on the latest technologies of this rapidly moving field.

Want Ad: Fundamental knowledge of the medical specialties, with an emphasis in cardiology. Ability to scrub, circulate, and perform hemodynamic monitoring preferred. Communicates effectively with patients, physicians, and other medical center personnel. Excellent telephone technique and triage skills. Bilingual preferred. Ability to function as a team member. Uses culturally sensitive good manners, respect, and polite communications. Open to creative and innovative approaches to providing care.

Professional Association

■ American Radiological Nurses Association (*www.arna.net*)

Professional Journal

■ *Journal of Radiology Nursing* (*www.radiologynursing.org*). This journal aims to make all nurses equipped to provide the absolute best care by being informed and inspired by the field of radiology.

Media Coverage

Approximately 400,000 Americans have multiple sclerosis (MS) and about 200 are diagnosed every week, according to the National Multiple Sclerosis Society. With confirmation of lesions using magnetic resonance imaging, MS is now often diagnosed after only one episode, eliminating the need to wait for a second flare-up that affects a different part of the central nervous system. Early diagnosis can significantly speed up treatment, especially given that years can pass between first and second attacks. Disease-modifying drugs such as beta interferon have also proven to be highly beneficial if given in the disease's earliest stages.[39]

---

39 MR Imaging Accuracy Questioned in Diagnosing MS," Radiological Society of North America Magazine Web site, *www.rsna.org/Publications/ rsnanews/july06/mr_july06.cfm* (accessed August 16, 2006).

REHABILITATION NURSE   *Also Known As:* REHAB NURSE

Definition: Nurses in this field provide physical and emotional support to patients and the families of patients with illnesses or disabilities that affect their ability to function normally and that may alter their lifestyle.

Want Ad: When children or adolescents experience a traumatic injury, their lives become dramatically altered. The resulting physical, cognitive, and behavioral problems interfere with numerous aspects of their lives. Normal activities of childhood—participating in school, relating with peers and contributing to family life—pose special challenges to children with physical or brain injuries. The program serves infants, children and adolescents who have neurological or musculoskeletal impairment resulting from traumatic injury, illness or malignancy. Individualized programs are offered to those whose disabilities are of recent onset and who demonstrate an ability to improve in such areas as self-care, mobility, safety, communication, cognition, and behavior.

Professional Associations

■ Association of Rehabilitation Nurses (ARN) (*www.rehabnurse.org*). ARN's mission is to promote and advance professional rehabilitation nursing practice through education, advocacy, collaboration, and research to enhance the quality of life for those affected by disability and chronic illness.

■ International Association of Rehabilitation Professionals (*rehabpro.org*)

Professional Journal

■ *Rehabilitation Nursing (www.rehabnurse.org/ profresources/index.html)*. This journal is rated by members as one of the most valuable benefits of belonging to ARN. It provides up-to-date information on a broad spectrum of rehabilitation nursing topics; articles ranging from administration and research to education and clinical topics; nursing perspectives, resource reviews, and product information; and continuing education opportunities in every issue.

Media Coverage

After suffering a stroke, General John Shalikashvili, chairman of the Joint Chiefs of Staff under President Bill Clinton, received treatment at Harborview Medical Center in Seattle, Washington. A video of his description of his recovery, narrated by him with his son Brant, was played at ARN's 31st Annual Educational conference. Shalikashvili's son said: "The ones that really work with you are the nurses… Whatever the therapy was, that was their focus…It is truly a noble field. It has brought my Dad back."[40]

---

40 "A Message of Thanks," Association of Rehabilitation Nurses home page, *www.rehabnurse.org* (accessed August 16, 2006).

KAPLAN

SUBACUTE NURSE

Definition: Nurses in this field provide comprehensive care for patients who have been hospitalized with an acute illness or injury. Oftentimes, this care is more intensive than long-term and traditional nursing home care, but less intensive than acute care

Want Ad #1: Performs specific patient care procedures (such as, phlebotomy, wound care, gastric and urethral tube insertion, and bedside testing) under the direction of a licensed nurse and performs specific support-procedures for the operation of a nursing or clinical department. Operates patient monitoring systems.

Want Ad #2: This position requires a current registered nurse license issued in the state where the person will practice, and the candidate must be a graduate of an approved school of nursing. Up-to-date physical assessment skills and comprehensive knowledge of nursing principles are also required. Recent experience in geriatric or rehabilitative nursing and experience in supervisory capacity are preferred. Prior experience with medical-surgical, ICU, and/or ventilator preferred, but not required.

Want Ad #3: This position is responsible for the assessment of patients' conditions, monitoring responses to treatment, and consulting with medical staff to plan nursing care. Administration of medications and IVs according to policy. Supervision of LVN and nursing assistants in accordance with nursing practice.

- Education: BSN preferred.

- Requirements: Six months experience in acute care setting and subacute. RN license and BLS required.

  Professional Association

- National Association for Subacute/Post Acute Care (*www.naspac.net*)

SURGICAL NURSE

Also Known As: PERIOPERATIVE NURSE or they are identified by their function in the Operating Room process: SCRUB NURSES pass sterile instruments and supplies to surgeons, CIRCULATING NURSES work outside the sterile field, and RN FIRST ASSISTANTS deliver direct surgical care to patients.

Definition: Nurses in this field provide care and support to patients before, during, and after surgery.

Want Ad #1: NP experience as a surgical first assistant with suturing skills strongly preferred. Participates in the coordination of urgent, complex, and routine admissions, transfers, and discharges. Educates patients/families regarding medical and surgical procedures related to specialty and plan of care. Develops educational material to be utilized by patients, families, and ancillary staff involved in the care to the surgical patient. Maintains accessibility and availability to provide ongoing consultation/education to health professionals regarding patient care issues. Develops and collects data in trends utilization/lab/diagnostics/procedural interventions. Develops and/or presents educations programs to hospital staff, members of the community, and professional organizations. Supports, facilitates, and participates in clinical research within specialty area.

Want Ad #2: Performs admission evaluation: obtaining basic medical information and history, reviewing patient's medical record, and reporting deviations from normal findings to attending physician. Provides preoperative and blood transfusion information. Assists with procedures consistent with practice guidelines. Transcribes standard post-operative orders. Assists with patient discharge in conjunction with social worker, pharmacist, and physical therapist. Dictates discharge and transfer summaries.

Professional Association

■ Association of Perioperative Registered Nurses (AORN) (*www.aorn.org*). The professional organization of perioperative registered nurses, whose mission is to support registered nurses in achieving optimal outcomes for patients undergoing operative and other invasive procedures.

Professional Journal

■ *AORN Journal (www.aorn.org/journal).* One of the most visible benefits of AORN membership is a subscription to the AORN Journal, an award-winning source of perioperative nursing information. The journal is published monthly and provides articles on clinical management and research topics; updates on clinical issues, and OR nursing law and legislation; and features such as book reviews, practical innovations, board reports, conference reports, and home study programs.

Members of the AORN have developed the Perioperative Nursing Data Set (PNDS)—the only American Nurses Association (ANA)–recognized, standardized language that meets the specific needs of the perioperative nurse clinician. The PNDS is a nursing vocabulary that addresses the perioperative patient experience from preadmission to discharge. It consists of 74 nursing diagnoses, 133 nursing interventions, and 28 nurse-sensitive patient outcomes. The guiding premise of the language development effort was that it would assist perioperative nurses document nursing care while providing a foundation for examining and evaluating the quality and effectiveness of that care.[41]

---

41 "Perioperative Nursing Data Set," Association of Perioperative Registered Nurses Web site, *www.aorn.org/research/faqs.htm* (accessed August 16, 2006).

TELEMETRY NURSE   *Also Known As:* PROGRESSIVE CARE UNIT (PCU) NURSE, STEP-DOWN UNIT NURSE

Definition: Nurses who care for patients connected to machines that measure heart rate, blood pressure, and breathing rate, as well as blood-oxygen level and electrocardiogram information. The machines send data to computer screens. Telemetry nurses read and interpret this information to help better direct patient care activities.

Want Ad: The Telemetry nurse's responsibilities include:

- Assesses, plans, and evaluates patient care needs, including discharge planning.

- Administers medications, changes dressings, cleans wounds, monitors vital signs

- Serves as primary coordinator of all disciplines

- Instructs and educates patients and families

- Demonstrates critical-thinking skills, decisive judgment, and the ability to work with minimal supervision in a fast-paced environment

- Performs work that requires frequent standing, bending, reaching, squatting, kneeling, moving, and lifting of patients and/or equipment up to 50 pounds

Professional Association

- American Association of Critical-Care Nurses (AACN) (*www.aacn.org*)

Professional Contribution

AACN "lobbies" in the form of endorsing legislation and supporting coalitions' efforts that AACN joins. Priority is given to specific nursing issues; however, many of the public policy issues AACN addresses are global public health/community issues such as collaboration with organizations such as the American Red Cross, the United Network for Organ Sharing, the National Kidney Foundation, and the Coalition for Consumer Health & Safety.[42]

---

42 "Public Policy Overview," American Association of Critical Care Nurses home page, *www.aacn.org/AACN/pubpolcy.nsf/ad0ca3b3bdb4f3328825698100 6fa692/a7f172f2b72a6b1b88256a4c0062f92f?Open Document* (accessed September 23, 2006).

TRANSCULTURAL NURSE

Definition: Nurses who provide specific care to individuals and families of different cultural groups (often immigrants and refugees) based on the specific physical, emotional, and spiritual care needs dictated by those cultures.

> **Quotes from Transcultural Nurses:**
> *"In order for us to understand the issues of populations of color and provide culturally relevant care, we've got to have nurses from those communities working alongside other nurses and professionals to help educate them about the cultures."*[43]
>
> *"We want to play a role in building cultural bridges in the profession....It's not just the message that's important. It's the delivery and timing."*[44]

Professional Associations

- Cultural Diversity in Nursing (*www.culturediversity.org*)

- Diversity RX Organization (*www.diversityrx.org*)

- Ethnic Medicine Guide (*ethnomed.org*)

- The Cross Cultural Health Care Program (*www.xculture.org*)

- Transcultural Nursing Society (*www.tcns.org*)

Professional Journal

- *Journal of Transcultural Nursing (www.tcns.org/journal)*. This journal discusses and encourages a broad perspective on the issues of nursing as it relates to different cultures.

Media Coverage

The *New York Times* reports that one important goal of transcultural nursing is to engender respect for varying traditional approaches to medical care, partly to gain patients' confidence. ...Appearing overly critical may cause patients to stay away from clinics rather than seek treatment.

In one example, doctors in San Antonio noticed that one-third of Mexican-American preschoolers studied were already quite overweight. Medical staff realized that the mothers traditionally associated healthiness with heaviness, hoping to avoid having malnourished children. Doctors and nurses had to negotiate between two conflicting sets of values to convince parents that they were not trading in their "Mexicanness" by following nutritional guidelines.[45]

---

43 National American Arab Nurses Association home page. *www.americanarabnurses.org* (accessed August 16, 2006).

44 Barbara Marquand, "Public Works: Careers in Public Health Nursing." MinorityNurse.com, *http://minoritynurse.com/features/nurse_emp/08-02-05e.html* (accessed August 16, 2006).

45 Gina Maranto, "Nurses Bridge Cultures to Give Better Care." *New York Times* (online), October 1, 2002. *http://query.nytimes.com/gst/fullpage.html?res=9800E1D91538F932A35753C1A9649C8B63&sec=health&pagewanted=2* (accessed September 23, 2006).

TRANSPLANT NURSE

Definition: Nurses in this field work in the area of organ transplantation, providing support to recipients of organs, living-donor patients offering their organs for transplant, and their families. These nurses are responsible for coordinating and administering care throughout the transplantation process—before, during, and after surgery. These nurses are also instrumental in providing education to patients and their families.

Want Ad #1: Key responsibilities include:

■ Serve as clinician, educator, investigator, consultant, and leader.

■ Coordinate heart transplantation of all pediatric and adult organ recipients.

■ Provide follow-up and care across the continuum from pretransplant, during transplant, and post-transplant.

Want Ad #2: Experienced registered nurse for a prestigious teaching hospital. This person will work as part of the team encompassing both liver and kidney transplants. They will collaborate to enhance teaching, research, and clinical excellence at the Medical Center. They will manage post kidney and liver transplant care, including patient medications, ongoing patient education, and monitor lab results.

> **Quote from a Transplant Nurse:** *"As a transplant coordinator, I meet with families after they've already made the decision. They're letting me into their lives at the worst moment they've ever had. I want them to understand—and they want to believe—that this death was not in vain, that the life was not wasted. These family members have been given the opportunity to let their loved one live on and give life to someone else. It helps with the grieving process."* [46]

Professional Associations

■ International Transplant Nurses Society (ITNS) (*www.itns.org*). The ITNS is a worldwide professional nursing organization that represents all areas of transplantation. The ITCS is a society of both clinical and procurement coordinators, who provide a major portion of the infrastructure in which organ or tissue donation and transplantation occur.

■ NATCO: The Organization for Transplant Professionals (*natco1.org*). NATCO is committed to the advancement of organ and tissue donation and transplantation. Its vision is: "That there be a better quality of life for patients with end-stage organ and tissue failure…and a respect for those who shared."

Professional Journal

■ *Progress in Transplantation (www.natco1.org/ prof_development/progress_transplantation. htm).* The official journal of NATCO, Progress in Transplantation is a quarterly, indexed, peer-reviewed publication. The journal provides a professional forum that features original research, case studies, donor management issues, international papers, review articles, clinical practice issues, and policy papers of interest to medical professionals focused on transplantation.

Media Coverage

Children's Hospital and Regional Medical Center in Seattle, Washington has a Web site that features videos about its Transplant Center. Recent stories included:

Chronic Liver Failure Leads to Transplant, about a pharmacy student's healing process; The Heart and Soul of the Heart Center, about a transplant nurse coordinator's work; The Gift of Life, about a 10-month-old who received two liver transplants [47]

---

46 Candy Goulette, "The Gift of Life," *Advance for Nurses.* April 24, 2006: 12.

47 "Stories," on the Transplant Center page of the Web site of the Children's Hospital and Regional Medical Center in Seattle, Washington, *http://transplant.seattlechildrens. org/about/stories.asp* (accessed September 23, 2006).

UROLOGY NURSE

Definition: Nurses who work with individuals with conditions that affect their excretion system. These include acute and chronic cystitis, erectile dysfunction, and nocturnal enuresis (bed-wetting).

Want Ad: The pediatric urology nurse practitioner provides primarily outpatient care to patients and families in the management of urinary disorders with a clinical focus on childhood incontinence and complex congenital anomalies. The primary focus of the pediatric urology nurse practitioner will be the development and management of a specialized clinical treatment program for children with urinary incontinence and dysfunctional elimination syndromes.

Professional Associations

- Pediatric Urology Nurse Specialists (PUNS) (*www.duj.com/puns.html*). The Pediatric Urology Nurse Specialists are affiliated with the urology section of the American Academy of Pediatrics (AAP). Membership is open to RNs practicing in pediatric urology.

- Society of Urologic Nurses and Associates (SUNA) (*www.duj.com/suna.html*)

Professional Journal

- *Digital Online Urology Nurses Online (UNO)* (*www.duj.com/unohome.html*). The new, peer-reviewed, online nursing section of the Digital Urology Journal employs the technology of the Internet to facilitate education, collaboration, and exchange of information among nurses practicing in urology. UNO invites the submission of original articles pertinent to all areas affecting both adult and pediatric urologic nursing.

Media Coverage

A recent article published on *Urology Nurses Online* discussed the psychological discomfort common among men with self-reported sexual dysfunction. Successful treatment of the impotent man involves attention to the physical as well as the psychological aspects of his ailment. Many men with erectile dysfunction are past 50 and can be quite uncomfortable with sharing their situation with younger female nurses. Nurses who know how to establish a relationship where discussion is open, relaxed, professional, and relatively unembarrassed will have far more ease in treating their patients.[48]

---

48 Henry Intili and Desnese Nier, "Self Esteem and Depression in Men Who Present with Erectile Dysfunction," Digital Urology Journal Web site, *www.duj.com/Nier.html* (accessed August 16, 2006).

WOMEN'S HEALTH NURSE   *Also Known As:* REPRODUCTIVE HEALTH NURSE

Definition: Nurses in this field provide education and support to individuals, couples, and families regarding fertility, menopause, and other reproductive concerns. These nurses work in clinics that provide treatments, in centers that match egg donors with families, or in counseling programs that help individuals and couples who are having difficulty conceiving.

Want Ad: Seeking an experienced IVF nurse coordinator to join its rapidly growing private practice that includes a brand new main facility. Applicants should be able to oversee standard IVF, egg donation, and SART data entry. Responsibilities also include the opportunity for teaching nursing students. Our program offers a fully equipped clinical and laboratory service and includes a laboratory director, reproductive urologist, reproductive health psychologist, and acupuncturist. We are committed to the highest quality of patient care and we are looking for those who share our same compassion and dedication.

Professional Associations

- National Association of Nurse Practitioners in Women's Health (*www.npwh.org*)

- Society for Assisted Reproductive Technology (*www.sart.org*)

- American Society for Reproductive Medicine (*www.asrm.org*)

- Association of Reproductive Health Professionals (*www.arhp.org*)

- International Embryo Transfer Society (*www.iets.org*)

- Society for Reproductive Endocrinology and Infertility (*www.socrei.org*)

- Resolve: The National Infertility Association (*www.resolve.org*)

- Alexander Foundation for Women's Health (*www.afwh.org*)

- Global Reproductive Health Forum (*www.hsph.harvard.edu/Organizations/healthnet*)

- North American Menopause Society (*www.menopause.org*)

- Nurses in Reproductive Medicine Professionals Group (*www.npg-asrm.org*)

- The American Fertility Association (*www.theafa.org*)

- International Federation of Fertility Societies (*www.iffs-reproduction.org*)

Professional Journal

- *Journal of Midwifery and Women's Health (www.jmwh.org)*. This interdisciplinary journal covers several women's health issues.

Media Coverage

The Association of Reproductive Health Professionals reports that communication between nurses and patients can significantly benefit sexual health. Effective patient/provider communication has been correlated with increased use of condoms, whereas lack of communication about sex is a recognized risk factor for HIV and STDs. One reason to blame for this lack of communication is that 68 percent of patients surveyed stated that fear of embarrassing a provider prevented them from broaching sexuality issues.[49]

---

[49] "What You Need to Know: Talking to Patients about Sexuality and Sexual Health," Association of Reproductive Health Professionals Web site, *www.arhp.org/factsheets/sexandsex.cfm* (accessed August 16, 2006).

WOUND AND OSTOMY NURSE   *Also Known As:* WOUND CARE NURSE,
ENTEROSTOMAL THERAPIST, HYPERBARIC MEDICINE NURSE

Definition: Nurses who provide support and care for individuals with stomas, vascular and pressure wounds, draining wounds, neuropathic wounds, and fistulas and help patients manage these conditions.

Want Ad #1: In a collaborative relationship with physicians, nurses, and patients you will formulate, implement, and evaluate plans of care. The ostomy and wound care nurses will coordinate wound and ostomy therapy, and related patient and nurse education. This is a position that requires flexibility to meet patient care needs.

Want Ad #2: Clinical nursing experience in caring for patients with abdominal somas, draining wounds, fistulas, pressure sores, and incontinence. Demonstrated knowledge of pediatric and adult patient teaching principles. Extensive knowledge of the gastrointestinal, genitourinary, and integumentary systems, including pathophysiology. Ability to utilize communication skills. Fine motor dexterity. Good written and verbal skills; ability to function as a team member.

Professional Association

■ Wound Ostomy & Continence Nurses Society (WOCN) (*www.wocn.org*). WOCN promotes educational, clinical, and research opportunities to support nurses who care for individuals with wounds, ostomies, and incontinence.

Professional Journal

■ *Journal of Wound, Ostomy, and Continence Nursing.* This journal is published by the WOCN. This international journal is a resource devoted to the nursing care and management of patients with abdominal stomas, wounds, pressure ulcers, fistulas, vascular ulcers, and incontinence. Original, peer-reviewed articles examine these topics in hospital, home, and long-term care settings.

Media Coverage

Nursing Spectrum reports that global trends indicate that wound, ostomy, and continence (WOC) nurses are likely to be in great demand for the foreseeable future. Because WOC nurses care for all age groups, they are versatile across care settings, and will be increasingly valuable to American society.[50]

---

50 Janice Beitz, "Wound, Ostomy, Continence Nursing: A Career for the New Millennium," Nursing Spectrum Web site, *http://nsweb .nursingspectrum.com/cfforms/GuestLecture/ woundcare.cfm* (accessed August 16, 2006).

CHAPTER 5

Nursing Specializations Outside the Hospital

INTRODUCTION

This chapter is longer than its predecessor, Chapter 4 "Nursing Specialization inside the Hospital," for a good reason. The scope of possible career opportunities is much broader outside the traditional hospital setting, and it is expanding rapidly. Between 1996 and 2000, the number of registered nurses in community health settings, including home health care, rose by 155 percent. That increase was more than triple the growth of the previous four years.[1]

Because you're considering nursing as a second career, you should know from the start that you don't necessarily need to envision yourself working within a hospital. Although the majority of new nurses begin their careers in that setting, the current trend of health care has increasingly shifted to providing care in nonhospital settings for a variety of reasons:

- Some insurance companies will only pay for outpatient care for certain treatments, because it is less expensive than inpatient.
- Potential patients prefer not to have their lives interrupted with a hospital stay. They want easy-in and quick-out.

---

1 "Your Nursing Career: A Look at the Facts," American Association of Colleges of Nursing Education Center, *www.aacn.nche/education/Career.htm* (accessed September 23, 2006).

- A maturing population of over-65-ers wants care provided in their own homes, postponing or rejecting moving to assisted care living arrangements.
- A comparison of the working environments of nonhospital and hospital settings often finds the former less hierarchical and more open to flexible working hours. Creative solutions can be implemented faster, without going through layers of supervisors and committees on the way to final decision makers.

You might find listed in these pages a specialty that mirrors your previous career. For example, if you have experience as a travel agent, you might want to explore the idea of becoming a travel nurse, who makes sure that people traveling to exotic locations are protected from a host of nonexotic illnesses and diseases by vaccination and preventive medication. If you have experience with medications, such as a pharmacy technician, you might enjoy working with clinicians who write the prescriptions, or with an advanced degree of nurse practitioner, you might plan to one day write the prescriptions yourself.

ABUSE PREVENTION AND TREATMENT NURSE
VIOLENCE PREVENTION NURSE, CHILD OR ELDER ABUSE NURSE

Also Known As:

Definition: Nurses who work to support the rights and welfare of the spectrum of vulnerable populations: children, adults, and the elderly. They may work in clinics or shelters for the abused, or do research to prevent elder abuse, child abuse, or domestic violence.

Want ad: With supervision by the Older Adult Protective Services, the nurse provides specialized intake, intervention, assessment, and short-term case management services for clients age 60 and above who are exhibiting actions and/or behaviors that suggest lack of capacity to make reasonable judgments regarding their care and safety. Second language abilities preferred. Experience addressing complex psychosocial, medical, legal, and ethical client situations. Ability to work with difficult clients and skill in case assessment are essential. Collects information to determine eligibility for Medicaid long-term care programs.

> **Quote from an Abuse Prevention and Treatment Nurse:** *"The effects of domestic violence bleed out into our society, and our children and entire communities are influenced by violence every day. The whole point of screening is to get the victim of domestic violence out of a situation as early as she/he thinks she/he can! When children become immersed in the cycle of domestic violence, the cycle continues and these children are at high risk of becoming either victims or perpetrators of domestic violence themselves."[2]*

Professional Associations

■ International Nursing Network on Violence Against Women (*www.nnvawi.org*)

■ Family Violence Prevention Fund (*endabuse .org/programs/healthcare*)

Professional Journal

■ *Family Violence Prevention and Health Practice (endabuse.org/health/ejournal)*

Media Coverage

The National Center on Elder Abuse is dedicated to using media to educate the public about elder abuse, neglect, and exploitation and its tragic consequences. The Center is an internationally recognized resource for policy leaders, practitioners, prevention specialists, researchers, advocates, families, and concerned citizens. Its partners are the National Association of State Units on Aging (Lead Organization), the American Bar Association Commission on Law and Aging, the Clearinghouse on Abuse and Neglect, University of Delaware, the National Adult Protective Services Association, and the National Committee for the Prevention of Elder Abuse. Support for the National Center on Elder Abuse comes from the Administration on Aging, U.S. Department of Health and Human Services.[3]

---

2   L. Powers, "A Day in the Life…An Interview with Laura Stats, Emergency Room Nurse," HospitalSoup.com, *www.hospitalsoup.com/Day/ nurse/lstatsernurse.asp* (accessed August 16, 2006).

3   Source; National Center on Elder Abuse home page, *www.elderabusecenter.org* (accessed August 16, 2006).

AMBULATORY CARE NURSE   *Also Known As:* CLINIC NURSE, OUTPATIENT NURSE

Definition: Nurses who care for patients in either a clinic associated with a hospital (usually located on the same land) or a free-standing (meaning located elsewhere) building dedicated to care outside the hospital.

Want ad #1: A high-volume clinic offers comprehensive pediatric care for children and young adults with a wide range of developmental, congenital, neuromuscular, and post traumatic problems. Requires the ability to be flexible in a collaborative setting working with multiple specialists, surgeons, nurse practitioners, nurses, outpatient administrative staff, and inpatient staff.

Want ad #2: Under general supervision of providers, assists physicians by greeting and identifying patients, escorting patient to exam room; identifying purpose of visit; preparing patient for office visit by weighing patient, taking vital signs, administering medication including injections according to policies and procedures in a safe, accurate, and timely manner; performing minor medical procedures and other tasks associated with patient care.

Want ad #3: Accountable for the management and provision of patient care in assigned area. Assess patient's needs for nursing care and other services, using clinical skills and visual, aural, and analytical abilities. Collaborate with physicians, other services, patient, and patient's family to plan care and evaluate outcomes, requiring strong interpersonal skills. Demonstrate clinical competency and compassion in providing care, using technology, administering medications, performing procedures, and managing emergencies. Ensure integration of safety and quality standards into practice and delivery of team care. Assure continuity of care through appropriate discharge planning, patient education, and coordination of services.

Quote from an Ambulatory Care Nurse: *One nurse who works at a theme park says, "You have to be prepared for anything and everything that comes through the door. We do a lot of PR so that we can turn accidents into a positive [experience] so [the guests] can go back out to the park and enjoy the rest of the day."*[4]

Professional Association

- American Academy of Ambulatory Care Nursing (*www.aaacn.org*). Members are RNs, LPNs, LVNs, students, affiliates of ambulatory care, administrators, clinicians, directors, managers, nurse practitioners, and clinical nurse specialists.

Professional Journal

- *Journal of Ambulatory Care Management (www.lww.com/product/0,1255,0148-9917,00.html).* Because this area of medicine changes so rapidly, this journal seeks to provide readers with up-to-date information on the latest developments in ambulatory care. Each issue of this peer-reviewed, quarterly journal covers a single topic in great depth.

Media Coverage

At Wal-Mart, CVS and other chain stores, walk-in health clinics are springing up as an antidote to the extensive and inconvenience of full-service doctors' offices or the high cost and impersonal last resort of emergency rooms. For a $30 flu shot, a $45 treatment for an ear infection, or other routine services from a posted price list, patients can visit nurse practitioners in independently operated clinics set up within the stores. About 100 of these clinics, which typically lease space from the host stores, are operating around the nation. Hundreds more are in the works.[5]

---

4   Kristin Rothwell, "Nurses at Theme Parks Care for Thrill-Seekers", Nurse Zone Web site, *www.nursezone.com/Ads/Forwork.asp?articleID=9076* (accessed August 16, 2006).

5   Jennifer Barrett, "Want Treatment with Those Pills?", Newsweek (online), *www.msnbc.msn.com/id/14014782/* (accessed August 16, 2006).

APHERESIS NURSE   *Also Known As:* BLOOD BANK NURSE, BLOOD CENTER NURSE

Definition: Nurses who collect blood donated by adults (either paid or volunteer) who fit certain criteria for health. Their donation is used to replace blood, plasma, and platelets that are lost due to injury, surgery, or disease such as hemophilia.

Want ad #1: Nurse manager will provide leadership for the coordination of clinical and administrative activities for patients, donors, and staff. This position will oversee the blood-and-donor and therapeutic apheresis programs. The position is also accountable for the quality assurance program, development and maintenance of standard operating procedures, and the regulatory compliance of the department. As a part of the leadership team, the RN manager provides direction to the department while representing nursing in multidisciplinary projects and serving on committees.

Want ad #2: For-profit blood bank with many hospital affiliations nationwide has an immediate need for a mobile blood drive registered nurse. RN will travel to scheduled blood drives performing whole blood and platelet collections on healthy volunteer donors. Registered nurse will have charge nurse duties on mobile drives and oversee a small team the day of the drive. RN will also be responsible for regulatory (AABB and FDA) guidelines to be followed. Must have current registered nurse license and be in good standing with RN Board. Blood donor/Apheresis experience a plus and excellent IV/venipuncture and phlebotomy skills required.

Quotes from Apheresis Nurses:

"Some people come in with sad, heart-wrenching stories and they can be frightened or extremely anxious. We try to have donors leave with a smile and feel better about themselves, since they have just accomplished a heroic deed."

"Your assessment skills are important in the screening area where you are assessing the donors' health to determine if they are able to give blood. Nurses also use their leadership skills in blood bank nursing. They are team leaders, managers, and counselors. So, they need the ability to communicate well and use their teaching skills. It was the atmosphere in the blood center and [the interaction] with the donors that I found appealing."[6]

Professional Association

- American Association of Blood Banks (*www.aabb.org*). Nearly 2,000 institutions (community and hospital blood banks, hospital transfusion services, and laboratories) and about 8,000 individuals are members, including physicians, nurses, other health care providers, scientists, administrators, medical technologists, blood donor recruiters, and public relations personnel.

Media Coverage

A video featuring a caped crusader is found on the "Blood Saves" Web site, part of their media campaign to educate the public about the need to increase blood donations. The facts are evident: Every two seconds, someone in America needs blood. About 38,000 pints are needed every day. Every year nearly five million people in the U.S. owe their lives to blood donors. Donating one pint of blood can save up to three lives.[7]

---

6   Stephanie Adamow, "Link to Life: Blood Bank Nurses May Not Care for the Injured, But They're Saving Lives," *Advance for Nurses,* 2, Issue 18, Page 33.

7   Blood Saves home page, *www.bloodsaves.com* (accessed August 16, 2006).

BUSINESS PERSON   *Also Known As:* PHARMACEUTICAL REPRESENTATIVE, MEDICAL SALES PERSON

Definition: Nurses who apply skills and training toward establishing, promoting, or consulting for business ventures in the health care industry. They can build on their nursing knowledge to develop medical devices or computerized systems for delivering health care. They can educate hands-on clinicians about the latest developments in medications, equipment, or services available to health care workers or patients.

Different from managed care nurses: Business persons work for a wide range of profit-making organizations; managed care nurses work for hospitals or insurance companies.

Different from nurse entrepreneurs, independent contractors, and contract nurse consultants: Business persons work for organizations as their employees, usually with benefits; nurse entrepreneurs, independent contractors, and contract nurse consultants are self-employed or temporary employees of organizations, usually without benefits.

Want ad #1: Nurse to serve as a clinical educator to interact with health care professionals to improve treatment adoption for diseases frequently underdiagnosed, misdiagnosed, or undertreated. Field-based position will call on health care providers to deliver educational programs regarding an osteoarthritis program. Will provide educational programs to clinical staff and to consumers-at-large in community settings.

Want ad #2: Nurse consultant for our infusion therapy and pain control, and product lines. Responsible for providing prompt and accurate information via incoming phone calls from inquiring customers, sales reps, and clinicians. These callers have concerns about existing or new products, including venous access devices, infusion sets and pumps, needle-free products, and pain control products.

Quotes from Business Persons:
"Working for a corporation is definitely less stressful than working at the patient's bedside. We work regular hours, can telecommute, and never have to work weekends or holidays."

"When a drug finally goes to market to fill an unmet medical need, you feel proud knowing you helped and that it's going to benefit many patients."[8]

Professional Association

■ National Nurses in Business Association (*www.nnba.net*)

8   Linda Childers, "Trade Your Scrubs for a Business Suit!" MinorityNurses.com, *http://minoritynurse.com/features/nurse_emp/11-18-04a.html* (accessed August 16, 2006).

CAMP NURSE

Definition: Nurses who provide care for healthy kids at camps, or for children with chronic conditions such as diabetes or HIV/AIDS. Whether the focus is on wellness or on patient self-care education, the camp nurse makes improved health an achievable goal.

Want ad #1: A summer camp for people with physical disabilities is seeking a nurse. Applicants work with a team. Duties include supervising the nursing students, catheterization, wound care, medication administration, and basic first aid. Nurses are provided with room and board. Nurses work six days per week.

Want ad #2: Nurse needed to work at a private residential children's summer camp nestled among the rolling hills and situated along a beautiful river. Campers and staff enjoy swimming, rafting, canoeing, hiking, mountain biking, horseback riding, and crafts. Our resident nurses enjoy room and board, on-site air-conditioned accommodations, regularly scheduled free time and days off, and a competitive salary with benefits.

Professional Association

■ Association of Camp Nurses (ACN) (*www.campnurse.org*)

Professional Journal

■ *CompassPoint* (*www.campnurse.org/ compasspoint/index.html*). The CAN's quarterly publication, featuring articles related to camp nursing and camp health, along with ACN member information.

Media Coverage

CompassPoint magazine reports that people who had mononucleosis during the school year prior to summer camp are at greater risk for fatigued-based illnesses than their healthy classmates. The camp nurse author recommends that "all potentially big impact activities should be reviewed for physician approval: bicycling, contact sports, ropes courses, horseback riding, rock climbing, diving... Rupture of the spleen is a rare complication, only occurring in one or two cases out of 1,000."[9]

---

9   Mary Marugg, "Clinical Commentary: Infectious Mononucleosis," Association of Camp Nurses Web site, *www.campnurse.org/edcenter/ infectiousmono.html* (accessed August 16, 2006).

CASE MANAGEMENT NURSE

Also Known As: WORKERS' COMPENSATION

MANAGER

Definition: Nurses who coordinate care for patients receiving long-term therapy, providing for optimal timing in all aspects of treatment. For cancer patients, for example, case management nurses coordinate primary care visits, surgery, radiation, and chemotherapy. A nurse case manager usually specializes in one specific area, such as AIDS, geriatrics, or children. Another area in which they practice is workers' compensation. These nurses coordinate care of patients who are discharged from a hospital or rehabilitation center, or who have been injured on the job.

Want ad: Responsible for assessment, planning, coordination, implementation, and evaluation of injured/disabled individuals involved in the medical case management process. Works as an intermediary between carriers, attorneys, medical care providers, employers, and employees to ensure appropriate and cost-effective health care services and a medically rehabilitated individual who is ready to return to an optimal level of work and functioning.

> **Quote from a Case Management Nurse:** *"I love to learn new things and seek out new challenges. Case management encompasses the best of both worlds. As a case manager, you assist members not only while they're in the hospital or in the acute phase of their illness, but you also have the opportunity to follow their care through a continuum."* [10]

Professional Associations

- Case Management Society of America (CMSA)(*www.cmsa.org*). CMSA is an international, nonprofit organization founded in 1990 dedicated to the support and development of the profession of case management through educational forums, networking opportunities and legislative involvement. Unique in its composition as an international organization, over 70 affiliated and prospective chapters (including Australia, Hong Kong, and London) in a tiered democratic structure, CMSA's success and strength is its structure as a member-driven society.

- Commission for Case Manager Certification (CCMC) (*www.ccmcertification.org*). Case management has evolved as a profession; more than 26,000 case managers have been awarded the CCM credential. CCMC has led the movement toward research-based certification, as well as the development of a uniform Scope of Practice and Code of Professional Conduct. All these advances have been subject to a peer-review process.

Professional Journals

- *The Journal of Nursing Administration (www.jonajournal.com)*

- *American Journal of Nursing (www.ajnonline.com)*

Media Coverage

CMSA reports that approximately 10 percent of all hospital admissions and 23 to 40 percent of all nursing home admissions are caused by noncompliance with patients' prescribed medications. This costs about $100 billion a year in the United States alone. CMSA has designed a set of Case Management Adherence Guidelines designed for case managers to help patients take their medications correctly. Reducing noncompliance by even 1 percent would save the health care system $1 billion and would also benefit patients by enhancing their quality of life. [11]

---

10 Barbara Marquand, "On the Case." MinorityNurse. com, *http://minoritynurse.com/features/nurse_emp/03-01-05d.html* (accessed August 16, 2006).

11 "The Problem: Medications Non-Adherence," Case Management Society of America Web site, *www.cmsa.org/PROGRAMSEVENTS/CaseManagementAdherenceGuidelinesCMAG/tabid/90/Default.aspx* (accessed August 16, 2006).

COMMUNITY HEALTH NURSE   *Also Known As:* PUBLIC HEALTH NURSE

Definition: Nurses who work in government and private agencies, clinics, and other private settings. These nurses focus on populations, working with individuals, groups, and families to improve the overall health of communities. They educate about health care issues, disease prevention, nutrition, and childcare, and also work with community leaders, teachers, parents, and physicians in community health education.

Want ad: Promote, maintain, and improve individual and community health by assisting members, communities, and providers adopt and support healthy behaviors. Collect and analyze data to identify community needs prior to planning, implementing, monitoring, and evaluating programs designed to encourage healthy lifestyles, policies, and environments. Oversee quality improvement projects including: analysis of data, development and implement interventions, arrangement and facilitation of meetings with network clinicians and key community agencies, documentation of activities, and collection of data as needed to support projects.

Quotes from Community Health Nurses: *"Community health nursing is so diverse. It requires everything you learn [as a nurse]. It uses all of you, and you never get bored."*

"When I see families and communities empowering themselves to take care of their own health problems and advocating for themselves because we as nurses have helped them to do that, that is the most exciting thing."[12]

Professional Associations

- Association of Community Health Nursing Educators (*www.achne.org*)
- American Public Health Association (*www.apha.org*)
- Society for Public Health Education (*www.sophe.org*)
- Rural Nurse Organization (*www.rno.org*)

Professional Journal

- *Journal of Community Health Nursing*
- *Journal of Community Nursing* *www.jcn.co.uk*)

Media Coverage

The Centers for Disease Control offers a Web site on "Health Related Hoaxes and Rumors" that addresses the legitimacy of recent health concerns. The site separates fact from urban legend, including information on needle sticks in public places, contaminated commercial ice machines, and other potential health threats. For more information, visit *www.cdc.gov.*[13]

---

12 Barbara Marquand, "Public Works: Careers in Public Health Nursing." MinorityNurse.com, *http://minoritynurse.com/features/nurse_emp/ 08-02-05e.html* (accessed August 16, 2006).

13 "Health Related Hoaxes and Rumors," Centers for Disease Control and Prevention, *www.cdc.gov/ doc.do/id/0900f3ec80226b9c* (accessed August 16, 2006).

COMPLEMENTARY HEALTH NURSE   *Also Known As:* ALTERNATIVE HEALTH NURSE, HOLISTIC NURSE, MIND-BODY-SPIRIT NURSE SPECIALIST

Definitions:

Complementary. Nurses who provide alternative forms of health care, including acupuncture and massage therapy.

Holistic. Nurses who provide a multifaceted approach to health care, bringing together all available resources to facilitate patient self-care, and promoting a physical, psychological, social, and spiritual well-being.

Want ad: Psychiatric nurse for our holistic healing farm community for individuals with serious mental illness. We offer a comprehensive recovery program that addresses the mind, body, and spirit to achieve optimal wellness. You would provide medication and dietary supplement administration, record-keeping, smoking cessation support and be an active leader of our growing wellness and complementary activities.

> **Quote from a Complementary Health Nurse:** *"It isn't just about adding new therapies and products, but changing the philosophy and approach to health and healing."[14]*

Professional Associations

- American Holistic Nurses Association *(www.ahna.org)*
- Canadian Holistic Nurses Association *(mypage.direct.ca/h/hutchings/chna.html)*

Professional Journal

- *Journal of Holistic Nursing (jhn.sagepub.com)*

Media Coverage

The National Center for Complementary and Alternative Medicine (NCCAM) (*nccam.nih.gov*) conducts research aimed at broadening available therapies. There is evidence that people with fatal illnesses are already availing themselves of nontraditional medical approaches.

A recent outpatient survey found that 83 percent of cancer patients at the University of Texas MD Anderson Cancer Center in Houston, Texas, sought alternative solutions. Examples are meditation and prayer, traditional Chinese medicine, herbs, vitamins, special diets, exercise, and relaxation techniques such as guided imagery.[15]

---

14 Sally Parker, "Hot Jobs, Emerging Careers." MinorityNurse.com, *http://minoritynurse.com/ features/nurse_emp/02-12-04a.html* (accessed August 16, 2006).

15 "Annieappleseedproject: Current Research/Future Directions/CAM," *www.annieappleseedproject.org/ curresdir.html* (accessed September 26, 2006).

CORRECTIONAL FACILITY NURSE
JUVENILE DETENTION NURSE

Also Known As: JAIL NURSE, PRISON NURSE,

Definition: Nurses who provide care to inmates of correctional facilities such as prisons, juvenile homes, jails, and penitentiaries.

Want ad #1: Nurse needed to provides educational, vocational, and rehabilitative residential services for adolescents. Willing to provide high-quality medical care and make a difference in the lives of at-risk youth.

Want ad #2: A correctional nurse needed to provide nursing services to arrestees/prisoners in city jails. Duties include: assisting the medical staff with patient evaluations, treatment, and procedures; performing phlebotomy for forensic purposes; obtaining patient histories; performing patient assessments, physical examinations, and diagnostic testing such as EKGs and urinalysis; providing emergency care and performing CPR; conducting sick call rounds; testifying in court proceedings.

Want ad #3: Nurse needed with psychiatric nursing experience to work in an outpatient setting at a correctional facility. Will be responsible for comprehensive patient evaluation of possible and actual mental health patients in coordination with clinical team. Psychological services staff provide diagnostic assessment, group and individual psychotherapy and crisis intervention.

> **Quotes from Correctional Facility Nurses:** *"This job involves the whole spectrum of nursing. We're providing mental and physical health care to a population that normally wouldn't have received the same services on their own or on the outside."*
>
> *"This population is hidden from society, and society has formed certain attitudes about them. Caring for this population allows nurses to demonstrate an increased level of compassion and advocacy. Correctional nurses must move out of their personal experiences and prejudices to serve without judgment of a person's life choices. If a nurse is truly passionate about nursing, this is a place to live out that passion."*[16]

Professional Associations

- American Correctional Health Services Association (ACHSA) (*www.corrections.com/achsa*) The mission of the American Correctional Health Services Association is to be the voice of the correctional healthcare profession, and serve as an effective forum for communication.

- National Commission on Correctional Healthcare (NCCHC) (*www.ncchc.org*) This organization is supported by 38 major national organizations, including the American Nurses Association.

- Academy of Correctional Health Professionals (*www.correctionalhealth.org*) The Academy of Correctional Health Professionals' mission is to create a professional community for the advancement of correctional health care.

Professional Journal

- *Journal of Correctional Health Care* (*www.ncchc.org/pubs/journal.html*) is the only national, peer-reviewed scientific journal to address correctional health care topics.

Media Coverage

The Academy of Correctional Health Professionals offers members the opportunity to use the Internet to participate in shared interest groups (SIGs)—small, online discussions focused around specific themes related to inmate health care. These themes include: administration, infection control, legal issues, mental health, public health, quality improvement, and research.[17]

---

16 Anne Bave, "Spirits in the Dark," MinorityNurse.com, *http://minoritynurse.com/features/nurse_emp/02-12-04b.html* (accessed August 16, 2006).

17 Academy of Correctional Health Professionals Web site, *www.correctionalhealth.org/education/SIG.html* (accessed August 16, 2006).

DEVELOPMENTAL DISABILITY NURSE

Definition: Nurses who provide care and support for patients with physical or mental disabilities, either children or adults.

Want ad #1: Nurse needed to provide individuals with complex behavioral or medical conditions options for living in the community. Oversight of complex medical needs for individuals with developmental disabilities in group homes and residential settings. Necessary skills include the ability to assess the individual's health status and the ability to train unlicensed staff in basic medication administration.

Want ad #2: Nurse needed to work for a residential community that provides service to children with special needs. Will be responsible for collaborating with personnel, both internally and externally, to develop individualized patient care plans. Focus is on prevention, education, maintenance of good health, and being creative in meeting each person's needs. This position will be part of our management team.

Quotes from Developmental Disability Nurses: *"If you talk to most nurses [who specialize in developmental disability nursing] they'll tell you they just fell into it. They didn't say 'gee I think I'll go in to developmental disabilities nursing. [However] Once a nurse finds rehab, they tend to stay in rehab. When someone comes in who is unable to dress themselves, is unable to walk or to have mobility and we're able to help them regain that, it's very satisfying."*

"I've seen people [patients] come out of institutions back into the community and see them grow, light up and have a life. It's just amazing."[18]

Professional Associations

- Developmental Disabilities Nurses Association (*www.ddna.org*)
- Developmental Disabilities Community Nurses Coalition
- Developmental Disabilities Leadership Forum

Professional Journal

- *International Journal of Nursing in Intellectual and Developmental Disabilities (journal.hsmc.org/ijnidd/index.asp)* This journal is a new publication aimed at providing all nurses with free, ongoing learning opportunities. The journal focuses on information that is current and relevant to disabilities nurses' education and experience, enabling them to provide quality services to patients with developmental disabilities worldwide.

Media Coverage

The mission of the National Rehabilitation Awareness Foundation (*www.nraf-rehabnet.org*) is to host a media campaign to develop programs which aim to increase opportunities for the nearly 50 million Americans with disabilities, and help those who are disabled live up to their fullest potential. Their motto is "Positive Thinking: Positive Results."

The mission of the National Rehabilitation Information Center (NARIC) (*www.naric.com*) is to provide an online gateway to disability-and-rehabilitation-oriented information. It sees its audience as being both the public and researchers.

---

18 Robert Scally, "Nurses Caring for the Disabled and Chronically Ill Find Work Challenging, Fulfilling," NurseZone.com, *www.nursezone.com/Stories/SpotlightOnNurses.asp?articleID=11079* (accessed August 16, 2006).

DIABETIC NURSING EDUCATOR   *Also Known As:* DIABETIC CLINICAL SPECIALIST

Definition: Nurses who work with people who have either pre-diabetes, or Type I or Type II diabetes, a disease that affects the body's ability to create insulin. They can also function as specialists in illnesses of the endocrine system (namely the hypothalamus, pituitary, thyroid, parathyroids, adrenals, pineal body, and the reproductive glands) and often work in close collaboration with a nutritionist or an endinocrinologist.

Want ad: The nurse educator/certified diabetes educator will assess, plan, implement, and evaluate the patient-centered diabetes education program at the clinic. Plans and conducts continuing education program in diabetes for professionals and the general public. Collaborates with other educators and providers in the areas of program development, implementation, marketing, and review of clinical programs/services. Participates in the development of education curricula and materials by writing original material and/or reviewing the work of others.

Professional Associations

- Endocrine Nurses Society
  (www.endo-nurses.org)
- Society for Endocrinology
  (www.endocrinology.org/default.htm)

Professional Journal

- *Journal of Diabetes Nursing*

Media Coverage

According to the World Health Organization, at least 171 million people worldwide suffered from diabetes mellitus in 2006. Incidence of the disease is increasing rapidly, and it is estimated that by 2030, this number will double. Diabetes occurs throughout the world, but is most common (particularly Type 2) in the more developed countries. However, the greatest increase in prevalence is expected to occur in Asia and Africa, where the majority of diabetics will likely be found by 2030. The increase in incidence of diabetes in developing countries correlates with the trend of urbanization and lifestyle changes, including a shift towards Western-style diets.[19]

---

19 "Diabetes: Epidemiology and Statistics," Wikipedia, *http://en.wikipedia.org/wiki/Diabetes_mellitus* (accessed August 16, 2006).

DISEASE MANAGER

Definition: Nurses who work with people whom insurance companies have identified as subscribers who would benefit from continued education about their illness, e.g. asthmatics and diabetics. They employ nurses to contact these specific subscribers to help them become aware of lifestyle habits and self-care measures to insure maximum health. Their purpose is to eventually reduce healthcare costs for all subscribers.

Want ad: Nurse needed with an interest in disease management for an internally managed program. Our goal is to help members work with their physicians to improve their quality of life and reduce the symptoms and complications associated with their specific disease. The disease manager will make proactive outbound calls to potential candidates for a specific program.

> **Quote from a Disease Manager Nurse:** *"Communication is the key to success in disease management. If you can't communicate with your patient, you are not able to effectively deliver your message. One of the most rewarding things about disease management is when you are able to give information to people who do not understand their condition and tell them what the condition is and what they can expect."[20]*

Professional Association

- Disease Management Association of America (DMAA) (*www.dmaa.org*) The mission of the Disease Management Association of America is to represent all stakeholders in disease management and care coordination. These stakeholders include the health care industry, government agencies, employers, and the general public.

Professional Journal

- *Disease Management. (www.dmaa.org/dmho. asp)* The office journal of the DMAA. A bimonthly, international, peer-reviewed publication that features articles about the practical implementation of disease management initiatives, insights from professionals, and clinical research and case studies.

Media Coverage

In the United States, disease management is a growing industry with numerous vendors. Disease management is especially important to health insurers, agencies, trusts, associations, and employers who offer health insurance. A Mercer Consulting study indicated that the percentage of employer-sponsored health plans offering disease management programs increased from 41 percent in 2002 to 58 percent in 2003. Illnesses targeted include: coronary artery disease, renal failure, hypertension, congestive heart failure, obesity, diabetes, asthma, cancer, and arthritis.[21]

---

20 Aaron Dalton, "Management Team." MinorityNurse.com, *http://minoritynurse.com/features/nurse_emp/10-25-05a.html* (accessed August 16, 2006).

21 Adapted from "Disease Management (health)," Wikipedia, *http://en.wikipedia.org/wiki/Disease_management_%28health%29* (accessed August 16, 2006).

ENTREPRENEUR   *Also Known As:* INDEPENDENT CONTRACTOR OR CONTRACT NURSE CONSULTANT

Definitions:

Entrepreneur or contract nurse consultants: Nurses who create a successful business venture, often in the health care industry. As founders and owners, they leverage their nursing knowledge to make sure the same values and principles that contribute to good patient care and education are present in their enterprise.

Independent contractors: Nurses who provide nursing care to hospitals or long-term care facilities when a facility's nurse staffing is low. These nurses contract with facilities to provide nursing services, usually charging by the hour. Nurse contractors practice across all aspects of the health care industry, including home health, nursing homes, hospitals, rehabilitation centers, and doctors' offices.

Different than business persons: Business persons work for organizations as employees, usually with benefits; nurse entrepreneurs, independent contractors, and contract nurse consultants are self-employed or temporary employees, usually without benefits.

According to *Merriam-Webster's Dictionary,* an entrepreneur is "one who organizes, manages, and assumes the risks of a business or enterprise." In some sense, all nurses function as entrepreneurs. They organize and manage their time, regardless of where they currently work. Some assume responsibility for life-and-death actions.

Want ad: Contract Nurse Consultant: Experience working with social workers and serving the elderly or disabled populations is preferred. Extremely well organized with high-energy level. Well-developed interpersonal and communication skills. Ability to quickly acquire needed knowledge; reviews a high-volume of consumer files with attention to detail within mandated timeframes. Second language abilities preferred.

> **Quote from an Entrepreneur:** *"I have contracts with these places [where she works] and I know they hired me because I was a nurse first. I'm not saying someone with [just] a fitness background couldn't have done it, but the way I got in there was through my contacts in nursing."[22]*

Professional Associations

- National Nurses in Business Association *(nnba.net/job_options_within_nursing.htm)*

- Nurse Entrepreneurs *(www.enursescribe.com/nurse_entrepreneus.htm)*

- NursingEntrepreneurs.com *(www.nursingentrepreneurs.com)*

- National Association of Independent Nurses *(www.independentrn.com)*

- Small Business Administration *(www.sba.gov)*

- National Association of Independent Nurses *(www.independentrn.com)*

- Independent Nurse Contractors *(www.independentrncontractor.com)*

Media Coverage

Today Vickie L. Milazzo, RN, MSN, JD, owns a $10 million business where she teaches other RNs to work for themselves. Vickie pioneered a whole new world where nurses can be independent business owners as certified legal nurse consultants (CLNCs). Over 20,000 nurses have become CLNCs through her home-study program or six-day seminars. As entrepreneurs, they earn $100 to $150 an hour working with attorneys on medical-related cases.[23]

22 Scott Williams, "The Wide World of Sports/Fitness Nursing," MinorityNurse.com, *http://minoritynurse.com/features/nurse_emp/03-03-05a.html* (accessed August 16, 2006).

23 "Vickie Milazzo Institute," National Alliance of Legal Nurse Consultants home page, *http://legalnurse.com* (accessed August 16, 2006).

ENVIRONMENTAL HEALTH NURSE

Definition: Nurses who educate members of the community about their environmental risks and rights. Issues include lead poisoning, pesticide exposure for migrant farm workers, pollution from medical waste incinerators, and the use of mercury in health care settings.

Quotes from Environmental Health Nurses: *"Environmental health nurses must have good listening and communication skills and an understanding of how the human body responds to stress—physically, mentally and emotionally. You need to have enough self-awareness and personal maturity to feel comfortable with yourself so that you will not be intimidated or react defensively."*

"Often what you find is that these communities not only don't know their rights but are not even aware that they are being exposed [to environmental hazards.]"

"Nurses are in opportune places to address environmental health issues. Nurses are in schools, workplaces, home health care, and other positions where they are clearly visible."[24]

Media Coverage

In 1995, the Institute of Medicine, part of the National Academy of Sciences, published the results of the work of their Committee on Enhancing Environmental Health Content in Nursing Practice. Their book, *Nursing, Health, and the Environment: Strengthening the Relationship to Improve the Public's Health* is designed to help nurses understand environmental concepts, complete environmental health histories for patients and make assessments and referrals. They will also learn how to inform patients and communities about environmental risks, understand the policy framework for addressing environmental health and know the major environmental laws and regulations. The book can be read online without cost at *www.nap.edu/catalog/4986.html#orgs*.[25]

The University of Maryland School of Nursing, with support from the Kellogg Foundation, partnered with the National League for Nursing, the Southern Region Education Board, and Howard University School of Nursing to produce a Web site EnviRN (*www.envirn.umaryland.edu*). This site serves as a "virtual nursing village" for the sharing of teaching strategies, practice guidance, and consensus on future research needs for environmental health and nursing. The ultimate goal is to prevent environmental disease.

24 Barbara Marquand, "Toxic Avengers," MinorityNurse.com, *http://minoritynurse.com/features/nurse_emp/01/27-02b.html* (accessed August 16, 2006).

25 Andrew Pope, Meta Snyder, and Lillian Mood., *Nursing, Health, and the Environment: Strengthening the Relationship to Improve the Public's Health*, Institute of Medicine, Division of Health Promotion and Disease Prevention. National Academy Press, Washington DC, 1995.

ETHICIST

Definition: Nurses who serve on a hospital ethics committee, or work in a legal setting. The ethicist may be called on to give an opinion in an individual case or asked to compose or review policies and procedures. The ethicist ensures that appropriate education and follow-up accompanies these activities.

Want ad #1: Serve as resource regarding ethics laws affecting agency personnel. Monitor the state ethics commission's rules and advisory opinions. Monitor ethics legislation introduced in the legislature. Work for integration of the "ethics message" into all areas/programs of the agency. Lead ethics leadership classes for upper management and executive administration, as well as frontline. Provide confidential opportunities to hear employees' ethical concerns and questions.

Want ad #2: This university seeks applications for a joint appointment, beginning summer/fall. This position presents the selected nurse professional the opportunity to be responsible for education, clinical consultation, policy development, research, and interdisciplinary projects in health policy and bioethical issues. In addition to a minimum of a BSN, applicants should have earned a graduate degree (doctorate preferred) in nursing, philosophy, professional ethics, law, or related area with demonstrated contributions to the ethics of health care and policy.

Professional Associations

- The American Society of Law, Medicine, & Ethics (*www.aslme.org*)

- International Centre for Nursing Ethics (*www.freedomtocare.org/iane.htm*)

- American Nurse's Association's Center for Ethics & Human Rights (*www.nursingworld.org/ethics*)

Professional Journals

- *Nursing Ethics: An International Journal for Healthcare Professionals. It can be found at www.arnoldpublishers.com/Journals/pages/nur_eth/09697330.htm*

- *A recent article (September 2006) was "Nurses' Fears and Professional Obligations Concerning Possible Human-to-Human Avian Flu."*

- *Ethics and Medicine (www.ethicsandmedicine.com)*

- *Journal of Medical Ethics (jme.bmjjournals.com)*

Media Coverage

The Online Ethics Center for Engineering and Science at Case Western Reserve University has a site they call OnlineEthics.org (found at *www.oeccombo.cwru.edu*) that offers descriptions of actual situations faced by nurses in order to promote thoughtful discussion. They look at the hard decisions that need to be made, such as a nurse whistleblower at a private psychiatric facility who observed patient abuse in the context of research participation.[26]

---

26 Online Ethics Center for Engineering and Science, *http://oeccombo.cwru.edu* (accessed August 16, 2006).

FAMILY NURSE PRACTITIONER (FNP)

Definition: Nurses who have one to two years of advanced education beyond a bachelor's degree. Because FNPs are trained to provide care, promote health, and treat disease and injury in patients from infancy through old age, they are trained to diagnose and treat a wide range of diseases.

Want ad: Working in the Department of Medicine Adult Sickle Cell Center, you will diagnose illness and prescribe interventions through interview and physical exam, order specific labs and diagnostic testing, and prescribe medications, while still providing health care education, counseling, and supportive care to an individual, family, or community. Participate in performance improvement and research activities.

Quotes from Family Nurse Practitioners: *"How a nurse practitioner practices depends on the philosophy of the organization. The physician I work with is a collaborator. We are a team and we act as a team. He's accessible to me 24 hours a day. My job as a nurse practitioner is rewarding financially. But spiritually, I'm a millionaire because I have the opportunity to make a real difference."*

"The biggest reward [for NPs] is having the time to do what we were educated to do: talk to patients about disease prevention and health maintenance. Most physicians don't have the time to do that. [Compared to doctors], we do a lot more education and discussion with patients."[27]

Professional Associations

■ American Academy of Nurse Practitioners *(www.aanp.org/default.asp)*

■ American College of Nurse Practitioners *(www.nurse.org/acnp/index.shtml)*

■ National Organization of Nurse Practitioner Faculties *(www.nonpf.com)*

Professional Journal

■ *Advance for Nurse Practitioners (nurse-practitioners.advanceweb.com/main.aspx)*

Media Coverage

A article on SpokesmanReview.com described nurse practitioner (NP) Ed Gruber's work at Spokane's People's Clinic. Gruber, past president of the American College of Nurse Practitioners, has been an NP for over thirty years. He states "In the early 70's when I did it… it was kind of on the cutting edge." Now there are more than 100,000 NPs in the United States.

Gruber is an assistant dean for graduate programs at the Intercollegiate College of Nursing. He believes "The most important thing we can teach our nurse practitioners is to know what they don't know. You need to know what your limits are, what you understand, and what you don't understand."[28]

---

27 Debra Williams, "From Minority Nurse to Nurse Practitioner," MinorityNurses.com, *www.minoritynurse.com/features/nurse_emp/ 08-02-05c.html* (accessed August 16, 2006).

28 Heather Lalley, "Primary Care," SpokesmanReview. com January 6, 2004 *www.spokesmanreview .com/pf.asp?date=010604&ID=s1467094.* (accessed September 23, 2006).

FLIGHT NURSE   *Also Known As:* LIFE TRANSPORT NURSE

Definition: Nurses who provide intensive nursing care while transporting critical patients by helicopter or ambulance. These nurses may also transport less-critical patients via commercial airlines.

Want ad: Commission on Accreditation of Medical Transport Systems (CAMTS) certified company seeks critical care RNs for aeromedical transport of stable and critical patients between island and occasional long distance flights. Must have critical care and or emergency room responder experience. Flight experience a very big plus!

Quotes from Flight Nurses: *"A flight nurse must be self-assured, with somewhat of an aggressive nature. Leadership qualities are needed, coupled with a passion and kindness for patient care."*

"Most of us are type A personality people. You need drive to do this job. You have to be accepting of change and be able to go with the flow. Every day is exciting. You never know where you will go or what patient you will have today."

"The learning curve is constant. Safety is paramount in everything we do. Emotional intelligence is also crucial to be successful in this job. You also have to be healthy and in good shape."[29]

Professional Associations

- Air & Surface Transport Nurses Association (ASTNA) (*www.astna.org*)

- Association of Air Medical Services (AAMS) (*www.aams.org*)

- The International Association of Flight Nurses (*wwwflightnursing.com*) Their online education site is at FlightNursing.Net. Their logo is the outline of a compass, consistent with their slogan "Setting a Course for Excellence."

Professional Journal

- *Journal of Emergency Nursing.* The official journal of the Emergency Nurses Association.

Media Coverage

A recent article on NurseZone.com gave some career advice and used humor to make a point. "Aspiring flight nurses should start out in critical care," said Kathleen Montgomery, MSN, RN, assistant dean for student services and instructor at the Frances Payne Bolton School of Nursing at Case Western Reserve University in Cleveland, Ohio.

Speaking during a presentation on flight nursing at the recent National Association of Student Nurses Mid Year Conference in Kansas City, Missouri, Montgomery said one other critical requirement for flight nursing transcends medical training: "Make sure you don't get air sick."[30]

---

29 Flight Nursing home page, *www.flightnursing.com* (accessed August 16, 2006).

30 Robert Scally, "Flight Nurses: Nursing's High Altitude Calling," NurseZone.com, *www.nursezone.com/Stories/SpotlightOnNurses.asp?articleID=9674* (accessed September 24, 2006).

FORENSICS NURSE

Definition: Nurses who work with law enforcement officials to aid in the investigation of crimes, such as sexual assault, accidental death, abuse, and assault. They also treat the victims of these crimes.

Want ad: The Sexual Assault Nurse Examiner (SANE) provides an objective medical and legal evaluation for victims of sexual assault. The SANE provides and meets International Association of Forensic Nurses Standards of Nursing Practice concerning forensic examination. While assessing patient health problems and resources, that nurse takes a leadership role in the development, implementation, and outcome evaluation of a plan of care for victims of sexual assault.

> **Quote from a Forensics Nurse:** *"My focus is to help that victim get through that medical experience. I hope that as nurses get better at taking care of victims, collecting evidence, providing support, and linking them up with services, more victims will come forward and cooperate with law enforcement and there will be better outcomes in court."*[31]

Professional Associations

- American Forensic Nurses *(www.amrn.com)*
- International Association of Forensic Nurses *(www.forensicnurse.org)*
- Forensic Science Resource Center *(www.forensictrak.com)*

Professional Journal

- *Forensic Nurse Magazine Online (www.forensicnursemag.com)*

Media Coverage

Forensics nursing, first recognized as a specialty as recently as 1995, has grown tremendously over the past decade. By 2006, the International Association of Forensic Nurses had swelled to 2,800 members, up from 1,400 in 2000. Meanwhile, more and more graduate schools are offering programs for forensic nursing specialists—in 2005, Johns Hopkins University became the 13th to do so. This increase in demand is commonly attributed to improved evidence-collection technologies, the popularity of television shows like *CSI*, and recognition of the need to bridge the gap between the legal and medical worlds.[32]

---

31 Susan Wessling, "The Case for Forensic Nursing," MinorityNurses.com, *http://minoritynurse.com/features/nurse_emp/01-09-03b.html* (accessed August 16, 2006).

32 In-Sung Yoo, "Nurse as Sleuth," posted Tuesday April 11, 2006, Delaware Online, *www.delawareonline.com* (accessed August 16, 2006).

GERIATRIC NURSE   *Also Known As:* GERONTOLOGICAL NURSE

Definition: Nurses who provide care to older adults (usually defined as over 65 years old) in an ambulatory care center, assisted living facility, community center, or patient home. These nurses have extensive knowledge of the special needs of rehabilitating and maintaining the mental and physical health of the elderly.

Want ad #1: Nurse provides case management for members with dementia and related disorders. Responsible for assessment, planning, follow-up, individual and group counseling, education, and community resources. Provides in-depth clinical expertise. Provides advanced clinical practice education, consultation, research, and administration.

Want ad #2: Nurse needed for long-term care skilled nursing facility. Assessments, dressing changes, administer medication, treatments, and trach care, oxygen, nebulizers, glucometers, etc. Care of patients with diabetes, arthritis, pneumonia, COPD, cardiopulmonary, MIs, CHF, Parkinson's, etc.

> **Quote from a Geriatric Nurse:** *"Maybe that simple interaction with the patient will help ease the pain. Most of those depressions, most of those pains, can really be minimized by listening. Seeing a depressed [patient] smile after you've talked with them is rewarding."*[33]

Professional Associations

- Building Academic Geriatric Nursing Capacity (BAGNC) (*www.geriatricnursing.org*)

- John A. Hartford Foundation Institute for Geriatric Nursing (*www.hartfordign.org*)

- U.S. Administration on Aging (*www.aoa.dhhs.gov*)

- American Geriatrics Society (*www.americangeriatrics.org*)

- National Gerontological Nursing Association (*www.ngna.org*)

- GeroNurse Online (*geronurseonline.org*)

- American Society on Aging (ASA) (*www.asaging.org*)

- The Gerontological Society of America (*www.geron.org*)

- National Association of Geriatric Education Centers (*www.nagec.org*)

- National Institute on Aging (*www.nia.nih.gov*)

- American Association of Colleges of Nursing's Geriatric Nursing Education Project (*www.aacn.nche.edu/Education/Hartford/index.htm*)

Professional Journal

- *Geriatric Nursing Journal* (*www3.us.elsevierhealth.com/gerinurs*). An online journal about geriatric nursing.

Media Coverage

The U.S. Administration on Aging (AoA) estimates that every year hundreds of thousands of older persons are abused, neglected, and exploited by family members or other acquaintances. Often, these victims are frail, vulnerable, unable to help themselves, or dependent on others to meet their daily needs. In response, the AoA and related organizations support ongoing awareness campaigns, including World Elder Abuse Awareness Day, held annually in June. This event serves as a call-to-action for individuals, organizations, and communities to foment awareness about all forms of elder abuse.[34]

---

33 Sally Parker, "Hot Jobs, Emerging Careers." MinorityNurse.com, *http://minoritynurse.com/features/nurse_emp/02-12-04a.html* (accessed August 16, 2006).

34 "Elder Rights & Resources," U.S. Department of Health and Human Services, *www.aoa.dhhs.gov/eldfam/Elder_Rights/Elder_Abuse/Elder_Abuse.asp* (accessed August 16, 2006).

GERONTOLOGICAL NURSE PRACTITIONER

Definition: Registered nurse with a master's degree from a nurse practitioner program that specializes in the care of older adults. GNPs are educated to diagnose and manage acute and chronic diseases, taking a holistic approach to meet the medical, psychosocial, and functional needs of older patients.

Want ad: NP provides evaluation and management services for the medical management of elders with behavioral health conditions. Under supervision of a psychiatrist, will conduct clinical assessments. NP makes specific treatment recommendations to the primary care physician. Monitors patient progress by carrying out patient care services; maintaining patient records; consulting with supervising physician when patient's progress does not meet criteria; arranging consultations.

Professional Associations

- Conference of Gerontological Nurse Practitioners *(www.ncgnp.org/index.cfm)*

- American Geriatrics Society *(www.americangeriatrics.org)*

- National Gerontological Nursing Association *(www.ngna.org)*

- John A. Hartford Foundation Institute for Geriatric Nursing *(www.hartfordign.org)*

- American Association of Colleges of Nursing's Geriatric Nursing Education Project *(www.aacn.nche.edu/Education/Hartford/index.htm)*

- American Geriatrics Association's Foundation for Health in Aging *(www.healthinaging.org)*

Professional Journal

- *Geriatric Nursing Journal (www3.us.elsevier health.com/gerinurs)*. An online journal about geriatric nursing.

Media Coverage

In 2005, Congress approved a budget for Fiscal Year 2006 that eliminated funding for Title VII Geriatrics Health Professions Training programs. The American Geriatrics Society has an online media campaign to help restore the funding to 2005 levels ($31.5 million). In 2005, the Title VII–funded Geriatric Education Centers reported delivery of low-cost professional geriatric training interventions to over 50,000 health care providers who collectively reported over 8.6 million patient encounters.[35]

---

35 American Geriatrics Society Advocacy Campaign Web site, *http://ga1.org/campaign/TitleVII2* (accessed September 24, 2006).

HEALTH POLICY NURSE

Definition: Nurses in this field are analysts, usually prepared at the PhD level. They provide expert analysis on the potential or current impact of health and government policies. They may work with government policy-making bodies, think tanks, or schools.

Want ad: The successful candidate will have excellent analytical and writing skills with the ability to objectively examine a variety of current health policy issues, prepare position papers and briefing materials, assist drafting Congressional testimony, respond to proposed regulations, and otherwise help to develop and implement public policy positions of the nation's largest national medical specialty society. You will work closely with policy committee and other staff, but also must have the ability to work well independently. Experience in health policy analysis, excellent writing and computer skills.

> **Quotes from Health Policy Nurses:**
> *"Working at this level provides nurses with an opportunity to impact patient outcomes on a national scale."*
>
> *"We fund a variety of grants to cities, states, and community-based organizations that work with HIV/AIDS patients...We are often the last and only hope (for) poor and vulnerable patients."*[36]

Professional Associations

- National League of Nursing's Public Policy Action Center *(capwiz.com/nln/home)*. The mission of the National League of Nursing's Public Policy Action center is to get members involved in setting standards, advancing quality and innovation, and advocating for all types of academic and lifelong learning programs in nursing.

- American Nurses Association *(www.ana.org)*

- International Council of Nurses *(www.icn.ch)*

Professional Journal

- *Public Health Nursing.* A bimonthly publication featuring theoretical discussions, clinical reports, and commentary from health care leaders throughout the nation.

---

36 Linda Childers, "Careers in Red, White and Blue," MinorityNurse.com *http://minoritynurse.com/ features/nurse_emp/02-12-04c.html* (accessed September 24, 2006).

HIV/AIDS NURSE

Definition: Nurses in this field educate individuals on how to prevent the spread of HIV and help those infected cope with the physical, social, and psychological aspects of their disease—to minimize pain and maximize independence. They also educate and support loved ones and family members of those infected with the disease.

Want ad #1: Nurse with HIV/AIDS experience needed for a large licensed home care agency to do field visits. The nurse will visit and assess patients in their home and give new medication, and will be accompanied by a pharmaceutical company rep on these visits.

Want ad #2: The clinic nurse is responsible for assessing the physical, medical, and psychosocial needs of persons living with HIV/AIDS. The nurse is responsible for completing an initial nursing assessment, triaging phone calls, walk-in patients, and timely chart documentation, and has a strong ability to educate the patient in reference to his or her medical regime. The nurse works closely with the primary health care provider. The nurse provides case coordination and serves as the primary contact for assigned patients. The ability to perform chart reviews is essential in order to direct patients for appropriate clinical trials.

Professional Association

■ Association of Nurses in AIDS Care (*www.anacnet.org*)

Professional Journal

■ *Journal of the Association of Nurses in AIDS Care.* A peer-reviewed journal that serves as a forum for discussion of nursing issues in HIV/AIDS, including prevention, treatment, education, research, practice, clinical issues, policies, and program development.

Media Coverage

United Nations AIDS and the World Health Organization estimate that AIDS is responsible for the deaths of over 25 million people since it was first recognized in 1981, making it one of the most far-reaching epidemics in modern history. Despite access to antiretroviral treatment in many regions of the world, the AIDS epidemic claimed an estimated 2.8 million lives in 2005—more than half a million of which were children.

Health Action AIDS is an international campaign that engages the U.S. health professional community, as well as caregivers in AIDS-burdened nations, in an international education and advocacy effort to halt the global AIDS pandemic.[37]

---

37 "About the Health Action AIDS Campaign," Health Action AIDS Web site, *www.phrusa.org/campaigns/aids/about.html* (accessed August 16, 2006).

HOME HEALTH CARE NURSE   *Also Known As:* VISITING NURSE

Definition: Nurses who provide care for people in their homes, such as those recovering from illness, accident, or childbirth.

Want ad: Nurse to deliver high-quality care where patients are most comfortable, in their homes. Use a holistic approach considering physical, psych/social, spiritual, educational, and safety, considerations. Provide patient, family, and caregiver education. Coordinate care of the at-risk population, making assessments, planning interventions, and working closely with the entire patient care team. Facilitate the interdisciplinary plan of care as well as eliminate fragmentation of care/service.

Quote from a Home Health Care Nurse: *"I love the flexibility of working in home health and the bond you have with your patients and their families. I love having the time to teach patients about hygiene, nutrition, and coping skills. You work your schedule around what is convenient for both you and the patient. And the interaction with patients is priceless. They are all part of my second family."*

"Patients from different countries and ethnic groups have different attitudes toward the health care system,...While Asian immigrants from rural villages of China may be unfamiliar and fearful of Western medicine, patients from Hong Kong are usually very comfortable with American treatments and practices."[38]

Professional Associations

- Visiting Nurses Association of America *(www.vnaa.org)*

- National Association for Home Care *(www.nahc.org)*

- Home Healthcare Nurses Association *(www.hhna.org)*

Professional Journal

- *Home Healthcare Nurse* *(www.homehealthcarenurseonline.com)*. Serves the educational and communication needs of home healthcare nurses by presenting articles that address clinical and operational issues, and offer practical, up-to-date approaches to everyday situations and analyses of the effects of current trends.

Media Coverage

During the past two decades, the demand for pediatric home care has exploded. According to the federal Centers for Medicare and Medicaid Services (CMS), this is the fastest-growing segment of the home health care industry. CMS anticipates that the pediatric market will represent a $3.5 billion business in the next decade.[39]

---

38 Linda Childers, "Where the Heart Is," MinorityNurse.com, *www.minoritynurse.com/features/nurse_emp/03-21-06g.html* (accessed September 24, 2006).

39 Centers for Medicare and Medicaid Services, *www.cms.hhs.gov* (accessed August 16, 2006).

HOSPICE NURSE   *Also Known As:* PALLIATIVE CARE NURSE

Definition: Nurses in this field provide sensitive care and pain relief to patients in the final stages of life. They protect patients from unnecessary, painful therapies, and often provide care at home, in order to maximize meaningful time patients can spend with family and loved ones.

Want ad #1: The Palliative Care Nurse Coordinator is a key member of an interdisciplinary team comprised of physicians, nurses, chaplains, social workers, pharmacists, and dietitians. The team's goal is to relieve suffering and support the best possible quality of life for patients with advanced chronic or life-threatening illnesses. The team's objectives are to provide effective management of pain and other distressing symptoms, while integrating psychosocial and spiritual care.

Want ad #2: As a nurse, you will make a significant difference in many people's lives. You're the one knowledgeable individual who has contact with the client when they're at home. As a hospice nurse, you're the person the family and friends will remember. You will provide consultation to patients, their loved ones, and health care providers regarding hospice services, end of life treatment, and case management of the patient's needs.

Professional Associations

■ National Board for Certification of Hospice and Palliative Nurses *(www.nbchpn.org)*

■ National Hospice Foundation *(www.hospiceinfo.org)*

■ Hospice & Palliative Nurses Association *(www.hpna.org)*

■ The Initiative for Pediatric Palliative Care *(www.ippcweb.org)*

Professional Journal

■ *Home and Healthcare Nurse (www.homehealthcarenurseonline.com)*. Serves the educational and communication needs of hospice nurses by presenting articles that address clinical and operational issues, and offer practical, up-to-date approaches to everyday situations and analyses of the effects of current trends.

Media Coverage

A NurseZone.com article described a typical day for hospice nurse Yvonne Mabery. "No two days are ever alike. I may have seen 15 patients in a week. I'd see them depending on their acuity and need. We would tailor our visits to the family and let them guide the care. Sometimes I'd see a patient once a week, other times it would be two or three times a week. We really try to meet them at their needs. It's critical we don't come in with an agenda."

Mabery would typically see three or four patients in one day. "I listen, validate, and assess their concerns, then I will arrange for experts to come in."[40]

---

40 Julie Benn, "Career Series—A Day in the Life of a Hospice Nurse, NurseZone.com, *www.nursezone.com/Stories/SpotlightOnNurses. asp?articleID=9372* (accessed September 24, 2006).

INFECTION CONTROL NURSE
INFECTION PREVENTION NURSE

Also Known As: NURSE EPIDEMIOLOGIST,

Definition: Nurses in this field identify and control infections that occur in the community or in a hospital setting. They collect data and instigate infection control and prevention measures. They also work with childhood infectious diseases, sexually transmitted diseases, HIV, tuberculosis, and infections that occur during hospitalization.

Want ad: Nurse to plan, implement, and evaluate the Infection Control and Prevention Program. Conduct surveillance of nosocomial infections and other adverse events. Coordinate with occupational health nurse to develop policies and procedures, such as placement evaluations, health and safety education, immunization programs, evaluations of potentially harmful infectious exposures, and appropriate preventative measures. Establish an education program to prevent nosocomial infections.

Professional Association

- National Center for Infectious Diseases (*www.cdc.gov/ncidod/index.htm*).

- Association for Professionals in Infection Control and Epidemiology (*www.apic.org*).

- Infection Control Nurses Association (*www.icna.co.uk*).

- Community and Hospital Infection Control Association (CHICA)—Canada (*www.chica.org*). CHICA–Canada is a national, multidisciplinary, voluntary association of infection control professionals (ICPs) committed to improving the health of Canadians by promoting excellence in the practice of infection prevention and control.

Professional Journals

- *American Journal of Infection Control.* A source for peer-reviewed articles related to infection control, epidemiology, quality management, infectious diseases, occupational health, and disease prevention.

- Emerging Infectious Diseases (*www.cdc.gov/ncidod/eid/index.htm*).

Media Coverage

A recent Nurse Zone.com article reports that nurse epidemiologists have garnered a higher profile in recent years as public concern over pathogenic health threats has grown. Increasingly, bioterrorism, avian flu, West Nile virus, and severe acute respiratory syndrome (SARS) have heightened Americans' desire to get educated about preventative measures.

As a result, nurse epidemiologists are gaining respect and recognition for their contributions to public health and awareness. The NurseZone. com author alludes to their special role in his article opening: "Nurse epidemiologists are the front-line troops in the never-ending war against infectious diseases. They are often considered the Paul Reveres of the medical world, sounding the alarm when a new disease arises or formulating new strategies to fight familiar diseases."[41]

---

41 Robert Scally, "Nurse Epidemiologists on the Front Lines of Fighting Diseases," NurseZone.com, *www.nursezone.com/stories/SpotlightOnNurses. asp?articleID=10734* (accessed September 24, 2006).

INFORMATICIST *Also Known As:* COMPUTER NURSE

Definition: Nurses who merge their knowledge of information technology, computer science, and nursing science. They are much in demand as health care makes the transition from traditional record-keeping and care delivery to computerized and automated systems. They implement, teach, design and evaluate information systems to be more user-friendly for health care professionals. In addition, they make sure that systems are designed to provide clinical and administrative data for quality improvement and research efforts.

Want ad #1: Nurse to advise hospital executives and nursing management on clinical computer systems. Establish operational and financial benchmarks for technology. Conduct nursing department data-gathering of current processes and procedures. Act as subject matter expert for nursing. Demonstrate software in a live environment at health care organizations, key seminars, and tradeshows.

Want ad #2: The nurse informaticist will support the development of clinical information systems that assist clinicians in the delivery of patient care. This includes representing the needs of the physician community, as well as nursing. Also serve as an advocate of management in promoting information technology in clinical settings.

Quote from a Nurse Informaticist:
"[The nurse informaticist is] part educator, part scientist, part interpreter…There are still a lot of people who think that if it's technical, you lose the human touch. …but the reality is that computers can improve patient care and the delivery of health care services."[42]

Professional Associations

- American Nursing Informatics Association (ANIA) *(www.ania.org)*
- Capital Area Roundtable on Informatics in Nursing *(www.caringonline.org)*

Professional Journal

- *Nursing CIN: Computers, Informatics, Nursing (www.cinjournal.com)*

---

42 Sally Parker, "Hot Jobs, Emerging Careers," MinorityNurse.com, *http://minoritynurse.com/ features/nurse_emp/02-12-04a.html* (accessed August 16, 2006).

LEGAL NURSE CONSULTANT   *Also Known As:* NURSE PARALEGAL

Definition: Nurses in this field review medical records and help attorneys determine whether professional negligence has occurred in a given case.

Want ad #1: Large law firm seeking legal nurse consultant/nurse paralegal for immediate, permanent opportunity. Busy litigation practice focuses on catastrophic injury and toxic tort litigation. Very competitive salary and benefits. Qualified candidates will have BOTH nursing experience AND 2+ years of legal experience (either in a law firm or with an insurer).

Want ad #2: We seek a licensed practical nurse or a registered nurse with a legal nurse consultant certification/diploma. Experience in case management or arbitration. Candidates should be knowledgeable in CPT/ICD-9 coding, carepaths, and precertification. Excellent communication/computer skills a must. Ability to multitask and work in a fast paced environment both independently and as part of a team is necessary.

> **Quote from a Legal Nurse Consultant:** *"The attorneys send me the medical records and I sit down and go through them. It can take anywhere from four hours to three days. I read through every line. With the records comes a cover letter from the attorney, telling me what the plaintiff is complaining of. ...I make notes of what I see in the records...As I'm reading what's happening I'm there, I feel the excitement...In every chart you can find some mistakes. You're looking for something that really caused major problem in this person's life, that are really going to be devastating for the rest of their life."*[43]

Professional Associations

- LNC Resource, a national paper for Legal Nurse Consultants (*www.lncresource.com*)

- The American College of Legal Nurse Consulting (*www.aihcp.org/lnc.htm*)

- American Association of Nurse Attorneys (*www.taana.org*)

- American Association of Legal Nurse Consultants (*www.aalnc.org*)

Professional Journal

- *The Journal of Legal Nurse Consulting (www.aalnc.org/edupro/journal.cfm).* Published quarterly by the American Association of Legal Nurse Consultants.

Media Coverage

The American Association of Legal Nurse Consultants has an online resource featuring inspirational stories of how established LNCs successfully started their careers. To learn more, visit the "Personal Success Stories" page at *www.aalnc.org/becomelnc/stories.cfm.*[44]

---

43 "Interview with a Legal Nurse Consultant," All Criminal Justice Schools Web site, *www.allcriminaljusticeschools.com/faqs/legalnurse-consultant.php* (accessed August 16, 2006).

44 "Personal Success Stories," American Association of Legal Nurse Consultants Web site, *www.aalnc.org/becomelnc/stories.cfm* (accessed August 16, 2006).

LEGISLATIVE NURSE   *Also Known As:* GOVERNMENTAL WORKER

Definition: Nurses who are in the public sector, working in local, state, or federal government to affect public health legislation.

Want ad: The Public & Government Affairs staff will initiate an in-depth look at Medicare, as well as the current system of long-term care in the state. Primary responsibilities may include: helping to increase awareness of programs and services, assisting with developing and maintaining Public & Government Affairs Web site and legislator directory, and conducting research on other programs of interest.

Quote from a Legislative Nurse:
"We're making a national push toward use of computerized medical records. By utilizing information technology, the risk of medication errors will substantially decrease."[45]

Professional Journal

- Legislative Network for Nurses Journal of Professional Nursing. Bimonthly publication that focuses on changes in the legislative, regulatory, ethical, and professional standards that affect nursing. Each issue also presents observations by nursing leaders on the diverse roles of baccalaureate- and graduate-prepared nurses.

45 Linda Childers, "Careers in Red, White and Blue," MinorityNurse.com, *http://minoritynurse.com/ features/nurse_emp/02-12-04c.html* (accessed August 16, 2006).

LONG-TERM CARE NURSE
NURSE ASSESSMENT COORDINATOR

Also Known As: NURSING HOME NURSE, MDS NURSE,

Definition: Nurses who provide continuing care to patients who have been diagnosed with chronic diseases. The care usually involves elderly or disabled patients and their families.

Want ad: In conjunction with the unit director, the nurse utilizes a general understanding of the principles of nursing and basic physical assessment skills in the development and implementation of individualized nursing care plans to ensure that the needs of the customers are met. He or she assists in the orientation of new personnel, attends to the daily operations of the unit on a per shift and unit level, and assumes responsibilities of a leadership role.

Professional Associations

■ National Gerontological Nursing Association (*www.ngna.org*)

■ American Assisted Living Nurses Association (*www.alnursing.org*)

■ Canadian Gerontological Nursing Association (*www.cgna.net*)

■ National Association of Professional Geriatric Care Managers (*www.caremanager.org*)

■ American Association of Homes and Services for the Aging (*www.aahsa.org*)

■ American Health Care Association (*www.ahca.org*)

■ National Association of Directors of Nursing Administration in Long-Term Care (*www.nadona.org*)

■ American Association for Continuity of Care (*www.continuityofcare.com*)

■ American Association of Nurse Assessment Coordinators (AANAC) (*www.aanac.org*). Founded in 1999, AANAC is a nonprofit professional organization dedicated to providing accurate and timely information, opportunities for education, and representation of nurse assessment coordinators in long-term care. The mission of AANAC is to improve the quality of care for residents/patients by providing health care professionals with accurate and timely information, education, networking, and advocacy related to clinical assessment and completion of federally mandated instruments.

Professional Journal

■ *Journal of Gerontological Nursing* (*www.jogonline.com*)

Media Coverage

Researchers at the San Francisco VA Medical Center and the University of California, San Francisco, recently found that people aged 70 and older with limited literacy skills are up to two times as likely to have poor health and poor health care access as people with adequate or higher reading ability.

Elders with limited literacy—roughly equivalent to a reading level below ninth grade—were one and a half times more likely than other study participants to report poor overall health and diabetes, and twice as likely to report depression. Furthermore, the study found that among community-dwelling elders between the ages of 70 and 79, approximately 25 percent had limited literacy, meaning they might not be able to read pill bottle instructions or basic health information.[46]

---

46 "Low Literacy Equals Poor Health for Senior Citizens," May 26, 2006, SeniorJournal.com, *www.seniorjournal.com/NEWS/Health/6-05-26-LowLiteracy.htm* (accessed September 24, 2006).

MANAGED CARE NURSE   *Also Known As:* CLAIMS PROCESSING NURSE, MEDICAL
BILL REVIEW ANALYST

Definition: Nurses who work to keep health care costs to a minimum by educating individuals and families about illness prevention and self-care and by helping health care providers administer to the sick in an efficient manner.

Want ad: With supervision by the manager of Utilization Management, the medical loss review nurse (MLRN) conducts clinical claim reviews. Reviews may include durable medical equipment, procedures, inpatient hospital services, and home health services. After a claim review has been completed, the MLRN will provide direction to adjudicators for appropriate reimbursement of hospital, emergency room, targeted specialists, and ancillary provider bills. The MLRN will identify potential billing irregularities, trends in billing, and provide information to the appropriate resources, including Provider Network Management, Operations, and Fraud & Abuse. The MLRN will complete payment audits for identified high dollar claims and provide appropriate follow up in a timely manner.

> **Quote from a Managed Care Nurse:**
> *"Nurses in the managed care arena can intervene ... As nurses, we can direct members to the appropriate services available in their benefit plan, or if the plan doesn't cover specific services, we can refer them to our community liaison."*[47]

Professional Associations

- American Board of Managed Care Nursing (*www.abmcn.org*)

- American Association of Managed Care Nurses (*www.aamcn.org*)

Professional Journal

- *The American Journal of Managed Care* (*www.ajmc.com/Index.cfm?Menu=1*)

Media Coverage

Nurse Practitioners are mentioned in the American College of Surgeons Q & A about managed care. "To keep costs low, specific health care practitioners within the plan—who are often called "gatekeepers"—"manage" the amount and type of health care that is provided to patients. Sometimes these practitioners are primary care physicians; other times they are health care professionals who are not physicians, such as nurse practitioners. These managed care practitioners may be required by the plan to limit the number of times that patients with special medical problems may be referred to specialists. Managed care plans also may require specialists to get approval from the managed care practitioners before they hospitalize a patient or order expensive diagnostic services."[48]

---

47 Linda Childers, "Trade Your Scrubs for a Business Suit," MinorityNurse.com, *http://minoritynurse.com/features/nurse_emp/11-18-04a.html* (accessed August 16, 2006).

48 "Information on Patient Choice", American College of Surgeons Web site, *www.facs.org/public_info/patient_choice/ychoice.html#choice3*, (accessed September 24, 2006).

MILITARY AND UNIFORMED SERVICE NURSE

Definition: Nurses who provide medical care for soldiers in all branches of the U.S. military, including Army, Navy, and Air Force, as well as in the U.S. Public Health service.

Want ad: Clinical Liaison Nurse—This position is in a TRICARE Service Center (TSC) located in a Military Treatment Facility (MTF), most often on a military installation. It is a clinical and customer service type environment. The incumbent manages the activities of the TSC to ensure compliance with contractual requirements and maintenance of customer service standards. Serves as the primary liaison for the MTF staff regarding TSC operations, network providers, and the Hub Healthcare Services and Customer Service staff. Clinical advisor to the SAD, focusing on assisting in building and maintaining relationships between the Hub and MTF staffs and for support of MTF Optimization initiatives.

Quotes from Military and Uniformed Service Nurses: *"We're all about leadership. If you follow the career paths, you're able to progress to whatever level you choose."*

"I have my bags ready to go at any point in time. We have to realize we're officers first. When you come into the military, it's almost like you're answering a higher calling."[49]

Professional Associations

- Navy Nurse Corps Association (*nnca.org*)
- U.S. Public Health Service Commissioned Corps (*www.usphs.gov*)
- U.S. Public Health Service Nursing (*phs-nurse.org*)
- National Health Service Corps (NHSC) (*nhsc.bhpr.hrsa.gov*)
- Nurses Organization of Veterans Affairs (*www.vanurse.org*)

Media Coverage

Loretta Scott wrote a book, *Yes I Can*, about her experiences as an Army Nurse in the 1991 Gulf War and then her life afterward. Her description on her Web site (*www.gulfnurse.com/bio.htm*) is worth quoting: "It's my story, a story of survival …(including) the lack of human kindness I encountered during my tests….Survival is a choice with perseverance and a dedication tightly packed like a spool of thread. So when the seams began to come apart, we are able to escape the full magnitude of the loose threads, because we are able to hold on, and sew them back in place…While I was overseas serving in Desert Storm in 1991, I decided to keep a journal…So this is my story, my experiences, my trials and tribulations, my thoughts and the path to "Yes I Can."[50]

---

49 Barbara Marquand, "An Army (and Navy and Air Force) of Opportunities," MinorityNurses.com, *http://minoritynurse.com/features/nurse_emp/05-12-04b.html* (accessed August 16, 2006).

50 Loretta Scott, "Bio," *www.gulfnurse.com.bio.htm* (accessed September 24, 2006).

NURSE ADVOCATE   *Also Known As:* NURSING LEADER OR VISIONARY

Definition: Nurses who take concerted action to promote the nursing profession in the public eye through marketing political and social campaigns or in the health policy arena through legislation. Issues promoted include increasing diversity in the workforce, ensuring pay and benefits consistent with responsibility, and enhancing the image of nursing as a career.

> **Quote from a Nurse Advocate:** *"It is by our ongoing vigilance and lobbying that we will keep the care in health care. This means we need more nurses in politics, all nurses comfortable in the advocacy role, and more emphasis on communications and marketing in our organizations. Successful advocacy, whether for better health services, more opportunities for nurses, or better salaries and working conditions, calls for unity of the nursing voice. To lead the world to better health, we need the strength of our numbers."*[51]

Professional Associations

- The Center for Nursing Advocacy—Increasing Public Understanding of Nursing *(nursingadvocacy.org)*. The center staff summarize news on nurses in the media. Their goal is to positively shape media portrayals of nurses. For example, they have campaigns about the television shows "Grey's Anatomy," "House," and "ER."

- National League of Nursing's Public Policy Action Center *(capwiz.com/nln/home)*. Its mission is to get members involved in setting standards, advancing quality and innovation, and advocating for all types of academic and lifelong learning programs in nursing.

Professional Journal

- *Nursing Economic$, the Journal for Health Care Leaders*

Media Coverage

African Americans, Hispanic Americans, and Native Americans compose almost 25 percent of the total U.S. population, yet account for only 9 percent of its nurses. Although the percentage of African American students increased from 9.3 percent of students in 1993 to 12.4 percent in 2003, African American registered nurses represent just over 6 percent of all registered nurses. The numbers are fewer for other nurses as Hispanics represented 3 percent and American Indian/Alaskan Natives represented less than 1 percent.[52]

---

51 Kirsten Stallknecht, "American Nurses Association Convention Speech," June 24, 2000, NursingWorld.com, *www.nursingworld.org/ojin/keynotes/speech_1.htm* (accessed August 16, 2006).

52 Mary Maxwell, "It's Not Just Black and White: How Diverse Is Your Workforce?" *Nursing Economics Journal* 23, no. 3 (May/June 2005).

NURSE ATTORNEY

Definition: Nurses in this field have degrees in both nursing and law. They may represent health care professionals in court or give advice to hospitals or insurance companies as their legal counsel. They may teach at a college of nursing or school of law. They may be an independent legal consultant in private practice or be an advocate of improvements in health care policy in the public sector.

Want ad #1: Top plaintiff firm is seeking a registered nurse (RN)/attorney to assist in medical malpractice, pharmaceutical and medical device, and personal injury matters. Ideal candidate will possess nursing experience, as well as a law degree. Primary responsibilities will include examining medical records, and interviewing doctors and other medical experts.

Want ad #2: A law firm seeks to hire a nurse attorney/law student with zero to three years experience to handle the defense of medical malpractice and general liability cases. The firm will devote considerable resources to train the new hire to become an excellent trial lawyer. The associate will participate in all aspects of representing our clients including learning how to take depositions, drafting and arguing motions, witness and client preparation, legal research, trial preparation, making court appearances, as well as how to manage their own files. The associate will enjoy a true open-door policy, working directly with a partner to obtain advice, training, and guidance concerning all aspects of their work. The firm has a very collegial work environment.

Professional Associations

- The American Association of Nurse Attorneys *(www.taana.org)*
- American Society of Law, Medicine, & Ethics *(www.aslme.org)*

Professional Journal

- *The Journal of Nursing Law*. This journal is published for members of the American Association of Nurse Attorneys

Media Coverage

A NurseWeek article featured nurse lawyer Kathleen Lambert, JD, RN. Lambert uses her combined skills to educate nurses on avoiding lawsuits and to lecture Arizona's elderly on advanced directives, wills, trusts, and other medical/legal issues. She works as a solo practitioner from her Tucson home and takes only those cases that appeal to her. She said that as both a nurse and lawyer she can address a client's legal, physical, emotional and spiritual needs. "I'm a nurturing attorney, which is not what people generally think of when they think of an attorney," she said. "I feel a true lawyer is a counselor in the true sense of the word."[53]

---

53 Scott Williams, "Legal Eagles," NurseWeek, February 13, 2002, *www.nurseweek.com/news/features/02-02/legalnurse.asp* (accessed September 25, 2006).

NURSING EDUCATOR   *Also Known As:* INSTRUCTIONAL OR ADMINISTRATIVE NURSING FACULTY, ACADEMIC NURSE, STAFF DEVELOPMENT OFFICER, CONTINUING EDUCATION SPECIALIST

Definition: Nurses who are responsible for teaching and mentoring current and future nurses. Working within the classroom and in the clinical practice setting, they enjoy preparing lesson plans, inspiring, instructing, evaluating learning, counseling, and assisting with solving challenging learning problems. Often they serve as the first role model for nursing students.

Want ad #1: Plans, develops, and directs the orientation program for all employees; supervises and monitors nursing employees throughout individualized orientation period; develops in-service programs in response to staff needs and teaches staff current accepted customer care and center practices; and coordinates and teaches nurse aide certification courses.

Want ad #2: Ensure quality patient care through education of new and existing employees. Develop instructional materials to assist new personnel in becoming oriented to facility and operational techniques. Determine the effectiveness of orientation materials and procedures through direct observation, and in collaboration with the Director of Nursing Services and Medical Director. Maintain library of books and educational materials for facility personnel.

> **Quote from a Nursing Educator:** *"Two days a week, I'm in a hospital setting doing clinical experiences with students. We determine which patient(s) they've chosen to spend time with and what is the plan of care. So that would be a full day of clinical. Other days may involve doing class work, which is the theoretical class. There's time spent in the classroom, which may involve preparing and giving the lecture for that class."*[54]

Professional Associations

- National Nursing Staff Development Organization *(www.nnsdo.org)*
- American Society for Training and Development *(www.astd.org)*

Professional Journals

- *Journal for Nurses in Staff Development (www.nursingcenter.com/library)*
- *Journal of Continuing Education in Nursing (www.slackinc.com/allied/jcen/jcenhome.htm)*
- *Journal of Nursing Education (www.journalofnursingeducation.com/about.asp)*
- *Journal of Professional Nursing (www.aacn.nche.edu/Publications/jpn.htm)*
- *Nurse Educator (www.nursingcenter.com/library)*
- *Nursing Education Perspectives (www.nln.org/nlnjournal/index.htm)*
- *Nurse Educator Magazine (www.nurseeducatoronline.com)*
- *Journal of Nursing Education (www.journalofnursingeducation.com)*

Media Coverage

Elizabeth Dole and Luci Baines Johnson are honorary chairs of Nurses for a Healthier Tomorrow (NHT), a coalition of more than 40 organizations created to increase the number of nurses. NHT members believe that one key to alleviating the nursing shortage is to address a root cause: insufficient number of nursing faculty.[55]

---

54   GinaMaria Jerome, "A Day in the Life: An Interview with Professor Bethany Hoffman, *www.hospitalsoup.com/Day/Nurse/hoffman.asp* (accessed September 25, 2006).

55   Nurses for a Healthier Tomorrow Web site, *www.nursesource.org/campaign_news.html* (accessed August 16, 2006).

NURSE EXECUTIVE AND NURSING CHIEF EXECUTIVE OFFICER

Definition: Nurses who are primarily involved with ongoing high-level management and administration concerns. They provide leadership roles in designing care delivery, in planning and developing procedures and policies, and in administering budgets in hospitals, health clinics, nursing homes, and ambulatory care centers.

Want ad #1: The chief nurse executive is a member of the administrative team; functions as director of nursing services; oversees all medical and health-related services provided by professionals and technicians; assures consistency in the provision of quality care to residents and patients throughout the campus; provides direct supervision to the nursing managers, education/quality assurance staff, medical records staff, and clinical nutrition; and provides the human resource department staffing plans for nursing units. In addition, she or he is a resource to the clinical nurse manager and the administrator. This person directs quality improvement efforts related to the delivery of health care services. The chief nurse executive reports to the administrator.

Want ad #2: A chief nurse executive is needed for large hospital. The qualified candidate may now be a CNO or DON at a small hospital, may have been over multiple departments in an acute care hospital during a span of at least seven years, or may have attained the title of ACNO or DON. He or she will be a strong mentor, retainer of staff, and a strategic thinker. A Bachelor's and Masters are required, and one of these degrees must be in nursing. This is a fabulous job for someone who sees the bigger picture.

Professional Associations

- National Association of Directors of Nursing Administration in Long-Term Care *(www.nadona.org)*

- American Organization of Nurse Executives *(www.aone.org)*

- AONE Institute for Patient Care Research & Education *(www.aone.org/aone/institute/home.html)*

Professional Journal

- NurseLeader Journal *(www.nurseleader.com)*

NURSE MANAGER AND NURSING ADMINISTRATOR

Also Known As: NURSING DIRECTOR, CHIEF NURSING OFFICER

Definition: Nurses in this field include those with degrees in nursing, business, or nursing administration and work with the top levels of hospital and health care administration, overseeing and guiding an institution's nursing workforce. A nurse supervisor is often responsible for several nursing units or all units for a particular function, such as staffing or a shift, such as night supervisor. The first-line manager/head nurse assumes responsibility for the personnel, resources, and patient care on a nursing unit.

Want ad: Seeking a qualified chief nursing officer who is forward-thinking, a team player, and looking to make a difference in the community and their profession. This position will provide overall leadership to the delivery of health and clinical programs. Promote quality patient care and nursing services. Create policies and establish standards of performance. Ensure programs, services, and practices are compliant with professional standards, medical by-laws, and regulations. Set clinical priorities and goals. Manage professional staff. Develop, present, and manage the budget for nursing services. Participate in the hospital's leadership functions.

Professional Associations

- American Organization of Nurse Executives (AONE) *(www.aone.org)*. Founded in 1967, AONE, a subsidiary of the American Hospital Association, is a national organization of over 5,000 nurses who design, facilitate, and manage care. Its mission is to represent nurse leaders who improve health care. AONE members are leaders in collaboration and catalysts for innovation. AONE's vision is "Shaping the future of health care through innovative nursing leadership."

- National Association of Directors of Nursing Administration for Long-Term Care *(www.nadona.org)*

Professional Journals

- *Nursing Management Magazine (www.nursingmanagement.com)*.

- *Journal of Nursing Administration (www.jona-journal.com)*. Issues since 1996 are available online.

NURSE MIDWIFE

Definition: Nurses who provide total care for pregnant women, from prenatal visits through to labor and delivery in hospitals, private homes, and birthing centers. They follow up with postpartum care. They also can provide primary health care throughout the course of a woman's reproductive life.

Want ad: Providing care to woman's health and low risk OB/GYN patients, as well as hospital-based obstetrical care for inpatient population. Functioning as part of the in-patient OB team. Supervising and instructing OB/GYN residents and medical students in their assessment of low risk OB patients. Managing labor, delivery, and repairs on low-risk patients. Demonstrated skill in biopsies, IUD placement, hormone replacement therapy, OB care, and in-office ultrasound skills. Experience in a full lifespan practice is necessary. A commitment to obtain RN First Assist certification in future development is necessary.

Professional Associations

- American College of Nurse Midwives (ACNM) *(www.midwife.org)*. With roots dating to 1929, the ACNM is the oldest women's health care organization in the U.S. ACNM provides research, accredits midwifery education programs, administers and promotes continuing-education programs, establishes clinical practice standards, and creates liaisons with state and federal agencies and members of Congress. The mission of ACNM is to promote the health and well-being of women and infants within their families and communities through the development and support of the profession of midwifery as

practiced by certified nurse-midwives and certified midwives. The philosophy inherent in the profession states that nurse-midwives believe every individual has the right to safe, satisfying health care with respect for human dignity and cultural variations.

- National Association of Nurse Practitioners in Reproductive Health

- Midwives Association of North America

Professional Journal

- *Journal of Nurse-Midwifery & Women's Health*. The official publication of the American College on Nurse-Midwives, this is a bimonthly, peer-reviewed journal dedicated to the publication of original research and review articles that focus on midwifery and women's health. It provides a forum for interdisciplinary exchange across a broad range of women's health issues. Manuscripts that address midwifery, women's health, education, evidence-based practice, public health, policy, and research are welcomed.

Media Coverage

GotMom.org is a Web site created by the American College of Nurse-Midwives to provide breastfeeding information and resources for mothers and families. One unique feature is that they address the situations of working new mothers. They state that "In the United States today, over 50 percent of mothers with children less than one year of age are in the labor force. Clearly, any initiative to support breastfeeding must address the workplace." Thus, one resource they provide is a downloadable brochure "Supporting Your Breastfeeding Employees."[56]

---

56 "Resources for Employers," *www.gotmom.org* (accessed September 25, 2006).

NURSE RECRUITER

Definition: Nurses in this field scout for the highest quality personnel for large employers of nurses, such as hospitals.

Want ad #1: Nurse to coordinate the process of securing qualified candidates for organizational vacancies for assigned clinical areas. Participate in the marketing program for recruitment of staff. Serve as a liaison with management, staff, and external candidates to streamline recruitment procedures and accomplish organizational objectives.

Want ad #2: Looking for a nurse recruiter to add to our human resources team. This position reports to the human resources manager responsible for the recruitment, hiring, transfer, and retention processes for nursing and nursing support personnel. Accountable for the ongoing evaluation and improvement of recruitment, hiring, transfer, and retention processes, utilizing continuous quality improvement techniques.

Professional Association

- The National Association for Health Care Recruitment *(www.nahcr.com)*. This association provides leadership and support for the health care recruiting profession through advocacy, education, and professional development. It is a nonprofit, 1,050-member national association.

Professional Journal

- *NAHCR Directions.* This is a resource directory for members of the National Association for Health Care Recruitment. This bimonthly newsletter features regional information on a variety of topics, as well as center-spread articles on important topics for all health care recruiters. The newsletter also functions as a directory, containing not only members' addresses and telephone numbers, but also names of members willing to be resources on a plethora of topics. The newsletter is offered at no cost through membership.

OCCUPATIONAL HEALTH NURSE
COMPENSATION NURSE, ERGONOMIC NURSE

Also Known As: WORKMANS'

Definition: Nurses who provide on-the-job health care at work sites for employees, customers, and others with minor injuries and illnesses. For workers, their goal is to ensure the employee's health, safety, and productivity. For workers and customers, they can provide emergency care, prepare accident reports, and arrange for further care if necessary. They initiate safety and wellness education efforts, including health counseling, assisting with health examinations and vaccinations, and working on accident prevention programs.

Want ad: Nurse needed to develop favorable working partnerships and relationships with members, physicians, health care service providers, and internal and external customers to improve health outcomes for members. Participates in activities that result in member access to medically necessary, quality health care in the most appropriate and cost effective setting. Facilitates communication among members and the health care delivery system.

> **Quote from an Occupational Health Nurse:** *"Occupational Health is a great field for nurses who are entrepreneurial in nature and who want more autonomy in their practice. Occupational Health Nurses often set up their own prevention and case management programs and can work as independent consultants for large corporate settings, small businesses, or Occupational Health clinics....opportunities that can provide both variety and career advancement."[57]*

---

57 "Occupational/Environmental Health Nursing," *nurseweb.ucsf.edu, www/spec-oeh.htm* (accessed September 25, 2006).

Professional Associations

- American Association of Occupational Health Nurses *(www.aaohn.org)*
- American Board for Occupational Health Nurses *(www.abohn.org)*
- International Commission on Occupational Health *(www.icoh.org.sg)*
- American College of Occupational and Environmental Medicine *(www.acoem.org)*
- U.S. Department of Labor's Occupational Safety & Health Administration (OSHA)'s Office of Occupational Health Nursing *(www.osha.gov/dts/oohn)*

Professional Journal

- *AAOHN Journal.* The official, peer-reviewed journal of the American Association of Occupational Health Nurses. The journal supports and promotes the practice of occupational and environmental health nursing by reporting on current research findings, clinical and technical data, and state-of-the-art information on issues that relate to the practice.

Media Coverage

The University of California Center for Occupational and Environmental Health publishes a journal "Bridges." Online access is found at *www.coeh.berkeley.edu/research/bridges.* Topics featured include:

- Environmental and Occupational Epidemiology
- Ergonomics
- Exposure Assessment
- Infectious Disease
- Lung Biology
- Toxicology

OUTREACH NURSE   *Also Known As:* HEALTH PROMOTION NURSE

Definition: Nurses who market health programs to current and future patients. The nurse introduces patient education to the public to increase awareness of self-care and treatment options.

Want ad: A nonprofit social services agency serving the needs of the city's senior adults seeks to improve the quality of life for the elderly and assist them in achieving optimum levels of health, independence, and productivity. This position is responsible for planning, implementing, evaluating, and monitoring senior community center-based health promotion programs. Duties also include providing clinical oversight of all planned health promotion programs to assure that appropriate health and medical issues are included. Experience in public health nursing or community-based work with older individuals, families, and groups is desired. You will make a significant impact on the lives of the elderly. Persons bilingual in Spanish or Asian languages are highly encouraged to apply.

> **Quotes from Outreach Nurses:** *"At CDC [the Center for Disease Control and Prevention], we strive to recognize trends and to identify issues, such as obesity, that pose a threat to women's health. Our goal is to help all women lead healthier, safer lives."*
>
> *"Without programs such as ours [breast cancer screening education], a large segment of the population would fall through the cracks in the health system."*[58]

Professional Association

- American Academy of Health Behavior *(www.aahb.org)*. The academy was founded April 1, 1998, to transform the health promotion and health education field from a teaching- and service-centered profession to one with a stronger research foundation in which discovery would be valued as a means of improving practice and enhancing public health.

Professional Journals

- *American Journal of Health Promotion (healthpromotionjournal.com)*. The American Journal of Health Promotion, was launched in 1986 as the first peer-reviewed journal devoted to health promotion, and it remains the largest, with subscribers in all 50 United States and about 40 other countries.

- *American Journal of Health Behavior (www.ajhb.org)*. This is the official publication of the American Academy of Health Behavior.

Media Coverage

The Arthur Ashe Institute of Urban Health's Black Pearls: Health and Beauty Outreach for Black Women program is a media campaign that uses hair salons as sites for providing health education and screening to black women in inner city neighborhoods. The Black Pearls program uses community residents, local health professionals, and participating salons to teach women about health issues like breast cancer, sexual health, smoking cessation, heart disease, high blood pressure, nutrition, and organ donation. The participants watch a film while they are getting their hair or nails done, then listen as the educators discuss information about disease prevention and early detection.[59]

---

58 Linda Childers, "Careers in Red, White and Blue," MinorityNurse.com, *http://minoritynurse.com/features/nurse_emp/02-12-04c.html* (accessed August 16, 2006).

59 Susan Wessling, "Closing the Cancer Gap," MinorityNurse.com, *http://minoritynurse.com/features/nurse_emp/01-27-02d.html* (accessed August 16, 2006).

OVERSEAS NURSE *Also Known As:* DEVELOPMENT, VOLUNTEER, MISSIONARY, OR REFUGEE NURSE

Definition: Nurses in these fields work at home and abroad with nonprofit organizations, such as the Peace Corps, to bring basic health care to poor communities.

Want ad: Save the Children posts overseas job openings in crisis areas. An example is Child Protection Officer, Darfur, Sudan. Will design and implement psychosocial play programs for war affected children. S/he will establish peer networks, psychosocial support, livelihoods support, and social integration; field visits to assess program quality, identify vulnerabilities, and ensure follow up on specific cases of vulnerable children; and maintain regular contact with relevant United Nations agencies. This position requires field experience working with displaced populations and women's protection concerns; experience implementing psychosocial projects for children and youth; community work with a participatory approach; demonstrated success working in conflict areas with a multi-ethnic teams; ability to work independently, with limited resources. [60]

Professional Associations

■ Centers for Disease Control's International Emergency and Refugee Health Branch *(www.cdc.gov/nceh/ierh/default.htm)*

■ International Federation of Red Cross and Red Crescent Societies *(www.ifrc.org)*

Professional Journal

■ Journal of Transcultural Nursing *(tcn.sagepub.com)*

Media Coverage

InterAction: American Council for Voluntary International Action is the largest alliance of U.S.-based international development and humanitarian nongovernmental organization. With more than 160 members operating in every developing country, they offer media resources to help change agents function more effectively. An example is their "Advocacy Toolkit: Creating Campaigns that Change the World." *(www.interaction.org/library/detail.php?id=4946)*.

---

60 Save The Children: Jobs, *http://hostedjobs.openhire.com/onlinejobs/jobs* (accessed September 25, 2006).

PAIN MANAGEMENT SPECIALIST

Definition: Nurses who are responsible for assessing, treating, and monitoring pain, which is often referred to as the fifth vital sign. They educate patients about the management of pain, as well as make sure the patient is safe during the administration of treatment. Pain management specialists are advanced practice nurses with master's degrees and a nurse practitioner certificate. They may also have certification in palliative care or advanced oncology.

Want ad: Nurse needed to provide case management for people suffering from chronic and acute pain, assisting with treatment plans; and coordinating with the patient, family, and medical staff to meet the patient's needs. You need to have excellent assessment, communication, teaching, and interpersonal skills; the ability to work independently; a working knowledge of anatomy and physiology of the nervous system and the interdependency of various bodily systems.

Professional Associations

- American Society for Pain Management Nursing (ASPMN) *(www.aspmn.org)* The mission of the American Society for Pain Management Nursing is to provide education, standards, advocacy and research for nurses.

- American Pain Society *(www.ampainsoc.org)*

- The American Academy of Pain Medicine *(www.painmed.org)*

- American Pain Foundation *(www.painfoundation.org)*

- International Association for the Study of Pain (IASP) *(www.iasp-pain.org)*

Professional Journal

- *Pain Management Nursing.* This is the official journal of the American Society for Pain Management Nursing.

PARISH NURSE   *Also Known As:* HEALTH MINISTRY NURSE

Definition: Nurses in this field administer to a church community, providing public health information and basic patient care; often focusing on the needs of the elderly or homeless individuals.

Want ad: Coordinates the Parish Nurse Partnership program. Assists congregations and the community to learn about and develop health ministry. Working, hands-on knowledge of holistic health required. Able to communicate wellness education with a spiritual outlook. Some study in theology, ministry, or clinical pastoral education preferred. Public health nursing certificate and valid nursing license required.

> **Quote from a Parish Nurse:** *"I maintain office hours at the church two days a week, two hours each day, for anyone wanting weekly blood pressure checks, information on medical problems, referrals to community resources, etc. I keep a file card on each family I become involved with and add notes at each contact so I have long-term information on the family's health issues. All of my records are kept secured and all contacts are confidential. I feel wonderfully blessed to have this ministry. I love being a parish nurse."*[61]

Professional Associations

- International Parish Nurse Resource Center (*ipnrc.parishnurses.org*)
- Mennonite Nurses Association (*mna.mennonite.net/objectives.shtml*)
- Caring Congregations (*www.caringcongregations.org*)
- Emory University's Interfaith Health Program (*www.ihpnet.org*)
- Institute for Public Health and Faith Collaborations (*www.ihpnet.org/4iphfc.htm*)
- Nurses Christian Fellowship (*www.ncf-jcn.org*)

Professional Journal

- *The Journal of Christian Nursing* (*www.intervarsity.org/ncf/jcn*)

Media Coverage

The University of Maryland hosts a Web site "What is Parish Nursing?" that provides information resources about that nursing specialty (*www.parishnursing.umaryland.edu/whatis.asp*). It includes links to the Internaional Parish Nurse Resource Center; the American Nurses Associaton publication about the specialty's Scope and Standards; a Lutheran Church's pastor's manual; and a Methodist guide on how to establish a parish ministry.

---

61 "Barbara C. RN, MSN, Parish Nurse" Discover Nursing, *www.discovernursing.com/jnj-profileID_413-dsc-profile_detail.aspx*. Accessed August 16, 2006.

PATIENT ADVOCATE   *Also Known As:* FAMILY HEALTH ADVOCATE

Definition: Nurses who serve as a liaison between the physician and the patient/family, either in or outside the hospital setting. These nurses may monitor the patient during an inpatient stay to oversee medical and nursing care. They could negotiate problems with billing issues afterward. They make sure that an individual's or family's concerns and complaints are resolved.

Want ad: This position is the liaison between the center and the families to whom the center provide services. The family health advocate will ensure that the center's services and policies and procedures function to serve the needs of families. Will work with parents/caretakers to help engage the families in positive relationships with the treatment team and to provide information to families that will empower them to make informed decisions regarding their child's treatment.

Quote from a Patient Advocate: *"So if you've got a Wonder Woman, or Wonder Man, available to help you get what you need from the medical system, count your blessings. If not, consider hiring a private patient advocate."*[62]

Quote from Patient: *"The student patient advocate met with me, toured the medical facilities, attended appointments with doctors, and helped wade through red tape. She also helped us create reasonable expectations."*[63]

---

62 "What Our Clients Say…" The Center for Patient Partnerships Web site, *www.law.wisc.edu/ patientadvocacy/quotes.html* (accessed August 16, 2006).

63 Ibid.

PEDIATRIC NURSE PRACTITIONER (PNP)

Definition: Nurses in this field have extensive education in pediatric health care and nursing, and serve as health care providers for children and adolescents. They work with pediatricians and other health care providers to promote and advance children's health care.

Want ad #1: To provide specialized nurse practitioner care in pediatric and adolescent health. Advanced knowledge of the provision of primary care under nurse practitioner guidelines Standards of Practice required. Strong knowledge of family practice and/or pediatric nurse practitioner techniques related standards of practice.

Want ad #2: Performs comprehensive medical and nursing assessments to be used in the diagnosis and treatment/management of infants in the full-term nursery, select infants in the special care nursery through adolescents in the ambulatory or inpatient care setting.

Professional Associations

■ American Academy of Nurse Practitioners (*www.aanp.org*)

■ National Association of Pediatric Nurse Associates and Practitioners (*www.napnap.org*)

■ American College of Nurse Practitioners (*www.nurse.org/acnp*)

Professional Journal

■ *Journal of Pediatric Health Care*. This is the official journal of the National Association of Pediatric Nurse Practitioners and is a benefit of membership.

Media Coverage

Nursing Spectrum reports that evidence strongly suggests that health problems that lead to heart attacks and atherosclerosis in adults can begin as early as age 5. The increased prevalence of these heart-related problems is due to Americans' fondness for junk food and sedentary activities like watching television.

According to the National Health and Nutrition Examination Survey, obesity in children ages 6 to 11 increased from 4.2 percent in 1963–65 to 15.3 percent in 1999–2000, and obesity in adolescents 12 to 19 increased from 4.6 percent to 15.5 percent during the same time period.[64]

---

64 Scott Williams, "Helping Children Stay Young at Heart, June 5, 2006, *Nursing Spectrum*, *http://community.nursingspectrum.com/ MagazineArticles/article.cfm?AID=21874* (accessed August 16, 2006).

POISON INFORMATION SPECIALIST   *Also Known As:* POISON CONTROL
SPECIALIST

Definition: Nurses who provide information to individuals, schools, businesses, and medical professionals regarding poison prevention and treatment. These specialists often work in poison control centers providing phone triage to patients who may have ingested poison. These nurses usually have backgrounds in emergency rooms and intensive care units.

Want ad: Provides verbal and written clinical information and management advice regarding emergency and informational telephone calls received at the center. Obtains pertinent information from the caller to determine the seriousness of the poisoning incident and assess the caller's level of understanding/state of mind. Based on the seriousness of the incident and the caller's level of cognition, determines whether the poisoning incident can be handled by the over the phone or whether the poisoning victim should be seen by a health care provider. Answers inquiries with complete, concise, and relevant recommendations for action. Initiates follow-up calls to assess patient status.

Professional Associations

- Agency for Toxic Substances and Disease Registry *(www.atsdr.cdc.gov)*
- Pediatric Critical Care Medicine *(pedsccm.wustl.edu)*

- American Academy of Clinical Toxicology *(www.clintox.org)*
- American College of Medical Toxicology *(www.acmt.net)*
- National Institutes of Health's National Toxicology Program *(ntp-server.niehs.nih.gov)*

Professional Journal and Database

- *International Journal of Toxicology (www .actox.org/Journal/Journal.aspx)*
- TOXNET, the National Library of Medicine's database on toxicology, hazardous chemicals, and related areas *(toxnet.nlm.nih.gov)*

Media Coverage

Nursing Spectrum reports that 53 percent of all poison exposure cases involve children younger than six years old. Experts say that most calls to poison control centers take place between 4 PM and 10 PM—the hours immediately following many children's bedtimes. Instead of going straight to sleep, many children get into trouble exploring bathroom medicine cabinets.

Overall, more than 90 percent of all poison exposures occur in homes. Experienced nurses say that the most common poisonings involve the ingestion of bleach and other cleaning supplies, plants, markers and crayons, and flavored medications.[65]

---

65 Margaret Hawke, "A Call for Help," Nursing Spectrum, *http://community.nursingspectrum.com/ MagazineArticles/article.cfm?AID=13827* (accessed August 16, 2006).

PSYCHIATRIC NURSE PRACTITIONER   *Also Known As:* MENTAL HEALTH
NURSE PRACTITIONER

Definition: Nurses who are advanced practice registered nurses offering a full spectrum of psychiatric care: assessing, diagnosing, and managing the prevention and treatment of psychiatric disorders and mental health problems.

Want ad: The psychiatric NP assumes ongoing responsibility for each patient from discovery of the disorder to recovery and discharge. Perform psychiatric and physical assessments, including interviewing patients to obtain complete medical histories, as well as ordering, interpreting, and evaluating diagnostic tests and examinations. Establish and document the mental health service plan and prognosis, maintaining records of each case that are detailed and complete for any physician reviewing to evaluate the effectiveness of the plan. Under established Department of Mental Health protocols, initiate drug therapy, taking responsibility for appropriate dosage, indications, contradictions, side effects, and other reactions, as well as for therapy when performed prior to consultation with a physician.

Professional Association

- American Psychiatric Nurses Association *(www.apna.org)*

Professional Journal

- *Journal of the American Psychiatric Nurses Association*

Media Coverage

In the 1999 film *Girl, Interrupted*, Angelina Jolie and Winona Ryder play patients at Claymoore Hospital, a fictitious mental institution based on the real-life McLean Hospital psychiatric hospital in Belmont, Massachusetts. The film was adapted from the memoir by Susanna Kaysen who wrote about her experiences in that hospital in the 1960s. McLean is renowned for both its clinical staff expertise and groundbreaking neuroscience research, as well as the unusually large number of celebrities who have been treated there, including mathematician John Nash, singer-songwriters James Taylor and Ray Charles, and poets Robert Lowell and Sylvia Plath.[66]

---

66 "McLean Hospital," Wikipedia, *http://en.wikipedia.org/wiki/McLean_Hospital* (accessed August 16, 2006). "Girl Interrupted," Wikipedia, *http://en.wikipedia.org/wiki/Girl%2C_ Interrupted_%28film%29* (accessed August 16, 2006).

QUALITY IMPROVEMENT DIRECTOR   *Also Known As:* CONTINUOUS QUALITY IMPROVEMENT (CQI) ANALYST, ACCREDITATION COORDINATOR

Definition: Nurses who focus on improving quality of care and patient safety through taking evidenced-based practices (from computer information systems to different pain management protocols) and implementing them in the entire range of health care providers and facilities.

Want ad: The Medical Bill Review Nurse Analyst reviews medical and surgical bills for overutilization, unbundling, fragmentation, medical necessity, and excessive charges. Answer provider inquiries on bills being requested for reconsideration. Train medical bill review operators in recognizing bills that need nursing review. Consult with medical director as appropriate. Review case management notes as needed.

Professional Associations

- National Association for Healthcare Quality (NAHQ) *(www.nahq.org)*. NAHQ is the nation's leading organization for health care quality professionals. Founded in 1976, NAHQ currently comprises more than 5,000 individual members and 100 institutional members.

- Joint Commission on Accreditation of Healthcare Organizations (JCAHO) *(www.jcaho.org)*

- JCAHO's Quality Check program *(www.qualitycheck.org)*

- National Committee for Quality Assurance *(www.ncqa.org)*

- Centers for Medicare and Medicaid Services Hospital Quality Initiative *(www.cms.hhs.gov/quality/hospital/)*

- Consumer Coalition for Quality Health Care *(www.consumers.org)*

- Families USA: The Voice for Health Care Consumers *(www.familiesusa.org)*

- National Association of Medical Staff Services *(www.namss.org)*

- Partners in Care (PIC): An integrated approach to improving care for depression in primary care *(www.rand.org/health/pic.products)*

- National Quality Forum *(www.qualityforum.org/about/home.htm)*

- Illinois Foundation for Quality Health Care *(www.ifqhc.org)*

Professional Journal

- *Journal for Healthcare Quality (www.nahq.org/journal/online)*

Media Coverage

The National Association for Healthcare Quality publishes peer-reviewed articles from the *Journal for Healthcare Quality* as Web exclusives on the NAHQ Web site *(www.nahq.org/journal/online)*. These articles are selected based on their timeliness and relevance to the contemporary health care quality environment. Access is free for all visitors to the NAHQ site, not just NAHQ members.

RESEARCH NURSE   *Also Known As:* RESEARCH COORDINATOR, CLINICAL RESEARCH DIRECTOR OR ANALYST, NURSE SCIENTIST

Definition: Nurses who either conduct or coordinate clinical trials for research participants for pharmaceutical companies, universities, and other organizations, either profit or nonprofit.

Want ad: The Clinical Research Nurse (CRN) is responsible for the accurate and timely collection of data related to study participants enrolled in IRB-approved outpatient and inpatient clinical studies. The CRN utilizes knowledge and nursing-specific skills to ensure that interactions with study participants and the collection and documentation of data are in accordance with protocol-specific guidelines and IRB and FDA requirements. The CRN arranges scheduling of patients, staff, and supplies, and plans, directs, coordinates, performs, and controls the patient follow-up and the administration of study medications to ensure continuity, quality, and cost effective care. The CRN will work closely with the clinical research team, including physicians, other research nurses, and data manager to assure data points and assessments are done accurately and in accordance with specific protocol requirements.

Professional Association

■ Association of Clinical Research Professionals *(www.acrpnet.org)*

Professional Journal

■ *International Journal of Clinical Practice*

Media Coverage

Nursing Spectrum reports that Florence Nightingale is credited as being one of the first nurse-researchers. Nightingale dramatically reduced the death rate of injured soldiers in the Crimean war by recognizing that darkness, foul air, and unsanitary conditions led to infection and death.

Bilirubin light therapy, used to clear post-natal physiological jaundice, was also developed by early nurse clinicians. Decades ago, observant nurses noticed that among babies who were in bassinets that were closer to the windows, post-natal physiological jaundice cleared more quickly. Consequently, the nurses began rotating the bassinets to give all of the babies an equal share of time at the windows. These nurses' observations, along with subsequent studies, led to the development of bili light therapy.[67]

---

67 Maryanne Bezyack, "The Science of Study," *Nursing Spectrum, http://community.nursingspectrum.com/ MagazineArticles/article.cfm?AID=20691* (accessed August 16, 2006).

RISK MANAGEMENT NURSE

Definition: Nurses who analyze the events that could happen and have happened during the provision of health care. They look at contributing factors and implement plans to prevent reoccurrence of negative events.

Want ad #1: Reviews patient medical records and collects data for legal/risk management analyses; performs root-cause analyses. Performs analysis of clinical care to determine appropriateness, timeliness, and efficiency; assists departments in identifying clinical quality problems and in implementing improvements. Reviews all complaints, claims, and lawsuits.

Want ad #2: Nurse to be responsible for reviewing medical records, policies and procedures, and legal implications, and be capable of conducting educational in-services covering all aspects of documentation and internal procedures that will protect facilities against litigation.

Professional Journal

■ *Legal Medicine: The Journal of Nursing Risk Management. (www.afip.org/Departments/legalmed/lmof.html).* This annually published journal doubles as a continuing education tool for health care professionals.

Media Coverage

Information resources about nursing risk management can be found at *www.nursingworld.org/mods/archive/mod312/cerm3abs.htm.* The Web site has links to four articles: "The Importance of Professional Liability Insurance in Managing Risk," "Managed Care and Managing Risks," "Ethics and Managing Risk," and "Occupational and Environmental Risks in Nursing."

SCHOOL NURSE   *Also Known As:* COLLEGE HEALTH NURSE

Definition: Nurses in this field are dedicated to promoting the health and well-being of children of all ages in an academic environment. This also extends to young adults attending colleges and university, both at the undergraduate and graduate levels.

Want ad: For a boarding school nurse, which includes free housing and meals while school is in session. Organize and disperse prescription medication to students in the mornings and evenings. Be available to students each morning to make decisions on school attendance. Schedule visits to the doctor, as needed, and coordinate that transportation. Complete all forms following accidents or health care visits. Be available during off hours to faculty and staff during medical emergencies. Build a professional relationship with the school's health care providers. Stock first aid kits on campus and in school vehicles. Participate in school activities whenever possible, including camping, teaching, and advising students.

> **Quotes from School Nurses:** *"The biggest [reason why nurses choose this specialty] is the kids. Working with them, you know you make a difference. You're giving kids the ability to do their best."*
>
> *"School nurses need to be sensitive to the cultural and social differences among students. Each culture brings with it some differences."*
>
> *"I knew [school nursing was right for me] the minute I came in. I feel like I touch a lot of children's lives, and their parents' as well."*[68]

Professional Associations

- National Association of School Nurses (*www.nasn.org*)

- National Association of School Nurses for the Deaf (*www.nasnd.org*)

- Overseas School Health Nurses Association (*www.oshna.org*)

- National Association of State School Nurse Consultants (*lserver.aea14.k12.ia.us/swp/tadkins/nassnc/nassnc.html*)

- American School Health Association (*www.ashaweb.org*)

- American College Health Association (*www.acha.org*)

- California School Nurses Organization (*www.csno.org*)

- New York State Association of School Nurses (*www.nysasn.org*)

Professional Journal

- *The Journal of School Nursing* (*www.nasn.org/josn/journal.htm*)

Media Coverage

The American Federation of Teachers reports that there are approximately 45,000 school nurses employed in the United States, which means that there is only one school nurse for every 1,155 students. Nearly half of all school nurses are responsible for three or more different schools, and funding cuts often mean that school nurses are sacrificed to balance budgets.

Though the number of school nurses is dropping, the need for a registered nurse in every school is growing increasingly important. Children with special health care needs are being mainstreamed into public schools. Between 10 and 20 percent of American schoolchildren now have chronic physical, social, or emotional problems. Five percent of all students receive prescription medication while at school.[69]

---

68 Sally Parker, "School Days," MinorityNurse.com, *http://minoritynurse.com/features/nurse_emp/10-20-03b.html* (accessed August 16, 2006).

69 "Every Child Needs a School Nurse," American Federation of Teachers Web site, *www.aft.org/topics/school-nurses/index.htm* (accessed August 16, 2006).

SUBSTANCE ABUSE NURSE *Also Known As:* CHEMICAL DEPENDENCY NURSE

Definition: Nurses who help regulate medications and provide care for those addicted to drugs or alcohol, or who are suffering from other types of substance abuse, such as dependence on prescribed or over-the-counter medications.

Want ad: You can make a difference in someone's life—and while you're at it you can make a difference in your own! For more than a century, our organization has been helping people leave homelessness, addiction, untreated mental illness and intergenerational poverty behind for good. The registered nurse is responsible for the direction, provision, and quality of the health maintenance and monitoring services provided to the residents and staff of the facility.

Professional Associations

■ International Nurses Society on Addictions (IntNSA) *(www.intnsa.org)* IntNSA offers the IntNSA Mentor Program that provides educational guidance and support for professional nurses conducting research, developing theory, or engaging in clinical practice related to addictions. The program includes mentoring support for nurses who do not have appropriate faculty or supervisors available to aid them with advanced practice, theoretical, or research issues. IntNSA anticipates that the program will help attract more nurses to the field of addictions.

■ Substance Abuse and Mental Health Services Administration *(www.samhsa.gov/index.aspx)*

■ American Society of Addictions Medicine *(www.asam.org)*

■ Nursing Council on Alcohol *(www.nursingcouncilonalcohol.org)*

Professional Journal

■ *Journal of Substance Abuse Treatment*

Media Coverage

Tobacco Free Nurses (*www.tobaccofreen urses.org*) is the first national media campaign focused on helping nurses and student nurses to stop smoking. The statistics are startling: Five times as many nurses smoke as doctors. For nurses, the percentage is 15 percent, while only 3 percent of physicians smoke.

The Web site has downloadable promotion materials (posters, brochures, flyers) that can be printed. Funded by the Robert Wood Johnson, the group won the 2005 American Academy of Nurses Media Award.

TELEPHONE TRIAGE NURSE *Also Known As:* CALL CENTER NURSE, PHONE ADVISE NURSE, TELEHEALTH NURSE

Definition: Nurses in this field support, advise, and consult by phone with patients, consumers, and clients. They assess the seriousness of the symptoms, using a series of questions designed to gather the needed data. They may give advice using an approved protocol or transfer the calr to a physician. This approach can reduce the number of visits made to offices of health care providers, clinics, and emergency departments. Telehealth nursing uses technology to transmit data across geographical spaces. Cameras can take pictures, and computer monitors can record blood pressures, pulses, heart rhythms, and blood sugar levels.

Want ad #1: We want to hire a telehealth RN to provide after-hours nurse triage services to physician's practices. The telehealth RN we are looking for has excellent communication skills, a current NC RN license, and a minimum of three years recent acute care experience. They can handle stressful situations effectively, multitask, function independently, and document meticulously. Our nurses take calls from home using nationally recognized protocols. Training is provided for all nurses prior to starting work. Each nurse must maintain currency in Healthcare Provider BLS (CPR/AED) and provide his or her own computer with Internet access.

Want ad #2: We provide telephone triage throughout the country for hospitals, providers, colleges/universities, and companies for employer/employee health benefits. We have openings for telephone triage nurses. Bilingual is a plus. The telephone triage nurse will: assess patient demographic information per telephone interview; demonstrate ability to perform complex telephone interviewing skills in a reasonable amount of time (7–12 minutes); effectively adapt to unit influx (e.g., increased number of calls, technical issues); utilize constructive conflict resolution through direct communication; identify resources and mechanisms to use in dealing with difficult or unusual patient calls.

Quote from Telephone Triage Nurses:
"Huge technical advances are driving the growth of telehealth. We're doing things now that weren't possible five years ago. We can do so much more than we even imagined. Telehealth has been tremendously useful for patient education."

"It's expensive to come to Anchorage, particularly if you have to accompany children or elderly patients. It can cost thousands of dollars just to come in for an earache. The alternative used to be no care. Telehealth makes it possible to get quality care to remote villages."[70]

Professional Association

- Association of Telehealth Service Providers (*www.atsp.org*)

Professional Journal

- *Physician Referral and Telephone Triage Times.* A national publication for the health care professional working, consulting, or managing services that relate to physician referral, health information call centers, telephone nurse advice, and telephone triage.

Media Coverage

The Natick Visiting Nurses Association in Massachusetts has provided patients with tele-monitoring devices. The devices, which mainly are used by patients with heart or respiratory conditions, prompt patients to check vital signs such as oxygen level, blood pressure and weight, and then ask a series of personalized questions. The information then is sent by a telephone line to a VNA computer and nurses analyze the results and identify any abnormal data. The VNA also sends a weekly report displaying trends to each patient's physician.[71]

---

70 Anne Ericksen, "Distance Nursing," MinorityNurse. com, *http://minorynurse.com/features/undergraduate/11-24-04b.html* (accessed August 16, 2006).

71 The Association of Telehealth Service Providers, *www.atsp.org* (accessed May 14, 2006).

TRAVEL NURSE

Definition: Nurses who work with people who are going on international trips. Topics of discussion and action include vaccines, self-care advice, and preventive medications. Advice includes information on current global health and illness situations from the Centers for Disease Control and Prevention.

Different from a traveling nurse: The travel nurse helps others go on trips and the traveling nurse goes to different destinations across the country for a finite time to supplement regular nursing employee staffing.

Professional Associations

- National Association of Traveling Nurses *(www.travelingnurse.org)*

- GoTravelNursing *(www.gotravelnursing.com)*

- Nurse Village *(www.nursevillage.com/nv/index.jsp)*

- Highway Hypodermics *(www.highwayhypodermics.com)*

- U.S. State Licensing Boards *(www.highwayhypodermics.com/state_ boards_of_nursing.htm)*

- Healthcare Traveler Magazine *(www.healthcaretraveler.com)*

- Cross Country Travel Corps *(www.crosscountrytravcorps.com/index.jsp)*

- Ultimatenursing.com *(www.ultimatenurse.com)*

- Accessnurses.com *(www.accessnurses.com)*

Nurses are also welcomed as members of the International Society of Travel Health Medicine and the American Society of Tropical Medicine and Hygiene.

Media Coverage

Nursing Spectrum reported that since its inception in the 1980s travel health nursing has been growing in the United States and worldwide. It is estimated that today more than 1,000 nurses in this country help prepare international travelers for safe and healthy journeys. With a focus on prevention and health promotion, travel health nurses provide their patients with many services, such as pretravel health assessments that identify health risks for a given trip itinerary, routine and travel immunizations, customized health education, recommendations for travel medical kits, instructions for self-care "on the road," and referrals for health services here and abroad.[72]

---

72 Gail Rosselot, "Protecting the International Traveler: A New Role for Nurses," Nursing Spectrum guest commentary, *http://nsweb.nursingspectrum. com/cfforms/GuestLecture/travelnursing.cfm* (accessed September 25, 2006).

UTILIZATION REVIEW NURSE

CARE REVIEW NURSE

Also Known As: INTAKE UTILIZATION NURSE,

Definition: Nurses who examine data about patient admission characteristics, length of stay, and other statistics to evaluate use of health care resources

Want ad #1: Facilitate the admission/intake process for the client, physician, and payors. Obtain clinical data for admission review to coordinate and implement activities in order to provide for appropriate admissions and placement of clients through the continuum of care. Responsible for optimizing revenue flow by communicating required information to payors as needed.

Want ad #2: Nurse is responsible for conducting the authorization and clinical review process. Nurse will provide short-term care coordination for members who are identified through the concurrent, prospective, and retrospective review process. Nurse works directly with the primary and other care providers, maximizing plan benefits, utilizing community resources, creating access, and meeting the targeted needs of the individual patient and their families.

Media Coverage

NurseWeek reports that "In the coldest terms and in many ways, what the federal Patients' Bill of Rights is all about is patient care versus dollars. And smack dab in the middle of that equation are RNs who, as utilization review staff, help managed care providers determine appropriate interventions and judicious use of health plan resources.

For consumers, enactment of a patients' bill of rights would represent guaranteed emergency room care, access to specialists including pediatricians and obstetricians and gynecologists, and the right to sue for damages—in some amount—resulting from the denial of care."[73]

---

73 Phil McPeck, "Balancing Act." *Nurse Week*. April 30, 2002. *www.nurseweek.com/news/features/ 02-04/utilization_web.asp* (accessed September 25, 2006).

WELLNESS NURSE   *Also Known As:* FITNESS NURSE, SPORTS MEDICINE NURSE

Definition: Nurses in this field work with individuals who want to live healthier lifestyles. Exercise, nutrition, and stress management are often the major parts of the prescription. They work in hospital fitness centers or sports injury clinics, and teach fitness classes in the community. They can also find positions with professional sports teams, college athletic departments, and orthopedic practices.

> **Quote from Wellness Nurses:**
> *"Patients respect it when the person who is taking care of them actually does the exercises. They're much more willing to listen if they see it's important to you."*
>
> *"...not only are you taking care of the patient, but there's usually a parent involved and sometimes a coach, depending on the player's level of expertise."*[74]

Professional Association

■ Aerobics and Fitness Association of America *(www.afaa.com)*

Professional Journal

■ *The Physician and Sportsmedicine Online (www.physsportsmed.com)*

Media Coverage

Nurse Julie Tupler with Andrea Thompson wrote a book, *Maternal Fitness: Preparing for a Healthy Pregnancy, an Easier Labor, and a Quick Recovery* (Simon & Schuster, 1996). It features exercises that focus specifically on the muscle groups used in childbirth labor. Called the transverse abdominals, those stomach muscles play a critical role during delivery. If they are strong, the results should be favorable to both mother and baby.

---

74 Scott Williams, "The Wide World of Sports Fitness Nursing,", MinorityNurse.com, *http://minoritynurse.com/features/nurse_emp/ 03-03-05a.html* (accessed August 16, 2006).

WRITER   *Also Known As:* AUTHOR, WEBMASTER, NURSING HISTORIAN

Definition: Nurses who write textbooks, articles for journals and newspapers, and books about historically important nursing leaders. They may also consult for or write television shows or films about nurses.

Want ad: We have an exciting opportunity for a health writer/editor to work on natural-health newsletters, articles, product descriptions, and informative web content. Essential responsibilities include: writing and editing original health-related content on a variety of health conditions, as well as natural therapies and treatments; transforming medical jargon into accurate and interesting copy the average person can understand; selecting and supervising staff, as well as coordinating with subcontractors and vendors in preparing print and electronic health communications; establishing relationships with health professionals and learning institutions throughout the country to obtain health content that can be disseminated to online and print consumers; supervising fact-checking staff and coordinating with staff on web and print production; managing long-term and short-term research assignments; establishing and maintaining weekly and monthly editorial production schedules.

> **Quote from a Medical Writer:**
> *"Medical writing is a great career! The work is interesting and often lucrative, and the demand for medical writers is high. Few people start out to be medical writers; most of us fall into it."[75]*

Professional Associations

- American Association for the History of Nursing, Inc. *(www.aahn.org)*
- American Medical Writers Association (AMWA) *(www.amwa.org)*
- National Association of Science Editors *(www.nasw.org)*
- Society for Technical Communications *(www.stc.org)*

Professional Journal and Resource

- *AMWA Journal.* A quarterly publication that includes articles on medical writing, book reviews, and news on association activities.
- American Medical Writers Association, Delaware Valley Chapter's Toolkit for New Medical Writers *(www.amwa-dvc.org/toolkit/index.shtml)*

Media Coverage

Nurse Kristen Baird wrote a book, *Journaling to Reclaim the Passion: a Writing Guide for Nurses,* that was designed to be a companion workbook for her book *Reclaiming the Passion: Stories That Celebrate the Essence of Nursing.* The accompanying CD has piano music composed and performed by a hospice nurse.

---

75 "Toolkit for New Medical Writers," *www.amwa-dvc.org/toolkit/index.shtml* (accessed September 25, 2006).

PART THREE

Getting into School

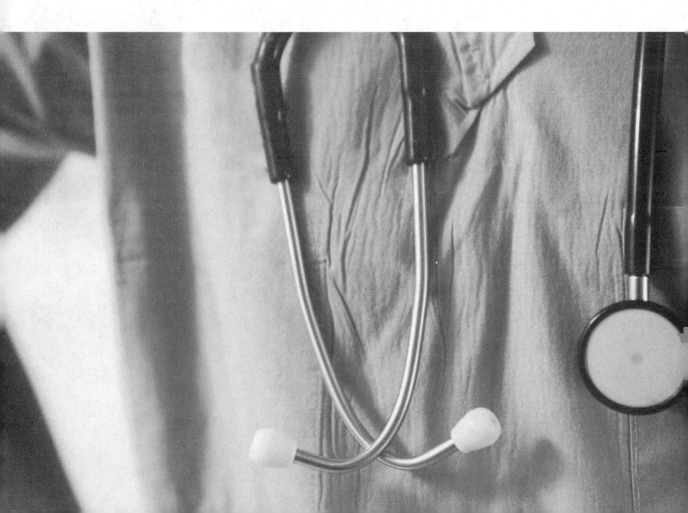

CHAPTER 6

Identifying Your Transferable Skills and Talents

YOUR BEST ATTRIBUTES WILL TRANSFER TO YOUR NEW NURSING CAREER

You've made the decision to change your career to nursing. You have sorted out the facts and fiction connected with the image of nursing. You have discovered the many choices of specialties for which nurses can train, both inside and outside the hospital.

Now, before you go on to apply to nursing school, recognize that you are proceeding from a position of strength. You have abilities and expertise that you discovered, grew, and refined as a result of your education, training, jobs, and volunteer activities. They are a definite plus to be highlighted in your nursing school application process.

You can review your specific abilities and expertise by using a special advanced assessment tool designed for second career people. To use formal career counseling language, the tool helps you clearly identify all your *transferable skills and talents*. You need to recognize your strengths and acknowledge their value. Then you can document those assets in applications and mention them in interviews. You have a natural head start with confidence-building. If a personal essay is required or if you include a cover letter, you will have assembled personal details to include in your narrative.

To use the tool, go through the list below which is adapted from a state of Wisconsin resource.[1] Check each skill or talent you have had the opportunity to demonstrate. At this time you can ignore the lines following the items—we will use some of them later.

Don't be overly modest; this is not the time to worry about bragging. If you have the skill or talent, check the box beside it. If you are an expert in it, put a star in the box instead of a checkmark. This allows you to single out your special achievements.

☐ Adapt to situations

_____

☐ Advise people

_____

☐ Analyze data

_____

☐ Anticipate problems

_____

☐ Assess situations

_____

☐ Budget finances

_____

☐ Calculate numbers

_____

☐ Chart information

_____

☐ Check for accuracy

_____

☐ Communicate

_____

---

1   Adapted from "Wisconsin Job Center Transferable Skills," Wisconsin Department of Workforce Development. *www.wisconsinjobcenter.org/publications/8961/8961.pdf* (accessed August 16, 2006).

☐ Compile statistics

_____

☐ Consult with others

_____

☐ Coordinate activities

_____

☐ Cope with deadlines

_____

☐ Correspond with others

_____

☐ Delegate

_____

☐ Detect

_____

☐ Direct others

_____

☐ Dispense information

_____

☐ Do precision work

_____

☐ Endure long hours

_____

☐ Evaluate

_____

☐ Examine

_____

☐ Explain

_____

☐ Explore

_____

☐ File records

_____

☐ Find information

_____

☐ Gather information

_____

☐ Guide/lead

_____

☐ Handle complaints

_____

☐ Help people

_____

☐ Imagine solutions

_____

☐ Implement

_____

☐ Improvise

_____

☐ Inform people

_____

☐ Initiate actions

_____

☐ Interpret data

_____

☐ Interview people

_____

☐ Investigate

_____

☐ Listen

_____

☐ Log information

_____

☐ Make decisions

_____

☐ Make policy

_____

☐ Manage people

_____

☐ Memorize information

_____

☐ Mentor others

_____

☐ Monitor progress

_____

☐ Motivate others

_____

☐ Observe

_____

☐ Operate equipment

_____

☐ Organize

_____

☐ Perceive needs

_____

☐ Perform routine work

_____

☐ Persuade others

_____

☐ Plan

_____

☐ Prepare

_____

☐ Process information

_____

☐ Read reference books

_____

☐ Recommend

_____

☐ Record data

_____

☐ Recruit people

_____

☐ Refer people

_____

☐ Remember information

_____

☐ Report information

_____

☐ Research

_____

☐ Resolve problems

_____

☐ Run meetings

_____

☐ Schedule

_____

☐ Set goals/objectives

_____

☐ Set up equipment

_____

☐ Speak in public

_____

☐ Supervise

_____

☐ Support

_____

☐ Take instructions

_____

☐ Test

_____

☐ Think ahead

_____

☐ Think logically

_____

☐ Tolerate interruptions

_____

☐ Track

_____

☐ Train/teach

_____

☐ Troubleshoot

_____

☐ Unite people

_____

PUTTING YOUR TRANSFERABLE SKILLS AND TALENTS IN A NURSING CONTEXT

Now that you have identified which transferable abilities you possess, you are ready for a creative career-planning activity. For the oral part of the exercise, read aloud just the name of the items that you starred to see if you find any patterns in your expertise. Then read aloud all the items you marked, both starred and checked. Is it any clearer what career niche would best suit you? For example, does the word *data* appear in more than one selection? You might consider how you could utilize your computer or statistical expertise in nursing.

For the written part of the exercise, choose at least three checked or starred abilities that you most enjoy using. Imagine how you might use those skills in a nursing career. Then come up with a phrase or two that describes your potential future role using your abilities. Don't worry if you're not totally familiar with the work environment of nurses; think about what you do know about their tasks from your reading or interviews. Here are some examples:

☐ Unite people
  help people feel like part of a patient care team, serve as link between doctor and patient

☐ Tolerate interruptions
  able to focus on giving patient care regardless of distractions, can multitask

☐ Write technical work
  design patient education brochures for elderly people taking medications

☐ Adapt to situations
  adjust to different patients based on their needs and personalities

☐ Analyze data
  use measurements to determine proper course of action and/or treatment for patients

☐ Perceive needs
  be able to take appropriate course of medical interventions/provide health care solutions

This list of your skills and talents will come in handy in several settings beyond applying to nursing school. When you interview nurses about their work, you can ask specific questions about how they think you could use your abilities in that clinical setting. If you had checked *tolerate interruptions,* for example, you could ask the nurses about what kind of day-to-day interruptions they experience on their particular job. Or you could compare notes on what kinds of coping skills have led to successful completion of tasks.

Finally, when it's time to put your résumé together for your first nursing job, don't forget to revisit your list of transferable skills and talents. You will impress your future health care employer with your self-knowledge and experience. You have a lot to offer and you want to make sure it is documented.

CHAPTER 7

Nursing Degrees, Exams, and More

Though there may be a shortage of nurses, there's certainly no shortage of nursing schools: more than 2,000 nursing programs are available nationwide. Even when you limit the number of programs by location, size, and a few other key factors, you still have a lot of schools and a number of different degree programs to choose from. This chapter will help you decide which program is best for you and where and how to apply. You'll also learn about the nursing exams you may need to take to obtain your license once you've earned your degree.

CHOOSING YOUR DEGREE PROGRAM

One of the wonderful things about a nursing career is that there are so many ways to enter the profession. If you have only a GED, there are programs for you. If you already have a bachelor's degree, there are programs for you. Whether you want to be an LPN or RN, earn an Associate Degree in Nursing, BSN, MSN, or doctorate—there are programs for you.

Licensed Practical Nurse (LPN) or Registered Nurse (RN)?

Your first step is to determine whether you want to become an Licensed Practical Nurse (LPN) or a Registered Nurse (RN). An LPN diploma or certificate entitles you to take the NCLEX-PN® and become a fully licensed LPN. An associate degree in

nursing or bachelor of science in nursing (BSN) enables you to take the NCLEX-RN*
and become a fully licensed RN.[1]

There are many differences to consider, including the basic ones of training, duties,
and responsibilities (see Chapter 2 for a full discussion of LPN and RN roles). Here
are some key factors that may substantially influence your decision

An LPN certificate will:

- Get you into a nursing job in as little as one year (approximately half the time
  of an associate degree in nursing).
- Enable you to work as a nurse while you pursue your RN licensure.

An associate degree in nursing will:

- Make you eligible for RN licensure in approximately two years.
- Put you in a higher earnings bracket.
- Open up many more job opportunities.

A BSN will:

- Get you RN licensure in two to four years (or one year if you're eligible for an
  accelerated BSN program).
- Put you in an even higher earnings bracket.
- Open up the most job opportunities.

LPN Diploma/Certificate

These are typically one-year, full-time training programs at hospitals, community
colleges, or vocational technical schools. Once you receive an LPN certificate or
diploma, you will be eligible to take the NCLEX-PN exam and become a fully-
licensed practical nurse.

---

1   Since only two states, California and Texas, use the term "Licensed Vocational Nurse (LVN) instead of LPN,
    the chapter will proceed using the more widely-known term of LPN.

Nursing Degrees and Programs—The Quick List

- Licensed Practical Nurse (LPN) diploma or certificate
- Associate degree in nursing
- LPN to associate degree in nursing

Bachelor of Science in Nursing (BSN)

- LPN to BSN
- RN to BSN
- Second-degree BSN
- Accelerated BSN

Master of Science in Nursing (MSN)

- RN to MSN
- Direct Entry MSN
- Accelerated MSN
- Joint-Degree MSN

Professional Certification Programs

Doctorates

- Doctor of Nursing (ND)
- Doctor of Nursing Practice (DNP)
- Doctor of Nursing Science (DNSc)
- Doctor of Philosophy (PhD)
- MSN/PhD Dual Degree
- Accelerated BSN to PhD

Typical Admission Requirements

- High school diploma or GED
- 3.0 (out of 4.0) or better grade point average in high-school college preparatory chemistry, biology, and algebra classes
- NET (Nursing Entrance Test), TEAS (Test of Essential Academic Skills), or NLN PAX-PN (National League for Nursing Pre-Admission Examination for Practical Nursing)—see "Nursing School Entrance Exams" later in this chapter for more information.

Associate Degree in Nursing

The associate degree in nursing provides basic technical training in nursing and enables graduates to take the NCLEX-RN exam. Typical programs are two years (full time) and include general education courses (e.g., English and algebra), foundation courses (such as anatomy and physiology), and nursing courses and clinical rotations. A hands-on, learn-by-doing approach is emphasized. For many students, the associate degree in nursing is a stepping stone to the BSN once they've already become an RN. This allows them to earn money in their new career, making a higher degree more affordable. Remember, many health care employers offer tuition reimbursement programs.

Typical Admission Requirements

- High school diploma or GED
- 3.0 (out of 4.0) or better grade point average in high-school college preparatory chemistry, biology, and algebra courses
- SAT, ACT, NET, TEAS, and/or NLN PAX-RN
- Completion of prerequisite courses with a minimum grade of C

Prerequisite courses typically include:

- Anatomy and/or physiology
- Microbiology
- Introduction to nursing/health care
- Algebra
- Psychology
- English

Alternative Associate Degree in Nursing Programs

- *LPN to ASN.* These programs give students who already have an LPN credit for nursing skills they've gained through work experience or study, allowing them to earn their associate degree in nursing in as little as one year.

Bachelor of Science in Nursing

This four-year (full-time) degree is a longer course of study than the associate degree in nursing, but offers the best opportunity for placement and advancement in a nursing career. It is often considered the basic rung to ascend the career ladder through increasingly challenging leadership positions. Most BSN programs focus on general education requirements in the first two years and nursing courses and clinical rotations in the second half of the program.

Typical Admission Requirements

Admission requirements vary depending on the kind of BSN program. RN to BSN programs, for example, require current RN licensure, a C average or above in college-level coursework, and completion of specific prerequisite courses. Some also require at least one year of clinical practice (nursing school clinical rotations apply). Again, admission requirements may include minimum scores on the SAT, ACT, NET, TEAS, and/or NLN PAX-RN.

Prerequisite courses typically include:

- Anatomy/physiology
- Microbiology
- Chemistry
- Introduction to nursing/health care
- Nutrition
- Algebra
- Psychology
- English
- Statistics
- Sociology, history, or other humanities elective

Alternative BSN Programs

- *LPN to BSN.* These programs give LPNs credit for their previous studies and work experience, enabling students to earn their BSN in four semesters rather than four years.
- *RN to BSN.* For RNs who are graduates of an associate degree in nursing or nursing diploma program, the RN to BSN also offers credit for nursing knowledge and skills already attained through work experience or previous coursework. These programs are typically designed to meet the scheduling demands of working RNs, and some even have "RN-only" classes to separate RNs from prelicensure students. RNs can often attain their BSN in less than four semesters (full time). RN to BSN programs may also go by the following names: BSN for RNs, Completion Program, Nursing Mobility in Education Program, Advanced Standing, Advanced Placement, and Transition Options.
- *Second-degree BSN.* In this program, students who hold a bachelor's degree in another field will earn credit for general education courses and only have to complete the nursing-specific coursework to earn a BSN in approximately two academic years. A minimum 3.0 GPA is often required.
- *Accelerated BSN.* Also for students who already have a bachelor's degree in another field, the accelerated BSN degree is a shorter, more intensive program that confers the BSN in less than two years. Most accelerated BSN programs run 12 months, although some take 16 to 20 months to complete. Again, a minimum 3.0 GPA from prior BA/BS coursework is often required.

Master of Science in Nursing

The MSN provides advanced training in a range of specializations including family nurse practitioner, clinical trials research nurse, acute/critical care advanced nurse practitioner, nursing informatics, leadership and management, and education. The number and type of specializations will vary from school to school. Most MSN programs are 18 to 24 months and typically require a BSN degree, an RN license (or licensure eligibility), and clinical work experience.

Typical Admission Requirements

- BSN with a grade point average of 3.0 (out of 4.0) or better
- Current RN licensure or eligibility for licensure in state

- 1+ year work experience as an RN
- GMAT or GRE
- Undergraduate coursework in statistics and one or more business courses

Alternative MSN Programs

- *RN to MSN.* These programs are designed for RNs with an associate degree in nursing who want to earn a BSN and MSN consecutively. The curriculum allows as much advanced placement credit as possible to prevent overlap between BSN and MSN courses.
- *Direct entry MSN.* Designed for students with a bachelor's degree in a non-nursing field, direct entry MSN programs give credit for general education courses and offer an abbreviated series of undergraduate nursing courses (approximately one year) so students can prepare for RN licensure while taking master's-level courses in a specialty area (approximately two additional years).
- *Accelerated MSN.* Same as the Direct Entry MSN but designed to be completed in two years rather than three.

Joint-degree Programs

Many MSN students opt for a joint degree in a related field. Typical joint-degree programs include:

- MSN/MPH: Master of Science in Nursing and Public Health
- MSN/MBA: Master of Science in Nursing and Business Administration
- MSN/MSHA: Master of Science in Nursing and Health Administration

Professional Certification Programs

Once you hold an MSN, you can enroll in post-master's certificate programs to qualify to take an American Nurses Credentialing Center (ANCC) certification exam. The ANCC offers generalist, advanced practice, and clinical specialist exams in nearly 30 different areas, such as acute care, nursing administration, pain management, advanced diabetes management, and family nurse practitioner. (See the ANCC's Web site at *www.nursingworld.org/ancc* for details.) ANCC certification can help advance your career. It demonstrates expertise in a specific field, as well as a commitment to continued education and quality of care.

Doctoral Programs

Finally, there are many doctoral programs for nurses who wish to become leaders in nursing administration, teaching, research, or practice. These programs typically take three to six years, depending on research and clinical requirements. Doctoral degrees include:

- *Doctor of Nursing (ND).* Emphasis is on advanced practical nursing skills and effective decision making in various nursing environments.
- *Doctor of Nursing Practice (DNP).* Emphasis is on leadership development in clinical care delivery and outcomes, research, and systems management.
- *Doctor of Nursing Science (DNSc).* Preparation as nurse scientist; emphasis is on investigative research skills and leadership.
- *Doctor of Philosophy (PhD).* Nurse scholars and researchers; emphasis is on the theoretical foundation of the nursing practice and profession.

Typical Admission Requirements

Admission requirements vary depending on the doctoral program. When you are researching schools, be sure you know the admission requirements for the program to which you are applying.

Alternative Doctoral Programs

- *MSN/PhD Dual Degree.* It typically takes five years to complete this intensive, accelerated program.
- *Accelerated BSN to PhD.* This is a rare, accelerated, and intensive program combining coursework to achieve a BSN, MSN, and PhD in nursing.

NURSING SCHOOL ENTRANCE EXAMS

There are three main entrance exams required by nursing programs: the Nursing School Entrance Test (NET), the Test of Essential Academic Skills (TEAS), and the National League for Nursing Pre-Admission Exam (NLN PAX). Not all programs require these tests; many simply use your SAT or ACT scores submitted for general admission to the college or university. However, the number of nursing schools requiring a nursing-specific entrance exam is on the rise. Here's a brief overview of each exam.

The NET

According to Educational Resources, Inc. (*www.eriworld.com*), which develops the NET, one fourth of all LPN, associate degree in nursing, and BSN programs require the NET. This two-and-a-half hour, computer-based exam consists of six parts, with an optional seventh writing portion:

1. *Math:* Whole numbers, decimals, fractions, percentages, system conversions, and algebra. 60 equations, 60 minutes. No calculators are permitted.
2. *Reading comprehension:* Comprehension of mostly scientific material at a tenth grade reading level. 33 questions, 30 minutes.
3. *Reading rate:* One-minute assessment of reading rate.
4. *Test-taking skills:* 130 questions, 20 minutes.
5. *Stress level profile:* 50 items, 12 minutes.
6. *Learning style profile:* 30 questions, 20 minutes.
7. *Written expression:* One essay, 30 minutes.

It is important to note that *only the first two sections count* toward your admissions eligibility (50 percent each). The other four sections are used as predictive indicators of your success in a nursing program.

You must complete all six required sections of the NET. The test typically costs $25 to $40 (check with the school requiring the exam). You may retake it after 60 days, up to three times in one year.

The TEAS

The Test of Essential Academic Skills is also a computer-based test administered by the schools and programs requiring it for admission. This three-and-a-half hour, multiple-choice aptitude test consists of four sections:

1. *Math:* Whole numbers, metric conversion, fractions and decimals, algebra, percentages, and ratio/proportion. 45 questions, 56 minutes.
2. *Reading comprehension:* Paragraph and passage comprehension, drawing inferences and conclusions. 40 questions, 50 minutes.
3. *English:* Sentence structure, grammar, vocabulary in context, punctuation, and spelling. 55 questions, 65 minutes.
4. *Science:* Biology, chemistry, anatomy and physiology, physics, and general science. 30 questions, 30 minutes.

Content is at a high school level. Cost varies from school to school, and typically ranges from $25 to $40. Check with the offering institution regarding retake policy. More information about the exam is available at *www.atitesting.com.*

Kaplan's Entrance Exam Edge

You can prepare for all three of these exams with Kaplan's *Nursing School Entrance Exams: Your Complete Guide to Getting into Nursing School.* The book includes a diagnostic test, hundreds of practice questions, two full-length exams, and complete answer explanations. You'll also find proven strategies for increasing your test score.

NLN PAX

The National League for Nursing Pre-Admission Exam comes in two versions, PN and RN. Both consist of three main sections:

1. *Verbal ability:* Vocabulary and reading comprehension.
2. *Math:* Basic calculations, word problems, algebra, geometry, conversions, graphs, and applied mathematics.
3. *Science:* General biology, chemistry, physics, and earth science.

You'll have one hour for each section, and all three sections must be taken consecutively in one testing session. The exam fee runs a little higher than the TEAS and NET (typically $50 to $75). Also you must wait at least six months before retaking the exam. Contact the school requiring the exam for cost and scheduling details. More information on the exam is available at *www.nln.org/ testprods/PreAdmin/index.htm.*

CHOOSING THE RIGHT SCHOOL

With so many schools to choose from, it is essential to determine exactly what you want from your nursing program. Some considerations, such as location and cost, are obvious, but there are many other important factors to consider as well. We've listed 12 criteria to use in evaluating schools and programs to help you select the one that is right for you.

1. Location

The real estate mantra "location, location, location" is as apropos for prospective nursing students as it is for prospective homebuyers. As much as you might want to attend a particular school, if it's too far away and your circumstances don't allow you to live on campus or move close enough to commute, you won't be able to earn your degree from that institution.

As you consider your criteria, determine how far you're willing to travel. Do you need to stay local? Within a how-many-mile radius? Keep in mind that, depending on the program and your course requirements, you might make the trip back and forth to campus five times a week and perhaps during the rush hours.

Remember that many schools now offer online courses and that "meetings" with other students and faculty can often take place online. A few even offer the entire degree online. See Chapter 8 for a full discussion of online nursing degree programs.

Checklist to Finding Your Top School Choices

- Determine your criteria.
- Find schools that meet those criteria.
- Research those schools.
- Rank those schools according to your criteria.
- Narrow down to your top three to five programs.

Visit the top schools, if possible. Then rerank them and apply to at least two. (Even if one program stands out far and above the others for you, you'll want to apply to more than one program to have at least one back-up.)

---

2. Accreditation

An accredited program has officially met the educational standards set by a national accrediting organization—in this case, the National League for Nursing Accrediting Commission (NLNAC) or the Commission on Collegiate Nursing Education (CCNE). (See Chapter 2 for more details.) Specialized programs for midwives and anesthesiologists can also be accredited by the American College of Nurse-Midwives (ACNM) Division of Accreditation and the Council of Accreditation of Nurse Anesthesia Educational Programs, respectively.

Accreditation is voluntary, but because of the numerous benefits of accreditation, the vast majority of nursing programs are accredited—in fact, the NLNAC alone monitors over 1,700 programs. Accreditation is your guarantee that a program has met or exceeded certain criteria for educational quality. While a nonaccredited program may be of equal caliber, an accredited program offers you the additional security of knowing that your course credits and degree will be accepted by another accredited program.

3. Flexibility

How important is it that the program be flexible, both in terms of its schedule and its curriculum? Can you attend a more-traditional full-time program with daytime courses? Or do you need a more flexible program geared toward working students who attend evenings, weekends, or even online? Do you want some flexibility in the curriculum—the ability to take electives that interest you or to determine the order in which you take some courses—or are you comfortable with a curriculum that requires you to take specific courses each term in a specific sequence? Will the program allow you to take time off (if necessary) without losing ground?

4. Size

How much does the size of the program and school matter to you? For example, are you comfortable being "lost in the crowd" at a large university or do you need the intimacy of a small school setting? Carefully consider the pros and cons of each type. Small programs typically offer more personal attention, as well as more student services and special programs. Large schools, on the other hand, often have a more diverse curriculum and student body and more student organizations and events.

Remember to consider the size of the department as well as the size of the school. A small department at a large school or a large department at a small school can often offer the best of both worlds.

5. Student-Faculty Ratio

For some students, personal attention from instructors in the classroom is essential. For others who are more independent learners, a high student-faculty ratio is of little concern. How important is student-faculty ratio to you? Find out about student-faculty ratios for classes, lectures, labs, and clinical rotations. Remember that smaller class size is typically more important once you get into your clinical rotations.

6. Clinical Rotations and Hospital Affiliations

Clinical rotations are at the core of every nursing program and provide you with the hands-on training you'll need to put what you learn in the classroom into practice. Find out as much as you can about the clinical rotations at the schools that interest you most. How many rotations do students complete? Where? With what hospitals, health care clinics, or health maintenance organizations is the school affiliated? How diverse will your clinical experiences be? You'll want to be sure to gain experience in a variety of types of care and a variety of care settings.

7. Personality

It's important to feel comfortable while you work towards your degree, so it's essential to consider the personality of the program you're interested in attending. If you're a quiet, introverted type who loves nature and the outdoors, for example, a bustling city school—no matter how prestigious—probably isn't for you. The best way to get a sense of the personality of a school and its nursing program is first-hand. But before you hop on the train or in your car, you can get a good sense of the personality of a school by considering:

- *The program's Web site.* What impression do you get from the Web site, both its text and its design? Rigorous? Traditional? Professional? Encouraging? Exciting? Cutting edge?
- *The location of the school.* Is it urban, suburban, or rural? What's in the surrounding area? What impression do you get from images of the campus environment?

- *The type of school.* Is it a liberal arts college, a technical university, a church-affiliated school? Public or private? Stereotypes aside, there are some general conclusions you can draw about the personality of each of these kinds of schools. A liberal arts college, for example, will place great value on a strong foundation in the humanities and elective courses.
- *Student services and programs.* What kinds of programs, activities, and organizations are available? What kinds of cultural and other events take place on campus?
- *Student demographics.* How many students are in the program? What's the male-female ratio? How diverse are the ethnic and cultural backgrounds of both students and staff? How many students are full time and how many part time?

8. Nursing Board Passing Rates

How do students in the program fare on the NCLEX-PN or -RN exam? Ask for pass rates for the last three to five years. The NCLEX pass rates often reflect how well students are prepared for nursing careers.

9. Job Placement

As confident as you may be in your ability to get a job when you graduate, a good job-placement program is an invaluable resource and attests to the quality of the program. What's the school's job placement program like? What job placement statistics and success stories are available?

10. Reputation and Rank

If a nursing school has a good reputation, you can feel confident that it's earned that reputation for good reason. But be careful not to put too much stake in rank.

There are two rankings of nursing schools: the *U.S. News & World Report* and the National Institutes of Health (NIH). *U.S. News* ranks nursing master's programs and specialties in NLNAC-accredited schools every three years, with the latest available rankings at the time of this writing from 2003. Specialties include nurse practitioner, nurse midwife, clinical nurse specialist, and others. *U.S. News* ranks schools based on a peer-review process in which deans and administrators at each institution evaluate schools based on specific criteria and standards. A copy of the current *U.S. News & World Report* nursing school rankings can be found in Appendix E.

The NIH, on the other hand, ranks programs solely by research dollars awarded. A high NIH ranking therefore indicates a high-quality research staff, usually at the graduate school level. Often doctoral programs will limit their research to one or two particular specialties to best use available resources.

Rankings always come with several caveats, however. For one thing, rankings emphasize statistics, not student experience. For another, rankings may emphasize one element more than another in a way that's contrary to your priorities. For example, student-faculty ratio may be one factor in the ranking while hospital affiliations and clinical rotations—which are more important to *you*—may not even be part of the equation. Further, rankings cannot take into account every aspect of a program, and there is much that matters—the personality of the program, student life, quality of individual professors and instruction—that should be more important to you than a school's rank.

11. Student Resources and Support

What kind of student resources and support systems are available? This is a great question to ask if you have the opportunity to interview current students at a nursing school. Consider availability of faculty and guidance staff, access to computer and science laboratory facilities, as well as counseling services, libraries, recreation centers, on-campus health care, and any other amenities that might improve your life as a student.

12. Cost

You should consider the factor of cost at the end of your exploration, not because it is an afterthought, but because you should not rule out a school because of cost—at least not yet. After all, you could actually end up paying *less* for your degree at an expensive private school than you would at a public school because of scholarships and grants awards. (See Chapter 9). While it's important to be realistic, for now, work under the assumption that you will maximize your financial aid and that no school is cost prohibitive.

Program Criteria Worksheet

Spend some time thinking carefully about the kind of program and school that will be best for you. Consider both what you *need* from the program and what you *want* from the program. For example:

I need a program that:

☐ Offers part-time study and night and weekend classes.
☐ Is local (less than 30 minutes travel time).
☐ Will accept most of my credits from my associate degree.

I want a program that:

☐ Offers a pediatric nursing specialization.
☐ Has a low student-faculty ratio.
☐ Is small and personal.
☐ Will allow me to work in a local clinic while attending.
☐ Has a diverse student body.
☐ Is accredited.

When you have chosen a school, it's time to begin filling out applications and drafting your essay or statement of purpose. Chapter 15 contains many tips that are targeted to nursing job applicants and are very useful for filling out nursing school applications.

NURSING LICENSING EXAMS: THE NCLEX-PN AND NCLEX-RN

Once you've completed your program and are ready for licensure, you'll need to "pass the boards"—the NCLEX-PN or -RN exam.

The NCLEX-PN and NCLEX-RN stand for the National Council Licensure Examination for Practical Nurses and Registered Nurses, respectively. These tests are developed and administered by the National Council of State Boards of Nursing (NCSBN). The goal of these exams is to determine whether it is safe for you to begin practice as an entry-level practical nurse or registered nurse. They are tests of *mini-*

mum competency based on the knowledge and behaviors required for entry-level LPN or RN work. The exams test not only your knowledge and nursing skills but also your ability to make competent nursing decisions in various health care situations.

The tests are based on job analysis surveys that the NCSBN conducts every three years to determine the duties, responsibilities, and type of care administered by entry-level LPNs and entry-level RNs around the country. The content and level of difficulty of the test are then adjusted to accurately reflect the knowledge new LPNs and RNs need to safely and effectively practice their craft.

How the Tests Work

Both exams are computer-adaptive tests (CAT), which means that the level of difficulty of the questions is continually adjusted throughout the exam to provide you with questions appropriate for your skill level. The first question will be relatively easy (below minimum competency level). If you answer that question correctly, your next question will be slightly more challenging; if you answer incorrectly, the next question will be slightly easier. The same process takes place after each question to allow the computer to calculate your level of competence.

You have up to five hours to complete the NCLEX-PN and six hours to complete the NCLEX-RN (including the beginning tutorial and the optional breaks).

Test	Time	Minimum # of Questions	Maximum # of Questions	# of Experimental Questions
NCLEX-PN	up to five hours	85	205	15
NCLEX-RN	up to six hours	75	265	15

You must answer a minimum number of questions (85 for the PN, 75 for the RN) and are allowed a maximum number of questions (205 for the PN, 265 for the RN). Fifteen questions on each exam are experimental questions being tested for future exams. They do not count toward your score.

Your test is complete when one of the following occurs:

- You have demonstrated minimum competency and answered the minimum number of questions (85 or 75).
- You have demonstrated a lack of minimum competency and answered the minimum number of questions (85 or 75).
- You have answered the maximum number of questions (205 or 265).
- You have used the maximum time allowed (5 or 6 hours).

Because the tests are computer-adaptive, every question counts. There is no warm-up time, so you must be ready to answer questions correctly from the very beginning. Remember that you are given plenty of time to take the test. Plan on testing for the full five or six hours, and focus on answering each question to the best of your ability.

What's on the NCLEX-PN and NCLEX-RN?

All content on the NCLEX-PN and NCLEX-RN is integrated, meaning you may need to pull together knowledge and skills from several different classes to answer correctly. The questions on both exams are organized according to the framework of "Meeting Client Needs."

The NCLEX-PN/NCLEX-RN *is*

- a test to determine your ability to provide basic, entry-level LPN/LVN or RN care.
- designed for entry-level nurses, not those with years of experience.
- a test of both nursing and decision-making skills

The NCLEX-PN/NCLEX-RN *is not*

- an intelligence test or indicator of your future success in nursing.
- a comprehensive exam covering everything you learned in nursing school.
- a hands-on exam with high-tech clinical nursing equipment.

Client Need Category	Percentage of Questions	
	NCLEX-PN	NCLEX-RN
1. Safe and Effective Care Environment, including two components:		
a) Coordinated Care (PN), Management of Care (RN)	11–17%	13–19%
b) Safety and Infection Control	8–14	8–14
2. Health Promotion and Maintenance	7–13	6–12
3. Psychosocial Integrity	8–14	6–12
4. Physiological Integrity, including four components:		
a) Basic Care and Comfort	11–17	6–12
b) Pharmacological Therapies	9–15	13–19
c) Reduction of Risk Potential	10–16	13–19
d) Physiological Adaptation	12–18	11–17

Integrated throughout each exam are several processes, the most important of which is *the nursing process*: data collection and analysis, planning, implementation, and evaluation of nursing care.

When you're ready for your boards, be sure to read the latest edition of Kaplan's *NCLEX-PN: Strategies for the Practical Nursing Licensing Exam* or Kaplan's *NCLEX-RN: Strategies for the Registered Nursing Licensing Exam*. Each book offers a complete review of question formats, general test-taking strategies, and specific techniques for the CAT, and an extensive practice test.

For now, you can turn to Chapter 8 to learn more about online educational opportunities.

Online Nursing Education

The Internet has dramatically changed the way nursing education is provided. Now you can go online to find a full range of Web-based continuing education, which ranges from a one-time class taken pass/fail to degree-granting institutional course-work. In this chapter, we explore the various ways in which you can achieve your educational goals in nursing by using the Internet. At the end of this chapter, you will find a list of available online programs, as well as a brief description of each.

USING THE INTERNET TO FURTHER YOUR NURSING EDUCATION

You may be skeptical of what an online learning program has to offer. However, you can expect many of the same things you would find in a three-dimensional classroom.

First, Web-based instruction is usually completed one course at a time, with each one requiring approximately 10 to 15 hours per week. The benefit though, is rather than having predetermined class times, online students can usually create their own schedules, choosing the hours that are most convenient for them.

Also, each class shares its own group mailbox or "student center." Typically, it's here that lectures, assignments, and discussions are conducted. Most schools use a system similar to e-mail or instant messaging so that students can receive timely feedback from peers or the professor. This is also how student assignments are submitted and how assessments are returned to students. Message boards, as well as non-Internet tools such as DVDs or videotapes, may also be a part of your online education.

If you go to school online, will you miss the warmth and closeness of having in-person classmates? Possibly. However, with active online communities, most students feel as though they have plenty of people to turn to for whatever reason. If you simply cannot imagine a classroom without four-walls, you should consider online education very seriously before applying.

CONTINUING EDUCATION

If you decide to make nursing your career, most likely you will have to take a significant number of continuing education classes on a regular basis to keep your licensure active. Requirements vary by state. The variety of their content is as varied as the nursing specialties in Chapters 4 and 5.

There is often a cost associated with continuing education classes. You may be reimbursed by your future employer, and you can usually choose to take these courses in person or online. However, there is a way for you to sample these courses without paying anything or even stepping out your door.

Take Advantage of Free Online Courses

To see an example of a free online course, take a look at the class on "Disaster Preparedness and Response for Nurses" that the American Red Cross and nursing honor society Sigma Theta Tau International collaborated to produce (*www.nursingsociety.org/education/case_studies/cases/SP0004.html*).

Tips for Online Students

As you browse through Web sites, be sure to add good ones to your Favorites or bookmarks; you want to be able to quickly go back to a Web site if you have more questions or if you need to check for updated information. Here are more useful tips to help you get the most out of the Internet:

- Create a folder to keep all printed information in one place.

- Set up a home office, even if it is a corner of a room in your house. You need to be as serious about your studies as those students who meet in a classroom.

- Take advantage of all the interactive, informational sessions offered, whether they are accessed via telephone or through chat rooms.

- Be persistent. If you don't feel as though your questions have been adequately answered, ask again or find another source for information.

You can find more examples of free online courses at the Meniscus Educational Institute (*www.meniscus.com*). Or, you can conduct an online search for "free nursing courses."

Because your credentials are not checked before you are allowed to take online courses, you don't have to be enrolled in nursing school to enjoy their benefits. Also, because you don't need the continuing education credit, you can skip the required tests, or challenge yourself by taking them, if you wish.

If you want to learn more but you don't want to complete an online course, check out Medscape Nurses (*www.medscape.com/nurses*). This site offers a variety of useful materials, including coverage of presentations from major nursing conferences such as the National Association of Pediatric Nurse Practitioners, Nurse Practitioners in Women's Health, National Association of Neonatal Nurses, and the National Conference of Gerontological Nurse Practitioners.

QUESTIONS TO ASK ONLINE EDUCATION PROVIDERS

When considering whether to pay for online courses, it is important to learn the essential facts about the program. Here are questions you should ask to make sure the online program is right for you. For ease, these questions have been separated into different categories.

Focus and Credibility

- Do they offer the degree I want to earn? Can I get a list of all the required and elective courses? After I complete that degree, do they offer a program for the next step up the ladder?
- Are they accredited? By whom?
- Are they experienced in online education? What year did they start their program?
- How many graduates have they produced? What is their graduation rate?
- Can I talk to alumni?
- What is the pass rate for their first-time test takers taking credentialing exams?
- Can I take all of my courses online? What kind of arrangements need to be made for any non-Web-based courses? Will I get assistance in making those arrangements?

- Are clinical practice sessions in my local community part of the requirements? How do they handle the need for an on-site preceptor at that location?
- Do they have a virtual library?
- Do they have an online student community?
- What is the faculty-to-student ratio? What are their faculty characteristics, such a minimum degree and years of nursing experience?

Technology

- What kind of computer set-up do I need? How fast does my connection to the Internet need to be?
- Do I need to buy additional software to complete my homework?
- Will any part of the coursework be delivered by mail, telephone, DVD, or videotape?

Admission Criteria

- What are the admission requirements? Get specifics, such as tests, GPA, and previous nursing work experience?
- Is there a toll-free phone number so that I can talk to an enrollment counselor?
- Can I transfer in credits from other institutions? Is there a time limit on that transferability?
- Can I get credit for life or work experiences? What is the mechanism for getting that credit? Is there a limit for how many credits I can earn this way?

Financial Considerations

- What financial assistance is available? How do I apply for it?
- Is financing available? What are the terms, such as interest and payback rate?
- How much is the application fee? Is it refundable?
- How much is tuition? Do their programs qualify for employer reimbursement?
- If I receive college credit for life or work experiences, will I still pay for those credits?

Timing

- Will online education fit my lifestyle and my current obligations? Do they have guidelines or requirements for how much time per week they expect to be spent on schoolwork?
- Can the program adapt to my sometimes-uncertain work, family, and personal schedules? Are there mechanisms for getting an extension on test-taking or homework deadlines?
- How long is their estimate for degree completion? Is there a limit for completing the requirements once I have started?
- Can I start anytime of the year or are there set times for beginning classes?
- Are they on the quarter or semester system? How long does each class last?
- Can I switch from full-time to part-time? Can I switch from part-time to full-time?

Residency Requirements

- Is any on-campus coursework *available*?
- Is any on-campus coursework *required*? How much and on what schedule?
- If I can't make it on-campus when expected, what does that do to my chances for graduation?

Be sure you have the answers to your most important questions in writing before making any final non-refundable decision.

ONLINE LPN -TO-ASSOCIATE DEGREE IN NURSING PROGRAMS

Associate degree in nursing graduates are eligible to take the NCLEX-RN exam. The following schools both have an online RN-to-BSN program, so they would be good options for you to advance your nursing education once you become a licensed nurse.

At Chamberlain College of Nursing (*www.deaconess.edu*)—formerly called Deaconess College of Nursing—you can take courses either on campus or online, and you can receive financial aid if you are qualified. They use the "portfolio process" to allow you to earn college credit based on your professional experiences. This means you would assemble a portfolio of documents that prove you achieved course objectives and outcomes on the job rather than by schooling.

Excelsior College School of Nursing (*www.excelsior.edu*) will evaluate credits you have already earned after you enroll in their program. They have been designated as a National League of Nursing Center of Excellence for "creating environments that promote student learning and professional development." Once enrolled, you will have access to their virtual library and an online student community. Degree completion takes about two years.

ONLINE RN-TO-BSN PROGRAMS

Although you will find some preliminary information here about these schools, do not forget to continue with your own research by asking the questions provided earlier in this chapter.

Florida Hospital College of Health Sciences (*fhchs.edu*) has an eight-semester RN-to-BSN online program that you can complete in less than three years. As a student, you are assigned a facilitator who has a graduate degree and responsibility for fifteen students. You will also receive support from your enrollment advisor, course instructor, program manager, e-learning helpdesk support, student services support, and peer group.

Grand Canyon University (*www.gcu.net*) is a liberal arts university that offers a bridge course to facilitate your transition from working RN to BSN student. The course focuses on differentiated nursing practice competencies, nursing conceptual models, professional accountability, integrating spirituality into practice, group dynamics, and critical thinking. The program has a message board and one-on-one professor feedback so that you can discuss and learn from other students as well as your teachers.

Jacksonville University (*dept.ju.edu/nursing*) has both an online and a campus-based RN-to-BSN program. Features of its curriculum include coursework in management concepts, research, and education, along with physical and behavioral sciences and community health. You can even enroll in online courses with labs such as chemistry and microbiology. The online lectures include streaming video clips and telephone calls between teachers and students, in addition to e-mail and message boards.

Kaplan University School of Nursing, Allied Health and Health Care (*www.getinfo. kaplan.edu/Microsite_B/nursing_healthcare.aspx*) has an online RN "degree completion" program. You can take classes in health promotion, risk reduction, disease prevention, information and health care technologies, ethics, human diversity, management theory, and health care system and policies. You must complete a laboratory and a clinical course in the state in which you will receive your licensure. The estimated time for completion is less than two years of full-time studies. The school offers help with your career planning as you design your own professional development plan. It is possible to receive credit for previous coursework taken elsewhere or work experience.

Keiser College (*www.keisercollege.edu/nursing*) has a Web-based RN-to-BSN program. Its curriculum includes coursework in critical thinking, leadership, management, research, advanced assessment, and health promotion. The college's goal is to provide you with a better understanding of the cultural, political, economic, and social issues that affect your patients and influence health care delivery. You will also learn how to allocate and manage physical, fiscal, and human resources. Electives in business and criminal justice are also offered.

National American University (NAU) (*national.edu*) offers an online RN-to-BSN program, and also has twelve campus locations across the United States, in South Dakota, Minnesota, Missouri, Kansas, Colorado and New Mexico. NAU considers the online student community to be their "13th campus." Topics in the curriculum include managed care, legal-ethical risk management, and caring for vulnerable populations. Just before you graduate you take a course in professional development or career management.

Saint Joseph's College of Maine (*sjcme.edu*) gives you a choice of online courses or print-based courses in their distance education program. They are based on the campus of a Catholic liberal arts college. Their focus is to give you "the knowledge and skills to practice as nurse generalists in a variety of settings." They allow you to progress through their system through a combination of transfer credits, earned credits, and challenge exams. You complete 39 semester credits, including six credits completed at a two-week summer program in Maine.

South University (*online.southuniversity.edu*) has a School of Health Professions that offers you a choice of on-campus or online learning for its RN-to-BSN program. Among the innovative health care concept classes you can take are ones in palliative care, gerontological nursing, and complementary and alternative nursing methods. You may receive up to 45 credit hours for your nursing experience, and financial aid is available for qualified applicants. They have accelerated five-and-a-half week courses, so that you can complete your degree in 18 months.

University of Phoenix (*www.universityofphoenix.com*) has instructors with an average of 15 years experience in its Web-based RN-to-BSN program. You can use your work experience to fulfill some credit requirements. Their programs qualify for employer reimbursement, and financing is also available. One hundred percent of the course-work can be completed online, and classes are offered one at a time, for five to six weeks each. They have over 180 campuses and learning centers across the country.

University of Wisconsin at Green Bay offers Web-based RN-to-BSN programs. They are unique in that they offer three separate education tracks: a national online pro-gram track for students outside Wisconsin (*bsnlinc.wisconsin.edu*), a track offered for Wisconsin and Upper Michigan students, and an on-campus program (both linked to *www.uwgb.edu/nursing*). You take one clinical class in community health nursing in your home state. It involves 112 hours, 40 of which are completed in a public health department.

ONLINE MS, MA, AND MSN PROGRAMS

These programs should also be subject to the questions found earlier in this chapter. Remember, if you can't find your answers on the program's Web site, be sure to con-tact an administrator by phone or e-mail.

American Sentinel University (*www.americansentinel.edu*) provides a Web-based MSN program. If your career goal is nursing administration, this program offers that dedicated coursework. Topics include management of resources, interdisciplinary collaboration, and application of technology, information systems, knowledge, and critical thinking.

Excelsior College School of Nursing (*www.excelsior.edu*) has two choices for its online MSN program. You can enroll in the MSN with a focus on clinical systems manage-ment, or you can move directly from an RN to work on both your bachelor's and master's degrees at the same time. In the latter case, you will be granted a minimum of 30 credits for completion of the NCLEX-RN. After you complete the undergradu-ate portion of the program, you begin the graduate portion. If you earn the grades to become an honor student, you can join their chapter of Sigma Theta Tau.

Florida State University (*www.fsu.edu*) has an online MSN program to develop nurse educators. If you take classes full-time, four semesters of work will earn the degree. If you attend part-time, you will need seven semesters to complete the work.

Frontier School of Midwifery and Family Nursing (*www.midwives.org/home*) has classes that start three times each year in its Web-based MSN program. Three specialties are offered: family nurse practitioner, certified nurse-midwife, women's health care nurse practitioner. If you have an ADN, they will allow you to proceed to the MSN without a bachelor's degree. You could study full-time for 24 months or part-time for 36 months. Their curriculum is designed in a modular format and they allow you to set your own pace of course completion within their guidelines. The school has over 600 preceptor sites for your clinical practice setting.

Grand Canyon University (*www.gcu.net*) offers a Web-based MSN program with a focus on Nursing Leadership in Health Care Systems. The first course is on "Advanced Nursing Issues and Roles." Its focus is the scope of practice, role behavior, and depth and breadth of knowledge in selected areas of advanced practice, nursing education and nursing leadership. A heavy emphasis is placed on caring, diversity, ethics, and spiritual aspects in nursing care delivery.

Gonzaga University (*www.gonzaga.edu*) has an online MSN program in their School of Professional Studies. Ethics, excellence, spirit, and community are their guiding values. You could complete the program within two years if you take two courses per semester. Courses are offered over an eight-week schedule, with each course divided into four two-week-long learning modules. Each module organizes your work around readings, teacher presentations, films, mentor statements, and class discussion.

Graceland University (*graceland.edu*) allows its online MSN students the opportunity to immediately enroll throughout the year. You can be granted up to 30 hours of credit for previous undergraduate nursing courses with no time limit on their transfer. Students take one course at a time, spending about ten to fifteen hours a week for seven to nine weeks. You perform your clinical rotation in your local community, but you need to commute to Independence, Missouri, for a two-day session at the end of the coursework. One additional on-campus session is required if you are taking the Family Nurse Practitioner and Clinical Nurse Specialist concentrations.

Indiana State University (*www.indstate.edu/distance/nursing*) offers an MS degree in a Web-based program. Four specializations are offered: Adult Health, Community Health, Family Nurse Practitioner, and Nursing Administration. You must have a grade point average of 3.0 in a NLN-accredited BSN program and a current Indiana RN license or an equivalent in your area. You also must supply evidence of one year of full-time work as an RN before you are admitted.

Norwich University (*msn.norwich.edu/grd/*) provides an online MSN in its nursing administration program. You would need to be able to devote 15 to 20 hours a week to take six for-credit seminars. Each seminar lasts about 11 weeks and you can complete the degree requirements in 18 months. The coursework is followed by a one-week residency and graduation on campus in Vermont.

Pace University's Lienhard School of Nursing (*pace.edu*) offers two types of master's degrees. An MS in Collaborative Nursing Informatics requires you to complete 36 credits, while an MA in Nursing Education offers you courses in adult learning theories, chaos theory, learning styles of the millennial student and Baby Boomer work force, use of technology for learning/teaching, educational policies, and key legislative issues. In both cases, your clinical time will take place in your local community.

Rush University (*www.rushu.rush.edu*) offers a Web-based MSN program with many choices for your concentration in advanced practice: Community/Public Health Nursing, Adult Critical Care, Gerontological, Medical-Surgical, Pediatric and Psychiatric-Mental Health. You can also study to be a nurse practitioner with an Acute Care, Anesthesia, or Neonatal focus. The faculty will prepare your local preceptor with tools to ensure your competency. You are required to take two compressed, weekend on-campus courses in Chicago, Illinois, to complete the online education program.

Saint Joseph's College of Maine (*www.sjcme.edu*) gives you a choice of online or print-based courses in their MSN distance education program. You must complete 39 credits with an overall grade point average of 3.0 or higher. You take six core curriculum courses, additional specialty courses, two practica within the specialty and a final thesis or professional paper. That thesis is graded as pass/fail.

Samuel Merritt College (*samuelmerritt.edu/nursing/msro_nursing*) offers a Web-based MSN program. You can specialize in three areas: Case Management, Family Nurse Practitioner, or Certified Registered Nurse Anesthetist. You must enroll in the first four semesters full time. A total of seven semesters that include two summers is needed for certain specializations, such as Case Management.

South University (*online.southuniversity.edu*) offers an online Master of Health Science in Nursing degree from its School of Health Professionals. You need to have a BSN from an accredited school and a GPA of 2.7 or better for the last 60 semester or 90 quarter hours. Courses focus on such current health care issues such as ethical decision-making strategies, multicultural educational needs, and the impact of the organization in the health care delivery system. You will learn to design teaching, curriculum evaluation, and testing plans.

The Midwifery Institute at Philadelphia University (*www.philau.edu/midwifery*) offers a post-bachelor's certificate program in Nurse Midwifery. You are required to have completed three trimesters of study and clinical experience in your local community before attending three on-campus sessions at Philadelphia University. Classes begin twice a year, in fall and spring, and clinical experience begins in your eighth month of your 21-month program. You can also earn an MS in Midwifery by adding 12 graduate credits beyond your ACNM certificate.

University of Cincinnati College of Nursing (*nursing.uc.edu*) has two online MSN programs. One produces nurse midwives, and the other women's health nurse practitioners. For these degrees you need to supplement online coursework with clinical work at a preceptor in your local community. Program faculty and staff will help you locate a preceptor. The university claims a 100 percent first-time pass rate for their graduates.

University of Michigan (*www.umich.edu*) offers an online master's degree with three focus areas. The first focus is on community care/home care nursing. This 22-month, 36-credit track is offered in a combined online/on-campus format. You need to come to campus in Ann Arbor for one long weekend (Thursday through Sunday) every other month. A second focus is nurse midwifery, with the following requirements for enrollment: completion of an advanced health assessment course, one year as an RN in maternal-child health care, and licensure in Michigan. However, other options are available if you are not a nurse. The third focus is on nursing business and health systems. In addition to coursework, you must complete a customized internship and a scholarly project. The time for degree completion is estimated as three to four terms if you attend full time.

University of Missouri-Columbia (*www.mudirect.missouri.edu*) offers an online MSN with a specialty in nursing education. You complete 39 to 42 semester credit hours to graduate, and you choose six of those hours in your concentration: adult health, mental health, women's health, or pediatrics.

University of Phoenix (*www.universityofphoenix.com*) provides online MSN programs that allow you to specialize in Health Care Education or Integrative Health

Care. In addition, you can enroll in two joint MSN programs, one that is combined with an MBA in Health Care Management, the other that is combined with a Master of Healthcare Administration (MHA).

University of Wyoming (*uwyo.edu*) offers a Web-based MSN program for nurse educators. It is a 100 percent online program, designed to increase educators in rural settings. Your courses include assessment of student learning needs, planning educational curricula, implementing educational methodologies, and evaluating both student learning and program outcomes.

Vanderbilt University (*www.msvanderbilt.info/grd/*) provides a Web-based MSN program in Health Systems Management. Courses include topics such as health care delivery systems and financial management, and transitioning to the advanced practice role. The degree calls for completing 15 courses, each lasting four to seven weeks. The time estimate is two years of part-time study. They offer live technical support around the clock every day of the year.

Walden University (*www.walden.edu*) offers an online master's degree program. You can begin with RN licensure or with a BSN. You can also choose between two specializations: Education (for a faculty position in nurse education, training, or staff development) or Management and Leadership. You will learn from expert faculty and contributing scholars via DVDs. You can complete the program within two years, with no campus visits required.

Wheeling Jesuit University (*wju.edu*) offers an online RN-to-BSN-to-MSN program, as well as a separate MSN program. The master's degrees can be obtained with three specialties: Nursing Education, Nursing Administration, and Family Nurse Practitioner. For the last specialty, multiple visits to the Wheeling, West Virginia, campus for face-to-face instruction are required.

ONLINE DOCTORAL PROGRAMS

Finally, these programs are for those looking for the highest level of education.

Indiana University School of Nursing (*nursing.iupui.edu/AcademicPrograms/ PhDNursingScience.htm*) has both an on-campus and a distance-accessible option. The distance-accessible option uses many technologies: Web-based courses, video conferencing, discussion dialogues, telephone conferencing. Admission criteria and curriculum are the same for both options. You must come to campus for two weeks every summer if you are not an on-campus student.

Rush University (*www.rushu.rush.edu*) offers two Web-based doctoral programs. One is for becoming a Doctor of Nursing Practice (DNP) with expertise in outcomes management. You can complete the DNP program of 39 credit hours in two years on a part-time basis. The other choice is to become a Doctor of Nursing Science (DNSc) who will function as a nurse scientist. You complete a minimum of 125 quarter hours of post-baccalaureate graduate study, along with a dissertation to earn the DNSc degree.

University of Arizona (*nursing.arizona.edu/doctoral*) has a BSN-to-PhD program. If you enter with a BSN, you first complete 15 hours of master's degree classes. You must go to Tucson for an intensive two-week research immersion presession each year for three years. You can only be admitted to a full-time program with a commitment to research in one of three focal areas: Understanding Mechanisms to Prevent and Treat Biological Injury, Reducing Risks and Promoting Health in Vulnerable Populations, Managing Consequences of Aging or Chronic Illness. You need to match the ongoing research interests of a current faculty member.

University of Northern Colorado (*unco.edu*) offers an online PhD in Nursing Education. You can start with a BS and move to the doctorate level with 95 credit hours. If you have a master's degree, the requirement is 65 credit hours. Your GRE scores (taken within five years) must add up to at least 1,000 total, and your GPA must be 3.0 or higher. Although nursing practice experience is not required for admission, your level of clinical expertise will be assessed and enhanced through further nursing employment, if needed, when school is not in session.

University of Phoenix (*www.uopxonline.com*) requires 19 days of residency in Phoenix, Arizona, for their Doctor of Health Administration degree. You can complete the requirements within three years. To keep your pace toward graduation on target, they have a standard for interaction that requires you to post comments at least four out of seven days each week. Any time of day or night is acceptable.

Please know that this is not a comprehensive list of every program available. You should complete your own research on programs that meet your specific needs.

Next it's time for a topic that can't be avoided—how to pay for your nursing education.

CHAPTER 9

Paying for Your Education

As with any career goal, becoming a nurse will require much of your time, effort, commitment, and, of course, money. This last resource is the one that could cause you to hesitate. Don't let it! Without proper information and planning, jumping right into nursing school can be an expensive proposition. However, if you take the time to plan, save, and learn about the costs, you can graduate without an insurmountable debt. In this chapter you will discover strategies you can use to effectively finance your education.

HOW MUCH DOES NURSING SCHOOL COST?

Today's college education comes with an expensive price tag, and the sticker shock for today's tuition can make even the hardiest feel faint. But you may be surprised by how affordable your nursing degree can be—even at one of the more expensive schools. That's because even though tuition and fees continue to rise, students have more opportunities for financial aid than ever before. In fact, the College Board recently reported that there is over $129 billion in financial aid for higher education. You'll find out later in this chapter how to tap into your share and minimize your personal contribution.

First, let's take a look at some tuition figures to see just how much you can expect your degree to cost.

According to the College Board's Trends in College Pricing 2005 (available at *www. collegeboard.com/prod_downloads/press/cost05/trends_college_pricing_05.pdf*, the average costs for the 2005–2006 academic year were as follows:

- Four-year private college: $21,235 per year, for a four-year total of $84,940
- Four-year public college: $5,491 per year for a four-year total of $21,964
- Two-year public college: $2,191 per year for a two-year total of $4,382

Of course, these are averages, and the prices for individual schools will vary. Still, there's a marked disparity between tuition for public and private schools, and an even bigger disparity between two and four year schools. This difference is the basis of a solid rationale for some people who do not have college degrees when they choose the two-year route to earn their nursing degrees.

Options are quite different for individuals who already have nonnursing college degrees. They can attend accelerated nursing programs, most of which lead to an advanced degree such as a master's. This means that their beginning salary will be even higher than those who enter with a BSN.

Despite these cost differences, you shouldn't rule out a school because of the tuition. Let's explore the reasons why in more depth so you can decide which school is best for you.

Public versus Private Schools

Private schools are often more expensive than public ones, with tuition often triple or even quadruple the cost of tuition of a public institution. The disparity in price comes from the fact that private colleges are funded by tuition, fees, gifts, and endowments, while public colleges are partially funded by tax dollars, which helps keep tuition costs down. Because public schools are partially funded by the public, they have an obligation to serve the needs of the population to the best of their ability, which often translates into more open admissions policies, more flexible scheduling, and, of course, lower tuition than private colleges. In contrast, private schools have the freedom to be more selective, limit their scheduling options, and charge significantly higher tuition and fees.

There are always exceptions and each school is unique, but, in general, you can expect the following differences between public and private schools.

Private nursing schools typically:

- Are more selective
- Have smaller classes
- Offer more personal attention
- Offer more special programs and services
- Offer limited scheduling options
- Have a less diverse student body
- Have mostly full-time students
- Have an undergraduate population consisting mostly of recent high school graduates

Public nursing schools typically:

- Have a more open admissions process
- Have larger classes
- Are more bureaucratic
- Offer more scheduling choices, including evening and weekend classes
- Have a more diverse student body
- Have a mix of full-time and part-time students
- Have more "nontraditional" students (people who have spent several years in the workforce)

Notice that these lists don't say private nursing schools are typically better than their less-expensive public counterparts. Despite the common misconception, pricier doesn't necessarily mean better. And just because private nursing schools cost more doesn't mean you can't afford to attend one.

Many students at private institutions pay only a small fraction of the published tuition price; scholarships and grants cover the rest. So don't rule out a school based solely on price. Financial aid is available. You may have to work to prove your eligibility, but it's an effort with a big pay off.

Full-Time versus Part-Time Costs

You really maximize your savings by going back to school full time when you enroll in more than the minimum number of credits. For example, by taking 18 undergraduate credit hours, you reduce the cost per credit to a much smaller number than the part-time cost per credit hour.

Sample Public College Tuition, 2006

The State University of New York–Westchester Community College (SUNY-WCC) and University of Washington (UWA)–Seattle are two public colleges with well-established nursing programs. SUNY-WCC is a good example of a program that offers a two-year AAS degree in nursing. In contrast, undergraduates in the four-year UWA-Seattle program earn a BS degree while graduate students can earn an MN, MS, PhD, or DNP.

State University of New York—Westchester Community College

Undergraduate full time (12 or more credits), resident: $1,675

Undergraduate part time, per credit, resident: $140

University of Washington—Seattle:

Undergraduate full time (10–18 credits), resident: $1,870

Undergraduate part time, per two credits, resident: $366

Graduate full time (7–18 credits), resident: $3,732

Graduate part time, per two credits, resident: $865

Sample Private College Tuitions, 2006

Gwynedd Mercy College, Gwynedd Valley, PA
Allied Health and Nursing Program

Undergraduate full time: $19,720

Undergraduate part time, per credit: $470

Graduate, per credit: $545

Boston College, Chestnut Hill, MA
William F. Connell School of Nursing

Undergraduate full time: $33,000

Undergraduate part time, per credit: $1,100

Graduate, per credit: $1,040

Let's take the cost of tuition at the University of Washington—Seattle as an example of how you can weigh the benefits of attending full-time:

- As a full-time undergraduate, if you take 10 credits of classes, each credit costs you $187.
- As a full-time undergraduate, if you take 18 credits of classes, each credit costs you $104.
- As a part-time undergraduate, if you accumulate any credits over time, each credit costs you $183.
- As a full-time graduate student, if you take 7 credits of classes, each credit costs you $534.
- As a full-time graduate student, if you take 18 credits of classes, each credit costs you $208.
- As a part-time graduate student, if you accumulate any credits over time, each credit costs you $433.

Under some circumstances, you might have to consider factors such as full- or part-time attendance qualifying you for more financial aid, even though attending on this basis costs more. Or, you might have to consider that attending part time might cost less, but it will delay your entrance into the well-paid nursing workforce.

Remember to Consider Fees

In addition to tuition, you can expect several fees on your bill each semester. These fees may run from several hundred to several thousand dollars, depending on the term. For the typical nursing program, you can expect the following kinds of fees:

- ID card
- Student activities fee
- Student services fee
- Laboratory fees
- CPR card
- Physical exam, including TB test (or chest X-ray) and vaccinations or immunizations
- Health insurance
- Malpractice insurance or other professional liability insurance that you carry while doing your clinical assignment
- Uniforms (while doing your clinical assignment)

- Clinical equipment
- Books
- School supplies, such as a computer, printer, Internet access, calculator, and notebooks
- Transportation to classes and clinical assignment, particularly in the community health nursing rotation

Be sure to include these figures when calculating costs per school.

Handy Online College Cost Calculators

Feeling overwhelmed by the numbers? Use these online tools to help you calculate your estimated college costs.

- The Web site *www.finaid.org* offers over a dozen different calculators, including a college cost projector, a savings plan designer, and a how-much-to-borrow calculator.

- The College Board's Web site (*www.collegeboard.org*) features a Financial Aid EasyPlanner that allows you to add up and estimate costs, as well as calculate how much financial aid you need and what you can expect to pay out of pocket.

- The Financial Aid Need Estimator on ACT's Web site (*www.act.org*) helps you estimate your expected contribution.

Investment versus Payoff

If the cost of your nursing degree is beginning to seem out of reach, or if you're wondering if that degree will be worth the investment, remember:

- there's a wealth of financial aid resources that you can tap into to finance your education, and
- the payoff when you receive your degree will be twofold: a career you enjoy and appealing salary potential.

First scenario: Let's say you'd like to attend part-time, taking two classes per term, with an average of $2,000 in tuition and fees per semester. If you take classes in the summer as well, you'll spend $6,000 a year (assuming you shoulder all the costs—an unlikely scenario) and still be able to keep your job, though you may have to cut back on hours. If you can complete your required courses in five years, you'll have invested $30,000. If half of that were in loans, and your current job pays you $25,000 per year, as an RN your starting salary could be $40,000, rising to $47,000 or more after just three years of experience. That extra $15,000-plus per year will help you pay off any debt you incurred.

KAPLAN

Figure 9.1 Investment/Payoff Worksheet

	School 1	School 2	School 3
A. Estimated tuition/fees per year:	_____	_____	_____
B. X number of years =	_____	_____	_____
C. Total estimated cost:	_____	_____	_____
D. Estimated current income per year:	_____	_____	_____
E. Estimated income after graduation:	_____	_____	_____
F. Annual increase in salary (subtract D from E):	_____	_____	_____
G. If you stop working: D × B = estimated income lost:	_____	_____	_____
H. How long it will take to "recoup" lost income (divide G by F):	_____	_____	_____

Second scenario: Of course, if you quit your job and go back to school full time, your investment projections change considerably because you'll lose your main income. However, you'll hold a nursing job in as little as two to three years. If your current job pays $25,000, you might "lose" $75,000 over three years, plus you'll have to pay tuition—a $100,000+ investment. But as a full-time student, (1) you'll be eligible for more financial aid and (2) you'll start earning that higher salary much sooner. With an extra $15,000+/year, you'll make up that $75,000 and more (pay back loans, etc.) in less than five years. Remember, the median salary of an RN is over $50,000, so you've got a great incentive to plow ahead, get that degree, and pay off your education bills.

The real scenario: You will benefit more from crunching your own numbers and looking at your own "what if's. So try the worksheet in Figure 9.1. Pencil would be the writing instrument of choice, since you might want to try out different financial situations.

Full-Time versus Part-Time Enrollment

Whether you attend full time or part time, going back to school to change your career brings a host of challenges; after all, you're not a fresh-out-of-high-school graduate anymore. You've got a job, perhaps a family, a mortgage or rent, car payments and credit card bills, and all the responsibilities that come with years of adulthood.

Some nursing schools will give you the option of enrolling as a part-time or full-time student; however, your circumstances might not offer you the same option. Perhaps you're the primary breadwinner for your family, for example, and it's simply not feasible for you to quit your current job to go back to school full time. However, if you do have the choice, consider the following pros and cons of each option.

Benefits of Full Time

- You'll finish faster and enter the job market sooner.
- Many financial aid opportunities are only available to full-time students.
- You'll be more focused on school.
- You'll have more networking opportunities and interactions with other students.

Drawbacks of Full Time

- You'll have a much larger annual investment and are more likely to incur debt.
- You'll either have to quit your job or cut back significantly on your hours. If you can somehow keep working full time and fit a full course load into your schedule, then you won't have much time for anything else.

Benefits of Part Time

- You can keep your job.
- Some employers offer tuition reimbursement.
- You'll incur less debt overall.
- You can choose how many courses to take to fit your needs each semester.

Drawbacks of Part Time

- It will take you significantly longer to enter the job market.
- You might have limited scheduling options.
- You may have more conflicts between work, home, and school.

Words of Wisdom: Advice from the Field

Michael Rogozinski, a second-year RN student at Gwynedd Mercy College in Pennsylvania, works and attends school full time after studying part time at Montgomery County Community College. His advice applies to anyone returning to school on either schedule:

> Balancing outside responsibilities is the most difficult part about returning to school. Mortgages must get paid, kids must be taken care of, and most people have to go to work. Squeezing in 12 credit hours is not easy. It takes time management and patience.
>
> If you are in a big rush, you are going to drive yourself crazy. You have to work within your own limits and not compare yourself to others. If you accept that having responsibilities is going to slow down the schooling process and that getting your degree may take longer things will go smoother for you.[1]

FINANCIAL AID: HOW TO GET YOUR SHARE

Whether nursing school will be your first foray into college life or you already have an advanced degree in another field, you'll want as much guidance as you can get for financing your education. Fortunately, there are many sources of aid and many resources to help you find the most effective way to subsidize your costs.

> Your Goal: Maximize Assistance, Minimize Costs

---

1   Michael Rogozinski, personal correspondence, July 2006.

Scholarships and Grants

Financial aid for higher education comes in the form of scholarships and grants, work-study programs, and loans. Obviously, scholarships and grants are the best form of aid because they don't need to be paid back. Scholarships are awarded for merit (e.g., GPA or other specific criteria) while grants are awarded based on financial need. Scholarships and grants can come from public or private sources and be as large as thousands of dollars from the federal government or as small as $100 from a local civic organization. The trick is to find as much of this free money as possible to minimize your costs.

You Don't Have to Duplicate Your Work

The process of finding financial aid may seem like a daunting task, but don't be discouraged by all the research and paperwork ahead. Remember that most applications will ask for the same information over and over. Once you've written one essay about why you'd like a career in nursing, for example, you simply have to customize it for other applications that ask a similar question. And once you've dug up your birth certificate or bank records, you'll have them on hand for other applications as needed.

The following are excellent sources for scholarships and grants. As you brainstorm possible avenues to pursue, make a list of the organizations or professions to which you belong or in which you are active. Find out if any of those organizations offer scholarships or grants for which you might be eligible.

The School(s) You Wish to Attend

All colleges offer scholarships, and you're likely to be eligible to apply for one or more awards, especially if there are scholarships or grants specific to the nursing program. Be sure to talk with a financial aid officer from the school(s) you'd like to attend. The officer can also be very helpful if you have special financial circumstances.

Federal Grants and Scholarships

Pell Grants are awarded by the government based on need. You'll have to fill out the Free Application for Federal Student Aid (FAFSA), which is available online (*www.fafsa.ed.gov*).

Fill out this form even if you think you are ineligible for federal aid, because this form is also required by most states and many colleges. The FAFSA uses a standard formula to calculate your estimated family contribution (EFC). If your EFC is below a certain number, you will be eligible for the federal Pell Grant.

The specific grant amount—from a few hundred to $4,050 for the year 2006—will be based on your EFC, the cost of attendance, whether you are full or part time, and whether you will attend for more than one semester.

In addition, Federal Supplemental Educational Opportunity Grants (FSEOG) are awarded to students with the lowest EFCs and greatest financial need. Grant amounts range from $100 to $4,000 per year.

Scholarships are also available from the U.S. Department of Health and Human Services Bureau of Health Professionals in exchange for at least two years of service after graduation at a health care facility with a critical nursing shortage. Other aid, including loans and loan repayment programs, are also available. See *www.bhpr.hrsa. gov/nursing/scholarship* for more information.

State Scholarships and Grants

Your state government is also an excellent source for scholarships and grants. For example, New Jersey offers a Tuition Aid Grant, an Educational Opportunity Grant, and a Garden State Scholarship Program. In addition, programs such as the New Jersey Volunteer Tuition Credit Program, which gives active volunteer fire and rescue workers and their spouses or dependent children $600 per year for higher education, offer smaller awards to eligible residents.

Check your state and local government official Web sites for more information. A list of state higher education agencies is available from the U.S. Department of Education at *wdcrobcolp01.ed.gov/Programs/EROD/org_list.cfm?category_ID=SHE*.

Local Organizations

These scholarships are often smaller but easier to obtain because the applicant criteria are more restricted (e.g., you must be a nursing student in a particular county) and there are therefore fewer applicants. You might be tempted to pass up a small scholarship from a local organization because it doesn't seem worth the effort, but remember, even a few hundred dollars can pay a year's worth of bookstore bills or lab fees.

Local organizations to check out include:

- Kiwanis or Rotary Club
- Local hospitals and health care centers
- Religious institutions
- Professional associations, chambers of commerce
- Ethnic and cultural groups
- Credit unions, banks, and businesses

Military

The U.S. military offers several scholarship, grant, and loan programs for full-time enlisted members. The programs include tuition assistance (up to 100 percent of tuition costs), the Montgomery GI Bill, College Fund Programs, and Loan Repayment Programs. Other opportunities are available for part-time reservists and National Guard members. Reserve Officer Training Corps (ROTC) programs are also available at over 1,000 schools for those who wish to enlist after graduation. Information is available at *www.todaysmilitary.com*. In addition, many scholarships are available to active members of the military. See *www.military.com/scholarships* for more information.

Beware of Scholarship Scams

If you spend a few minutes online looking for scholarships, you'll quickly realize that there are dozens scholarship search sites that will link you to thousands of scholarship opportunities. Unfortunately, not all of these scholarships are legitimate. Be aware of the following signs that a scholarship is a scam:

- *Fees.* Very rarely will a legitimate scholarship charge an application fee. A scholarship search service might charge you a fee per search or application, but before you go paying someone else to find scholarships, check out the free search services listed below.

- *Guarantees.* No source can guarantee that you will receive a scholarship or grant that you apply for.

- *Requests for credit card or bank account number.* Legitimate scholarships will not require a credit card or bank account number to "hold" a scholarship or application.

- *Third party applications.* A legitimate application must be filled out by you, not a third party.

KAPLAN

Scholarship Search Engines

The following free scholarship search services will help you find specific scholarships for which you are eligible to apply. Apply for as many as time will allow—after all, you have nothing to lose and free money to gain!

- American Student Assistance (*www.amsa.com*)
- BrokeScholar (*www.brokescholar.com*)
- College Board (*www.collegeboard.org*)
- College Data (*www.collegedata.com*)
- CollegeNET (*www.collegenet.com/mach25/app/*)
- FastWeb (*www.fastweb.com*)
- FreSch! (*www.freschinfo.com*)
- Go College (*www.gocollege.com*)
- Scholarship Experts (*www.scholarshipexperts.com*)
- Scholarships.com (*www.scholarships.com*)

Nursing Organizations

These nursing organizations offer dozens of links to scholarship and financial assistance programs specifically for nursing students. Some scholarships are open to all nursing students while others may have very specific eligibility criteria.

- The American Association of Colleges of Nursing (*www.aacn.nche.edu/Education/financialaid.htm*)
- Campus RN (*www.campusrn.com/scholarships/scholarships.asp*)
- Discover Nursing (*www.discovernursing.com/scholarship_search.aspx*)
- Minority Nurse.com (*www.minoritynurse.com/financial/scholarships.html*)
- Nurse Web Search (*www.nursewebsearch.com/nursing_scholarships.htm*)
- Sigma Theta Tau International Honor Society of Nursing (*www.nursingsociety.org/career/scholarships_opps.html*)

Work Study

The Federal Work Study Program pays you to work on campus as part of a financial aid package. For example, you might work 10 to 12 hours a week in the admissions office or 18 to 20 hours per week in the bookstore. The money you earn (minimum wage or higher) is paid directly to you unless you request that it be applied directly to tuition or fees. Whenever possible, work-study students are placed in positions that complement their career goals. A work-study nursing student, for example, might assist in the health center or nursing lab. Some schools offer off-campus work-study positions, too. Note that your work-study hours cannot exceed your total work-study award.

Contact the financial aid office of the school to which you are applying for more information on its work-study program.

Loans

While scholarships and grants can significantly reduce college costs, many students—especially if they attend full time—need student loans to cover the remaining balance. While student loans are less than ideal because you have to pay them back, they typically offer low interest rates with flexible repayment, deferment, and loan forgiveness options. The most common student loans are described below.

Federal Perkins Loan

This low-interest loan (currently set at 5 percent) comes directly from the college, which contributes some of its own funds to the federal monies it receives for these loans. Depending on when you apply and your need, you may borrow up to $4,000 per year for undergraduate study and $6,000 per year of graduate or professional study. If you're attending school at least half time, you will have a grace period of nine months after you graduate to begin making payments to repay this loan.

Federal Stafford Loan

This loan has a variable interest rate (not to exceed 8.25 percent) and can be either subsidized (based on need, and you won't be charged interest until you graduate) or unsubsidized (not based on need, and you'll be charged interest beginning with the date of disbursement). The amount you may borrow depends on what year and type of student you are. A six-month grace period after graduation or a drop below half-time enrollment applies.

Federal Graduate PLUS Loan

The PLUS loan allows you to borrow up to the full cost of your graduate education (minus other financial aid). The interest rate is fixed at 8.25 percent, but rate reduction programs are available.

Private loans

As a last resort, private loans can bridge the gap between your available financing and the cost of attendance. Most private student loans come from large lenders such as Sallie Mae or Wells Fargo. If you need a commercial lender, be sure to shop around for the best available rate. (Try a source like the Lending Tree at *www.studentloans .lendingtree.com* to compare loan amounts, rates, and fees.) Companies such as Next Student (*www.nextstudent.com*) and Sallie Mae (*www.salliemae.com*) will also help you with your federal loan applications, so you can do all of your loan applications through one source.

Employer-sponsored Tuition Grants

Due to the shortage of nurses and the willingness of organizational leaders to design innovative initiatives, employer-sponsored tuition grants are also available. Many are tied to current or future employment with a health care facility. Some examples of this financial incentive are:

- The University of Rochester School of Nursing in New York advertises on its Web site that full-time or part-time employees at the University of Rochester Medical Center and Strong Memorial Hospital may be given 100 percent tuition benefits for up to two courses per semester, including summer, after a one-year waiting period for full-time employees and a two-year waiting period for part-time employees. Because the 2006–7 summer semester tuition was $15,000 and the academic year tuition (September to May) was $30,000, this is a substantial benefit.
- The University of Colorado Hospital has a BSN Nursing Work Site Program. One day a week, individuals who meet eligibility criteria will be paid to attend nursing school classes. Hospital employees are given priority. (Additionally, employees can use their tuition reimbursement benefit.) Enrollees can receive

their BSN in two to three years. Enrollees made a commitment to work as an RN for the University of Colorado Hospital for 4,000 hours (about two years). They also have a loan forgiveness program.

■ If you are a state or local government employee in Maryland and you earn less than $40,000 gross annually, you may be eligible for a loan assistance or repayment program to study nursing. You should contact the Maryland State Scholarship Administration, 16 Francis Street, Annapolis, MD 21401, or phone them at 410-974-2971, extension 146.

Nursing Education Loan Repayment Program (NELRP)

The Nursing Education Loan Repayment Program is meant to repay, in exchange for two years of work at a critical shortage facility, 60 percent of the loan balance. Those registered nurses willing to work a third year at the same facility can receive an additional 25 percent of the loan balance. This is a win-win situation: nurses have a majority of their loans paid off, and underserved facilities have a dedicated staff.

To be eligible, you must have completed the degree-granting program and be licensed, working at least 32 hours per week at a critical shortage facility. Preference is given to applicants with the greatest financial need and working in facilities such as:

■ Specific hospitals
■ Nursing homes
■ Federally designated health centers
■ Federally designated migrant health centers
■ Public health departments
■ Rural health clinics
■ Indian Health Service health centers

For more information about this program, see *bhpr.hrsa.gov/nursing/loanrepay.htm.*

Tips for a Smooth Ride

As you apply for financial aid, you will have to juggle a number of different applications and deadlines, as well as the mounds of supporting paperwork (essays, bank statements, transcripts, etc.) that will accompany the different applications. These five tips will help keep this process running smoothly and ensure you don't miss any opportunities for aid:

1. Mark a calendar with each application deadline. Make sure this calendar is in a prominent place so you can refer to it easily and regularly.
2. Put a "send in" date for each application at least one week before the actual deadline. That way, if you fall behind or run into delays with paperwork, you'll still be able to get the application in on time.
3. Set up a filing system. Use a separate folder for applications to complete, applications in progress, and completed applications. (Make sure you keep a copy of everything you submit for your records.) File supporting papers in separate folders so you can locate them quickly and easily.
4. Keep copies of original essays so that it's easy to customize them for future applications.
5. Proofread each application carefully before sending it in. The last thing you want is to miss a scholarship opportunity because you forgot to fill in a section of an application or include an important piece of documentation.

There's no doubt that you have much work to do to figure out how to pay for your nursing degree. But the work you put in now will have both immediate and long-term benefits by helping to minimize your personal costs and future debt. Go for it!

PART FOUR

Getting through School

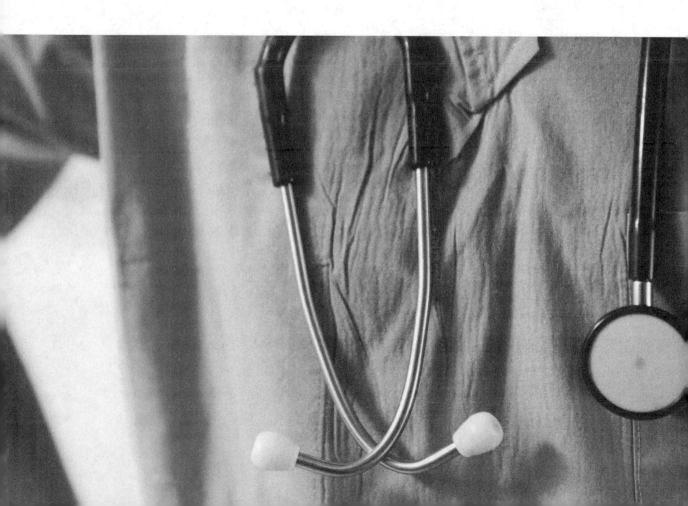

CHAPTER 10

How to Manage Going Back to School

Going back to school can be a daunting task for some people. However, being a second-time student is, in itself, a unique opportunity. In this chapter, you will learn about how school has changed since you were last a student. You will also learn the best tips for making the most of the resources available to you and for making the transition back to school a painless one.

GETTING USED TO YOUR STUDENT IDENTITY

Because the number of people going back to school has skyrocketed, a new vocabulary has arisen to describe these incoming students. Here are several examples of terms that various organizations, such as financial aid or admissions offices, might use to describe you:

- Re-entry student
- Mature student
- Adult learner
- Nontraditional student
- Career changer
- Second career student
- Back-to-school student
- Returning student

Tips for Academic Success from Nursing Students at Riverside Community College (California):[1]

- Never think you won't be accepted into the program. Prepare as if a position has already been offered.

- If you're going into the LVN program, take Anatomy & Physiology; you'll find it very helpful.

- Attend a nursing school preparation workshop so you can get all the details and plan ahead.

- Know fractions and decimals!

- Do all the prerequisites and suggested courses before entering, if at all possible.

- Discover what learning style is best for you before you start.

- Start an educational plan with a counselor.

- Learn to study and focus.

- If you're waiting to get into the program, take a medical terminology class. Pharmacology also helps.

- Talk to someone who knows how the Nursing Program functions. Don't assume things.

Recent statistics from the U.S. Department of Education show that if you decide to return to school, you will join the fastest growing educational demographic. The data is persuasive—you will definitely not be alone, no matter which label fits you.

In addition to being from many different backgrounds, second career or re-entry students can also be grouped by age. Here are some interesting facts for each group that might apply to you:

- *If you are over 25:* In 1970, people over 25 were 28 percent of all college students. By 1998, they were 41 percent. The Association for Nontraditional Students in Higher Education (ANTSHE) found that over-25ers now make up 47 percent of college students.

- *If you are over 35:* In 1970, about 823,000 people over 35 were in college. By 2001, their number was 2.9 million. That doubled the percentage from 9.6 percent to 19.2 percent of all students, according to the National Center for Education Statistics.

- *If you are over 40:* People over 40 on campus increased by 235 percent from 1970 to 1993, according to the Institute for Higher Education Policy.

- *If you are a single parent:* Numbers of single parents going to college have almost doubled, from 7.6 percent in 1993 to 13 percent today, according to the U.S. Department of Education.

---

1   Riverside Community College Web site, *www.rcc.edu/academicPrograms/nursing/tips.cfm* (accessed August 29, 2006).

Differences between "Then" and "Now"

The first time you went to school for your current profession was a time of new beginnings. Though you didn't know exactly what to expect, you knew you would face some challenges. Because you could not foresee how difficult some of those might be, you might have had an easier time entering school the first time around. Now, as a repeat adventure, you might feel the weight of awareness; you know how difficult it is to balance priorities and fulfill several roles.

Currently, educational institutions often offer special kinds of services that were originally planned for re-entry students. Examples of students who qualify for these special services are: undergraduates age 25 years and over and graduate students age 30 years and over; married students and those with children; divorced or widowed students; those who have worked full-time or are working full-time while in school; military veterans; commuters from out-of-town. You probably find yourself in one or more of these categories and should be aware that schools offer support for your unique needs. To help you feel at home in your new student life, make sure to find out about these services so you can take full advantage of them.

> The Association for Nontraditional Students in Higher Education (ANTSHE) was founded in October 1996 by a coalition of academic institutions throughout the United States and Canada to advocate for nontraditional students. They point out that these students "are pursuing careers, raising children and providing extraordinary service as volunteers in their communities while they go to school." Visit *www.antshe.org* for more information on this group.

Support Groups

You can usually find a staff person in the admissions or counseling offices who can help you locate a student support group for your particular needs. For example, if you are a commuter, you might want to join a student commuter support group. If you are a parent, you might ask about a support group for students with children. If the type of support group you seek has an official name, you can often find information about it directly on the school's Web site. The staff of the admissions or counseling offices can help you determine this. You might also find information on support groups on flyers posted around campus. Other groups can be located by reading the bulletins of the campus ministry program or ethnic cultural centers.

Some support groups are e-mail-only information sharing networks. Others, however, offer ongoing discussion groups, such as ALIFE at the University of North Dakota. Here is a description of how the support group operates and the issues they deal with:

> Discussion topics will reflect the needs of the group members and may include the challenges of juggling multiple roles, learning effective study techniques, adjusting to a new role and new environment, finding resources for specific needs, and many more. The group process will focus on empowering group members, so that group members will take primary responsibility to direct the group.[2]

As you can see, individual needs, questions, and issues are discussed in a friendly environment in which students provide support for one another. Support groups work for many people, and you might consider joining one to discuss your concerns and meet other students with whom you share common experiences.

ASKING FOR HELP WITH SCHOOL MATTERS

This might be the hardest change for some of you who are used to being independent, giving assistance whenever asked, and providing firm direction for others. Now, it might be your turn to ask for help or to request information that you might feel uncomfortable asking for because you expect to get along completely on your own. To make sure you have a solid understanding of everything from school policies to course material, you will need to quickly realize when you are just "not getting it" and ask for assistance at that moment. Don't wait until you feel completely overwhelmed, as you can avoid this by identifying what you don't understand and asking for clarification or more explanation.

Pay attention when you feel that some information is missing, and you'll know the right questions to ask. As a returning student, you might need some practice where asking questions is concerned. Rather than waiting for office hours, for example, consider approaching your instructor directly after class with your questions. If you need more time to reflect on what you want to ask, stick around for a few minutes after

---

2   University of North Dakota Web site, *www.union.und.edu/reentry/handbook/overview.htm* (accessed August 29, 2006).

class; chances are, other students might have questions for the instructor as well, and you could benefit from listening in on their discussions. This can be especially helpful right after pop quizzes, or before mid-term and final examinations.

You Are a Different Student the Second Time Around

If you had difficulty with math or with making oral presentations the first time through school, do not automatically expect these challenges to pop up again. Remember, you have more life experience now than you did the first time you were a student, and some of this experience can positively impact your academic performance. For example, you've been balancing bank statements and handling finances for many years, so your math skills might not be as rusty as you think. In other words, you might have outgrown your earlier academic weaknesses.

You Have More Resources

Another pleasant surprise for returning students is that education in nursing has changed dramatically over the past few years. Simulations are now available for many nursing practices. For example, simulation models allow you to practice giving injections and doing CPR using dummies. Computer tutorials are also available to help you identify areas of weakness where you need to brush up, provide you with more practice, and provide links to more information on a particular topic. This help is instant, which means that you get answers to your questions as they arise.

In addition to these resources, there is also the library, and a very important person known as a reference librarian. If there is a reference librarian at your school, familiarize yourself with the resources he or she can provide. Some schools offer formal tours of the library, computer tutoring, and reservations for group and individual study rooms, all of which can be accessed through the reference librarian. If no one at your school's library has this title, look for an administrative staff member at the library; they often function in the same way and can provide the same resources that a reference librarian can.

Don't Be Afraid to Start Slow

Especially at the beginning of your return to school, consider taking it slowly at first. Don't sign up for more courses than you can reasonably manage at one time. While your goal is most likely to keep your time in school before graduation to a minimum, remember that you might feel overwhelmed by the number of assignments due at once if you overload your class schedule.

Double-Check Your Work

Now that you're a more mature student, you're probably more focused than you were as an undergraduate and might even take the extra step to double-check your homework assignments before handing them in. This can help your classroom success tremendously, so take the time to proof your assignments at least twice before handing them in. You quickly do this by reading your work the next day, or by asking a colleague to review it for you.

Provide for Yourself First

If possible, make sure to have your own computer and printer. Having to negotiate time to finish your homework or complete your online research will only stress otherwise peaceful relationships and will put extra stress on you to plan your study time around another person's schedule.

Stay Focused on Your Goal

If you need reminders of the rewards of your new career path, think about using some kind of visual reminder of the benefits that await you upon graduation and post it in a place where you'll see it on a regular basis. This could be on your computer screensaver or on your bathroom mirror.

In her book, *Living the Possible Dream,* Julia Riley said, "I would say that it's not easy, but returning to college has been the best and most rewarding experience of my life. I had become a nonperson in my own life and coming to school has renewed my faith in life generally and myself specifically. When it seems tough, just stick it out. It's well worth it."[3]

---

3 Julia Riley, *Living the Possible Dream: The Single Parent's Guide to College Success* (Boulder, Colorado: Johnson Books, 1991).

KAPLAN

When All Is Said and Done

Returning to school and maintaining balance in your life can be difficult. If you feel overwhelmed, keep in mind this short fable about one re-entry student who seeks advice from a magician.

"Please give me some help, because I am about to give up—it is such hard work!" The magician said, "Magic words will help you make it through school more comfortably. Be sure to say them aloud when you need to. Say them as often as you need to. Say them with emphasis. Say: 'This too shall pass.'"

If your concern is not so much school itself, but how your "normal" life will change, Chapter 11 has more great tips and advice.

Returning Students Share Their Tips

- Use your time and energy wisely. At times you will have to make difficult choices: daily chores often can wait; studying cannot.

- Feeling guilty about the time you spend in classes and studying depletes your energy. Believe that you and your goals have worth and the people you are close to will believe it also.

- Keep your dreams, but set realistic short-term objectives that are not overwhelming.

- Be persistent. At times you may wonder what you are doing and why you are doing it. That's normal.

- Exchange phone numbers with classmates in case you can't attend class and need to know what went on.[4]

---

4 "Hints from Former Students,"Utah State University Online Re-entry Student Center. *www.usu.edu/stuserv/ womencen/Reentry/hints.htm* (accessed August 16, 2006).

CHAPTER 11

Managing Your Life outside of Nursing School

After all the effort you put into getting into nursing school, you may think that the hard part is behind you. Keep in mind, though, that your journey is just beginning and there are many more sacrifices to be made. But don't be overwhelmed. This chapter offers the best advice on how to create a balance between school and life, on how to incorporate nursing into your workplace, and most important, on how to minimize or overcome stress and burnout.

CREATING A BALANCE

As you consider becoming a nontraditional student, remember that you will be balancing the unknown demands of your education with your other responsibilities. These might include several important commitments such as marriage, children, work, community obligations, or the care of your elderly parents.

Get Your Feet Damp

This approach is the cousin of the old adage, "getting your feet wet." Because you have many other demands on your time and energy, you might want to find out how all the pieces of your life will fit together once you're in school. You can do this easily and inexpensively by enrolling in one class, anywhere, on any topic. The beauty of this experiment is that you do not need to limit your choice of topic to one that fits into your future plans. For example, the course could be a continuing education class at your neighborhood adult recreation department, or a college extension course. It could be a course on mosaics or beginning linear equations.

Tips for Personal Success from Nursing Students at Riverside Community College (California):[1]

- Learn to do without.

- Balance your life and get out of major stressors before getting into the nursing program (e.g., if you need to move, do it first!)

- Make sure you have a dependable vehicle.

- Organize your finances and use student aid.

- Know that your schedule will need to be very flexible if you must work during school.

The important thing is that you actually try a sample of basic student life to discover how going back to school will affect the rest of your life. You will be reading, researching, writing, studying, traveling to class, shifting plans to fit your new schedule, and spending less time with your family and friends.

To get the most out of the experience of sampling student life, take notes or keep a diary of how you feel about these adjustments. This will give you a sense of whether you're ready to fully immerse yourself in school.

Employer-Employee Issues

This is perhaps the most difficult of the challenges you will face if you need to continue working while going to school. Often, the employer is not as supportive as it would be if the employee were pursuing a degree in a field related to his/her job, both in terms of finance (tuition reimbursement) and morale.

Other people have shared their worries about the impact of their employer or colleagues even knowing about their educational pursuits. For example, here is one LPN student's view on this issue:

> Many working students are concerned whether or not they should let their boss or coworkers in on their secret. This is a highly individual decision which depends greatly on your work arrangements, how much school

---

1   Riverside Community College Web site, *www.rcc.edu/academicPrograms/nursing/tips.cfm* (accessed August 29, 2006).

will affect your work, and how well you get along with your boss. Bear in mind that a boss's job as well as yours is to act in the best interests of the company."[2]

Whatever your situation, you must decide how to balance your work life with your educational pursuits. Remember that this is something many people deal with, and that you do not face this challenge alone.

REMEMBER YOU ARE NOT ALONE

You are not the only person whose life will change if you enroll in school. Your relationships with your spouse, parents, friends, children, and employer might go through an adjustment period that can sometimes be unsettling. If you have kept them aware of possible changes from the beginning, they will have had time to become more comfortable with the situation by the time you register for classes.

Even if you must make rapid decisions to go back to school because of deadlines for enrollment or financial aid opportunities, make sure to keep those around you informed as much as possible. It's easy to become so immersed in the process that you inadvertently leave others out of the picture.

The need to communicate effectively will become greater the longer you are in school. For example, you'll need to keep your significant others up to date on both your short-term schedule and long-term timetable until graduation.

Here are some ideas for effectively communicating your schedule with those whose lives it will impact:

- Keep a wall calendar with activities color-coded by person for one month, or for the several months that make up your school quarter or semester.
- Use a dry-erase board to record messages about your whereabouts for the day.
- Use an agreed-upon procedure to communicate delays or last-minute changes in plans.

---

2   D. Bitritto. "Juggling Nursing School and Family." *Imprint Magazine* 45:4 (Sep-Oct 1997): 45-46.

Consider a Family Meeting

Having a family meeting is a good way to make sure everyone's needs are considered from the outset. This is a good time to brainstorm ideas to organize family and household responsibilities. Here are five suggested rules for the meeting that will help you communicate effectively:

1. Only one person speaks at a time. If this proves difficult to remember, use a prop that one must hold in order to talk. Pass it around on a regular basis. It might even be used to encourage a quiet person to speak up.
2. Set an agreed-on start and stop time. Stick to that timetable, since you are meeting because people have pressing obligations.
3. Rotate the leadership roles so that everyone feels part of the decision-making process.
4. Don't point fingers, accusing others of mounting obstacles to your career progress. Instead, share with them how situations make you feel. Use the format: "When I am (describe the situation), I feel (describe your reaction." Remember, your family and friends can't read your mind, so let them know what you need for support and what is not working as well as it could.
5. At the end of the meeting, do two things: evaluate how the current meeting went, and plan the timing for your next meeting.

Don't Make Unnecessary Comparisons

Returning to school is not a good time to compare yourself to others who do not have to make dramatic changes in their lives. This is a time when it's easy to look at your family and friends and wish you had their schedules. You might even become resentful that they seem to have so many fewer obligations than you do. However, you need to keep these feelings in check. If you do find yourself engaging in a "pity party," you need to redirect your attention to your goals and the choices you've made to achieve them.

Take Time for Fun—Even If Briefly

It's easy to forget the fact that your mind requires rest from time to time. This does not mean that you have to take whole days off to recuperate. However, it does mean that you need to plan for some down time.

You are probably multitasking in the rest of your life, and you can feel efficient if you do two things at once:

- Recreation and exercise. For example you can read a magazine while working out on a stationary bike, or listen to music as you run outside or on the treadmill.
- Household chores and relaxation. Fold the laundry, vacuum, cook, or wash dishes while listening to music or singing along with the lyrics.
- Relaxation and schoolwork. Do deep breathing exercises or muscle stretches between writing each page of an assignment.

Of course, you can always do two "nonfun" tasks at once to make more time for pleasurable activities, such as reading class materials while on a stationary bike.

Don't feel guilty about taking some time for yourself. You deserve it and it will help you stay focused on your goal.

OVERCOMING OVERLOAD, STRESS, AND BURNOUT

Everyone who undertakes new challenges, especially when those are added on to the everyday responsibilities in one's life, can become overwhelmed. People run the risk of overload, stress, and burnout when they don't take enough time out of each day to tend to their own needs. Though going back to school is tough, you don't have to burn out if you pay attention to how you feel and check in with yourself every now and then.

> ## Homework Alternatives
>
> It's easy to burn out when you're faced with the demands of life, school, and possibly even work. Here are some activities that require only 30 minutes of your time, but will help keep you less stressed through it all.
>
> - Visit your favorite Web sites
> - Listen to your favorite CD
> - Take a walk around the block.
> - Read the latest issue of your favorite magazine
> - Make a phone call to a friend you haven't spoken to in a while
> - Watch your favorite TV program
> - Spend some quality time with your family
> - Take a hot shower or bath
> - Enjoy a short nap

Burnout Can Be Conquered

To avoid burnout, you need to recognize the very early warning symptoms of burnout so that you can prevent it from progressing to a serious life-altering stage. Here are some thirteen "unlucky signs" you should watch for: [3]

1. Chronic fatigue—exhaustion, tiredness, a sense of being physically run down
2. Anger at those making demands
3. Self-criticism for putting up with the demands
4. Cynicism, negativity, and irritability
5. A sense of being besieged
6. Exploding easily at seemingly inconsequential things
7. Frequent headaches and gastrointestinal disturbances
8. Weight loss or gain
9. Sleeplessness and depression
10. Shortness of breath
11. Suspiciousness
12. Feelings of helplessness
13. Increased degree of risk taking

If you find yourself experiencing these early warning symptoms, take action.

---

3   Henry Neils, 13 Signs of Burnout and How to Help You Avoid It," Assessment.com, *www.assessment.com/ mappmembers/avoidingburnout.asp?Accnum=06-5210-010.00* (accessed August 29, 2006).

Overload Can Be Prevented

Keeping a visual aid to organize the tasks you must complete can help you look objectively at what you need to accomplish. Try using a table like this one to make plans (labeled ■) to accomplish your goals, as well as backup (labeled ✓)plans for when you can't follow through exactly as you planned.

Goal	Planned Course of Action	Revisions

1. A on exams	■ Study 15 hours per week
	  • Attend tutoring sessions
	  • Review material and attend class
		✓ Join study group (2 hours per week)

2. Paint living room	• Shop for new paint • Plan a time to do the actual painting	✓ Do this next month when I have time
3. Daughter will play volleyball	■ Attend all games	✓ Miss practices ✓ Make arrangements for daughter's transportation

---

Think Positive Thoughts

Create a list of self-affirming positive statements. These statements might include these thoughts:

- I am intelligent and I can pass this course.
- There is nothing better than a good challenge.
- My faculty cares about me.
- My family and friends support me.
- I can be successful and achieve my goals.
- I can pass this test.
- I love to learn.
- I will graduate.
- I can learn this material.
- I am kind and caring toward my patients.

Take out a piece of paper now and make a list of positive thoughts about yourself. Carry this list with you. When confronted with a stressful event such as an exam or clinical evaluation, refer to your list and perform successfully.[4]

Hopefully, just by reading this chapter you will have calmed your nerves and overcome any fears you may have about starting a new career. In the next chapter you will get some advice directly from nurses who have been exactly where you are right now.

---

4   Christine McMurtrie. "Nursing Education Program: *Success in Nursing Series* (Revised, April 1999): page 11, Howard Community College, Columbia, Maryland *www.howardcc.edu/health/PDF%20files/ Success%20in%20Nursing.pdf#search=%22Christine%20McMurtrie.%20%E2%80%9CSuccess%20in%20 Nursing%20%22*

CHAPTER 12

Succeeding in School and at Home: Peer Advice

You will find that your fellow nursing students are a terrific source for ideas on how to balance your new academic life with your personal life. They will share a tremendous number of hints and suggestions that helped them and that can also benefit you. While some of their "secrets of success" will not fit your unique situation, sharing ideas with your fellow nursing students can help you tremendously. This chapter includes examples of tips and strategies you might hear from your classmates to help you deal with the various aspects of being a nursing student.

GET THE MOST OUT OF YOUR CLASSES

- During even the most boring lecture, look interested. The secret to making a good impression is behaving the way you wish to be perceived.
- Remember, some teachers are just plain difficult and you will have to find ways to deal with them. Learning how to effectively interact with difficult people is a good skill to cultivate in any discipline.
- Introduce yourself to your instructors. You don't want to be just another face in the crowd.[1]

---

1 Unless otherwise noted, quotes in this chapter are from Angela Pearson, "Study Tips from Former Nursing Students," developed from the public parts of SNURSE-L, now in the public domain, *http://medismart.com/study-tips.htm*, accessed August 30, 2006.

- The first two weeks of class, you need to hit the ground running. Read everything you are assigned, and try to finish your assignments early. This will get you into a regular study routine that will carry you through the rest of the semester.
- Use colored index cards, which help you more easily recall information than plain white paper.
- Record your instructors' lectures (get permission first), and listen to them while exercising, laying in bed, driving in the car, or while waiting for class. Repetition helps.
- REVIEW, REVIEW, REVIEW! I can't stress how important it is to stay ahead of the game and review your material every night.
- I run after class to allow myself some alone time. This gives my mind a chance to rest and get reenergized. I run before I study so that I can get blood and oxygen pumping through my system. This helps me stay alert and focus on my studies, not to mention keeping me in shape.
- One of the things I have found most helpful is planning ahead. I go through my syllabi at the beginning of the semester and I write in my planner the due dates for everything. That way, I can anticipate which weeks will be rough and which will be more relaxed. This also helps avoid overscheduling. Make sure to leave some time in that busy schedule to sleep; it's something we could all use a little more of in nursing school![3]

Here are seven N-U-R-S-I-N-G tips!

N: Nutrition (Eat healthy)

U: Unity (Work together to help each other and to help our patients)

R: Rest (Plenty of sleep before clinicals, exams, and classes)

S: Study (To succeed in our classes and further our knowledge)

I: Imprint (Our favorite magazine to read for helpful hints relaxation, and new information)

N: Nurture (Top priority for our patients, ourselves, and each other)

G: Grades (Pass all our classes so we can move on to boards and finally become nurses)[2]

---

2 Reprinted from *Imprint*, Vol. 52, Number 4, September/October 2005, National Student Nurses' Association, Inc.

3 Ibid.

■ Purchase a full-size executive date book. This date book shows time slots for each day from 7 AM to 7 PM, and incorporates a block for every 15 minutes. When I receive my class schedule, I take a colorful highlighter and fill in the blocks of time that I am in school/clinicals. Using a different color, I then highlight family responsibilities. Lastly, I color in my time for study and exercise, along with mealtimes.

■ Keep up with your school work from the beginning of each course, and do not wait until the night before an exam to begin your reading. Get tutoring for anything you do not understand, and realize that material that is not on a test may help you save someone's life in the future. Beyond any test, you are preparing for a profession, so allow yourself enough time and opportunity to learn well.

■ For every topic studied, ask yourself "why?" or "so what?" This helps to clarify the meaning and purpose behind the topic and to develop ever-important critical thinking skills.

■ When you are studying, always keep in mind the steps needed to answer those questions:

   1. Airway, breathing, circulation are considered first.
   2. Nursing process (assessment, diagnosing, planning, implementing, and evaluating) in that order, are considered second.
   3. Maslow's hierarchy of needs is considered third. If all else fails, grab a chocolate bar and take a good guess!"[4]

Get organized and stay that way. When you are organized it gives you a sense of control, which boosts your confidence level. Keep a three-ring binder with side pockets and dividers for the syllabus, notes, handouts, projects, and grade sheet for each class. The syllabus usually contains a schedule of topics and when they will be covered, and I like to put a tab on that page so that I can refer back to it easily and stay on track. In addition, the syllabus has a breakdown of how you will be graded, and I use that to make myself a grade sheet. For the notes section, print out the PowerPoint file in handout form before class, and date it. You should also date any handouts you receive, and keep them in the folder's pockets until you have access to a hole puncher. A little extra work at the beginning of the semester will save you a lot of time and headaches later.[5]

---

4   Ibid.

5   Ibid.

GET THE MOST FROM YOUR BOOKS

- Take your materials out of the house to study. Get away from distractions, undone dishes, radio, and TV.
- Read nursing journals and magazines. Often, current articles will compliment your text and make the information easier to understand.
- Use individual sheets of paper or large index cards to make a file of diseases/conditions and their treatments. List etiology, signs and symptoms, diagnostic tests, interventions, and so on, and keep them in a binder for future reference as well as present study.
- Take notes from your notes! After taking notes in class or from the book, put away the book and outline your notes to help the information sink in.
- Use NCLEX review materials as your study guide. Sort questions by topic as you go through school and study those questions pertaining to your current lesson. This will help you learn and give you a head start for when it's time to take the NCLEX.
- Turn course objectives (as found in the beginning of each chapter or on the course syllabus) into questions—an instant study guide!

THRIVE IN CLINICALS

- Whether or not you've been an EMT for years, remember that everyone begins clinicals at different levels of experience. Focus on your goals and what you will learn, not on how much (or little) you know now.
- If you have trouble remembering protocols, lab values, or even your patient's name, write them down on index cards and keep them in your pocket. The more you use them, the more you study them.
- During Psych rotation, take a moment to center yourself before working with patients. Most respond best to a calm, focused approach.
- Get to know your instructors. The more you know them the more likely you are to understand them and what they are expecting from you.
- If you don't know how to do a procedure, look it up, check the protocols, and ask for help. Instructors would rather walk you through the procedure than fix the mess or hear complaints if you do something wrong.
- Be helpful to the nurse you are assigned to for clinical. Take all the vitals, never contradict publicly, and don't ask constant questions—that's what your instructors are for. The nurse will be glad of the help and be more likely to help you.
- Don't make your supervising nurse hold your hand. Even if you're scared and have never done something before, jump in and do anything suggested.

- Volunteer information! Instructors like to be informed about your patients. If they can trust you to keep them informed, they are likely to trust you to work independently.
- Explore volunteer opportunities in your area; these aren't just for candy stripers any more. Many clinics and outreach organizations are completely run by volunteers, and the experience can help you shine when you're out on the floor.

- Instead of creating an outline of each chapter, I write detailed questions. For example, if the text states, "The first step of the nursing process is assessment," I write on one side of a flashcard, "What is the first step of the nursing process?" On the other side of the flashcard, I write the original sentence. This method allows me to quiz myself in a style that forces me to recall the information. I think the key is recall—I was not having much success in writing an outline and just reading it over and over.

- I like to highlight my book as the instructor is lecturing. For each set of test materials, I use a different color highlighter. This way, when I flip through my book, I can tell at a glance which material goes with the test I need to study. This is also handy for finals, because you can easily study for the test you did worst on. Just look for the right color!

- Study in a brightly lit room, sitting up at a table or desk. Never study in bed. Light a citrus-scented candle to help keep your senses awake.[6]

> One of the biggest problems for nursing students is not getting enough sleep. I have found that taking a 15 minute power nap when returning home from school really helps to refresh me. And when I feel refreshed, I am able to hit the books for the evening. I know 15 minutes doesn't seem like a lot of time, but if you can train your body to do this, you will see how good you really feel! Try not to sleep past the 15 minutes, because I have found that just makes you feel groggy.

6   Ibid.

ACE THE TEST

- Take your tests in comfort and style. Wear comfortable, loose-fitting clothing on test day. Loose fitting does not mean sloppy; do your confidence level a favor and dress for success. Cardigan sweaters, full skirts, and stretch pants are comfortable without compromising your professional style and attitude. Layers can help you adjust if the test room is too cold or hot.

- If you need to discuss an issue on a test with your instructor, do it privately. To dispute a grade in public will embarrass them and make them want to be right in front of the crowd. Address the issue in the context of needing correct information, not that you're trying to gain one more point.

- When the instructor's viewpoint conflicts with what's written in the textbook, offer both answers on the test when possible. If this not possible (as on a multiple choice test), most instructors will allow you to approach them quietly during the test. You can display your knowledge and ask which answer is being requested.

- Ask former students about an instructor's testing style before taking the first exam.

- I have been a nursing student for three years, and therefore, have some experience in taking nursing exams. First of all, test-taking is not my best skill, so I have to study hard to successfully take an exam. I have learned that I benefit most by decreasing my anxiety before an exam. There are three main tactics I use to calm my pre-exam nerves. First, I give myself positive feedback and recognize the progress I make while studying. Second, I try to complete all of the assigned readings ahead of time. This way I only have to study my notes and reread problem sections. Third, it is helpful for me to start studying a few days in advance. This helps me feel less rushed and makes me more comfortable with the material.[7]

- I always have an NCLEX book with me while I study. This allows me to compare what I think are the most important points of a section to what I need to know for the NCLEX. My NCLEX books also contain NCLEX-style questions. I find this has better prepared me for classroom tests and for the licensure exam.[8]

---

7   Ibid.

8   Ibid.

■ After just one semester, I have learned how different studying for nursing exams is compared with our prerequisite courses. In addition to getting at least eight hours of sleep every night, exercising three to five times weekly, drinking plenty of water, and taking vitamins, it is imperative to make a study schedule and stick to it! At the beginning of the semester, I write all my exams, return demonstrations, projects, quizzes, clinicals, and finals in my day planner. I highlight those important dates and schedule the rest of my week around studying. Treating school like a full-time job helps me prioritize free time.

■ When I need to study for an exam, I get copies of all of the old quizzes and tests that I did earlier on the class, and make a note card out of each question. Then I quiz myself with the note cards and make two piles, one for the ones I get right, and one for the ones I get wrong. Once I go all the way though the pile, I keep going through the wrong pile until I get every single one right. Then, I go through the entire stack of note cards and repeat the process until I can get all the answers right.

■ One tip that helps students focus and think clearly when studying for examinations is to create a ritual of restfulness. This requires setting some "comfort cues" that trigger rest at about the same time each day and allow at least six hours of renewing sleep. Hygiene rituals, music, scented candles, journaling, massage, reading a "brain-candy" novel, and learning deep-breathing with head-to-toe relaxation and imagery, are all tips that can enhance the cycle of rest while creating a refreshed and focused mind for studying.

■ I make flashcards for the subject that I have a test on. I usually write down a key word or phrase on one side of the flash card and the answer on the other side. Sometimes, I even add a picture on the front to help me remember the card and what it relates to. Making flash cards makes you write the notes over again, and it is an easy way to study by yourself or with another student. This method is especially helpful if you are a visual learner![9]

---

9   Ibid

Blogging Success for Nursing Students

A nursing student created the Web site Mediblogopathy (*mediblogopathy.blogspot. com*), which has since become home to the most extensive list of nurse blogs on the Internet. The site also receives regular nominations from readers for "NurseBlog of the Month." The site's motto is "To Do What Nobody Else Will Do. In a Way That Nobody Else Can Do. That Is to Be a Nurse." The author started the site when she was looking online for homework resources during nursing school and says that Mediblogopathy now serves many purposes.

"In the beginning, I used it as an outlet to express my feelings toward nursing school and my instructors. Later I wanted to make a home base where I could go for links to blogs I liked. Now, I see it as a way to contribute to the nursing community on the Internet, both by helping other nurses connect and share stories from work and life, and also by giving nursing students a place to find information on what nurses really experience straight from the source—including all the joys and frustrations," she added. "My goal is to be a hub for the community—a starting place for people to explore and share."[10]

ADJUST YOUR ATTITUDE

- Dare to try. Fear can be difficult to overcome, but if you do not try, you will never know whether you could have succeeded. You might have many doubts, questions, and fears when you start college again—and no answers. But tell yourself: I just need to pass one class at a time!
- Buy a good personal planner and note all projects, deadlines, and tests in it. Plan a realistic schedule and follow it. Take one day at a time, confident that every day's tasks bring you closer to your goal
- Being a nursing student is harder than being a nurse in many ways. Just relax, don't sweat the small stuff, and be receptive to patient and staff needs.

---

10 Christina Orlovsky. "Trends in Nursing: Blogs Provide Window into the Profession." RN.com, (April 2006). *http://w3.rn.com/news_news.asp?articleID=15163* (accessed August 16, 2006).

- Replace your fear, anxiety, and worry with joy. Have fun with what you know. Have fun learning interesting new things. Enjoy your new role.
- Don't give up. Failure is not an option!
- Graduation is not a goal. It is simply the natural consequence of your actions.
- Set the tone of your clinical day right. Press your uniform, lay out clothes and shoes, get essential items together (always in the same place) and pack your bag the night before. You'll feel "with it" and together the next day. It's a great confidence builder.

FORM AND USE A STUDY GROUP

- Form a study group, especially one you can stick with through graduation. Develop a mutual, vested interest in each other, and divide and conquer the huge amount of info you're expected to learn.
- Go through your notes together. Sometimes someone else puts information down in an especially memorable way. Sometimes someone else catches something you missed.
- Sit in the front row. Most study groups form from those you associate with during classes. Select your lab partner with care and sit in the front row with the students who are (or want to be) brilliant.
- Divide and conquer! Assign a portion of each chapter or assignment to each member of your group. Each person is to make up study questions for their portion and distribute copies to the others. This is like creating your own practice exam.
- Network with students in classes ahead of you for information on courses and instructors. A little foreknowledge can go a long way.
- Make quizzes and ask each other questions about the subject your quiz covers. Reward yourself for the hard work and studying you have done along with a successful test—we all know they are not at all easy!
- Join a student nurse forum and share questions, tips, and experiences with other students as well as experienced nurses.

USE TECHNOLOGY

- Record lectures (request permission first), and then listen to them again while you rewrite your notes. You'd be surprised what you can miss the first time.
- Read your clinical notes into a tape recorder by topic in a concise, repeatable form. Ask questions on tape that you can answer when you listen to it. Listen to tapes on your way to clinicals in your car or on a headset walking to class. You can even save them to be used for NCLEX review.
- Seek out and use Web resources in your research papers. Also get the free learning software available from FTP sites online.
- Use your e-mail account to communicate with instructors. You are likely to get well crafted, concise answers to your concerns if they are expressed in writing. This also eliminates phone tag and the restrictions of office hours.
- Some software and database programs allow you to create templates for your specific needs. You can make forms for care plans, assessments, process recordings—any standard paperwork. Then all you need to do is fill in the blanks and print it up.

WHEN YOU ALSO HAVE A FAMILY

- Lower your standard of housekeeping. You don't need to make the beds every day as long as your sheets are clean. You want your home clean enough to stay healthy and organized enough to find your shoes in the morning. Every thing else is far less important.

> I am currently working toward a BSN. I have been an LPN for 21 years, but decided I wanted more, so I went back to school. All my prerequisites went smoothly. Then came pathophysiology and pharmacology, and no matter how I studied or how much I studied, I had a very difficult time passing weekly exams. My son, a college student himself, bought me a microrecorder. I tried taping the professor's lectures, but it still didn't help. Then I decided I would tape myself reading the set and listen to it while driving to and from work and school. I also listened to it an hour each evening. I started receiving excellent exam scores, and passed the course![11]

---

11 Reprinted from *Imprint*, Vol. 52, Number 4, September/October 2005, National Student Nurses' Association, Inc.

- Keep life simple. Do not permit clutter in your house. It's easier to dust, vacuum, and clean with all that stuff around. You can plan a menu and make one trip to the grocery store each week. You can do laundry during free moments and all the housework on the weekends.

- Care and upkeep of significant others is important. Tell your significant others how much you appreciate and count on them. When they do something you find helpful—*thank them*. Remember, you're in this together.

- If you have all-day (not hourly) care for your children, use it. Drop the kids off when the doors open and study.

- Shop around for reliable daycare. Most facilities will send a child home "sick" with a touch of diarrhea or have an arbitrary degree temperature as the "sick" point. Have a backup plan if your child is ill.

- Look around your community for activities your kids can enjoy while you are in class or studying. Little League, after school programs, and community events are all good possibilities.

- Set aside family time and protect it—even when you have a paper due the next day or even if it means hiring a babysitter or trading babysitting duty with a friend.

- Enforce a "family homework time" and let everyone study together at the table. You will set a good example of study habits and have some extra family time together.

Mom × 4 + School

Here's how one nursing student handles her dual roles of student and mother—of four!

"Trying to attend nursing school and raise four kids really is a challenge. People always ask me how I do it. Well, you have to be organized and have lots of patience. I never study when my kids are awake. My kids need me to be mom, not student, during the day. I do have schedules for them and 8:00 PM is bedtime. I do my studying from about 8:30 to 12:30 each night. I have no distractions then and I retain what I am studying. This really has been the key for me and I am proud to say I have one semester of school left. Stay focused and organized!"

If you consider the source of the advice in this chapter, people who are going through or have done what you are contemplating, you should cherish it. And just think, in a few years, you could be offering your own helpful hints for succeeding in school and at home. In the next chapter, you will find a brief review of the major nursing concepts you will need to know for success in school.

Tips on Being a Mom and a Nursing Student

I never realized before that I could do five things at once! I can do laundry, help my kids with their homework, organize dinner, and review the notes I've taped to kitchen cupboards to memorize immunoglobulins and their functions. It's amazing that I can memorize and make a great meatloaf at the same time!

When you are in nursing school, it can consume your life… But it is still important to me to be there for my family, and particularly, to be a good mom…It would be great to always fulfill my children's needs first, but there are times when studying for an exam has to take priority…. I try to do special things with my children when life isn't so hectic, like a pizza picnic in the living room, slumber party in mom and dad's room, … or just reading a book with them.[12]

---

12 Diane Brandsrud. "Tips on Being a Mom and a Nursing Student." National Student Nurses' Association Web site, *www.nsna.org/career/tipson.asp* (accessed August 16, 2006).

CHAPTER 13

Nursing Concepts You Need to Know for Success

You will learn many concepts throughout your nursing school education, and among the most important are the ones in this chapter. As you progress through your program, their definitions will become even clearer, because you will be able to put them in the context of what you learn in the classroom and during your clinical rotations.

THE NURSING PROCESS

For the practical nurse, the nursing process involves data collection, planning, implementation, and evaluation of nursing care. For the registered nurse, the nursing process includes assessment, analysis, planning, implementation, and evaluation of nursing care. Each step is essential to the performance of safe and effective care.

Data collection or *assessment* is the process of establishing and verifying facts about the patient. This gives you a basis of information with which to identify actual or potential health problems (LPN) or assess these problems (RN). You obtain either subjective or objective data by a variety of means: interviews, observation, review of the health history, performance of a head-to-toe assessment, lab results, and communication with other members of the health care team.

Analysis is the examination of the facts you obtained through data collection and assessment. This allows you to draw conclusions about the health problems you've identified. During analysis, you compare your findings with normal data to establish a nursing diagnosis of a particular health problem.

Planning is the next step, the outcome of which results in the formulation of the nursing care plan. You engage in planning by:

- Assigning priorities to nursing diagnosis
- Specifying goals
- Identifying interventions
- Articulating expected outcomes
- Documenting the nursing care plan

Implementation is the term for activating the plan. It includes assisting patients in their activities of daily living (ADLs), counseling and educating patients and their families, and giving nursing care to patients. For RNs, implementation also means counseling patients and their families and supervising and evaluating the work of other health care team members.

Evaluation measures the patient's response to nursing intervention. It examines the patient's progress in achieving the goals of the nursing care plan. To complete an evaluation, you compare the observed results to the expected outcome and answer the question, "Did the care plan work?"

MASLOW'S HIERARCHY OF NEEDS

Researcher Abraham Maslow used a triangle to illustrate five levels of human needs that were presented in the following order from the bottom of the triangle to the top: physiological, safety and security, love and belonging, self-esteem, and self-actualization. These needs are important to know and keep in mind as you begin your career as a nurse, as you will encounter patients at many levels of the hierarchy.

Physiological needs are necessary for survival, so they are placed at the base of the triangle. They have the highest priority and must be met first. These needs include air, water, food, temperate climate, excretion of waste, shelter, rest, and sex. If you don't have oxygen to breathe or food to eat, you are not in a position to care about self-esteem.

Safety and security needs are the next necessity, so are located directly above physiological needs on the Maslow's triangle. Examples of physical security needs include the prevention of illness (such as pneumonia), accidents (such as handling loaded guns), and environmental threats (such as drinking contaminated water). An example of a psychological security need is a patient who has had a stroke or heart transplant needing to know what to expect after these events.

Love and belonging needs are on the next level in the triangle. They are satisfied when individuals feel loved by family and friends and accepted by other people.

Self-esteem needs are just below the top level of the triangle. They are satisfied when individuals feel self-confident and useful.

Self-actualization needs are the highest level of the triangle. To achieve self-actualization, you must have satisfied all of the lower-level needs. Due to the stresses of life, this is not always possible. Many people never realize this sense of fulfillment and realization of their full potential because they are unable to satisfy all of the lower-level needs.

BODY SYSTEMS APPROACH TO NURSING

You will learn the fundamentals of caring for patients with problems or health promotion (wellness) needs related to their body systems. Each system has its own characteristic response to illness, injury, and positive self-care. Here are the names of each system and the parts of the body to which they relate:

- Musculoskeletal—bones, joints, muscles, tendons
- Integumentary—skin
- Gastrointestinal—mouth, pharynx, esophagus, stomach, small and large intestines, rectum, anus, liver, and biliary tract
- Genitourinary—kidney, ureters, bladder, urethra
- Respiratory—lungs
- Circulatory—heart
- Cardiovascular—arteries , veins, capillaries
- Neurosensory—central nervous system (brain and spinal cord), peripheral nervous systems (sensory and motor pathways)
- Endocrine—pituitary, thyroid gland, parathyroid, adrenal gland, testes, ovaries, pancreas

- Hematological—blood
- Immune—bone marrow, lymph nodes, spleen, thymus, tonsils
- Reproductive—ovaries, uterus

INDIVIDUALIZING PATIENT CARE

The best part of nursing is that you can treat each patient that you encounter as a unique individual. You will discover many innovative practices that allow you to customize your approach.

Critical Thinking

You will problem-solve for a particular patient by thinking creatively. This requires that you:

- Observe the situation
- Decide what's important to accomplish
- Look for patterns and relationships
- Identify the problem
- Transfer your knowledge from one situation to another
- Apply your knowledge
- Evaluate the outcome according to established criteria

Cultural Awareness

You will discover that different cultures have widely varied ideas about health, the healing process, medications, food, and lifestyle habits. You will be introduced to some basic concepts, so that when you encounter different cultures on-the-job, you will know to respond with respect and understanding.

Physical Assessment Skills

You will learn how to take and interpret vital signs, usually defined as the details of an individual's temperature, pulse, respirations, and blood pressure. Also, you will gather critical information from monitors such as an EKG machine, which is used for recording heart functioning.

Laboratory/Diagnostic Data

You will understand the meaning of laboratory and diagnostic data and will be able to use them to evaluate patients' responses to care.

Medication Administration

You will learn about pharmacology to safely administer medications following medical providers' orders. You will discover that the nursing profession has a long tradition of insisting on the five "rights." They are:

1. Right patient
2. Right drug
3. Right dose
4. Right route
5. Right time

You also will discover there is more to learn about drugs, specifically:

- Rationale for specific nursing care in relation to drug groups
- Observations related to desired drug effects, side effects, and toxic effects
- Education of the patient and family members
- Documentation of drug administration

You will have chances to practice in the major routes of medication administration: oral, intramuscular (IM), intravenous (IV), and subcutaneous (under the skin).

You will be tested on the essential mathematical calculations used by nurses in a clinical setting. You need basic math skills (knowledge of decimals, fractions, metric system, conversion between systems of measurement, ratio-proportion, and ability to do basic algebraic equations).

MOTHER AND CHILD HEALTH

You will adapt the nursing process to the assessment and nursing management of the childbearing family. Your emphasis will be on the biopsychosocial needs of the family during the phases of pregnancy, childbirth, and the neonatal period; this also includes awareness of abnormal conditions. You will learn the concept of family-centered nursing care that enables children and their families to prevent illness and disability and promote, protect, and restore health. You will be introduced to the unique biopsychosocial and health educational needs of the growing child, from infancy through adolescence. You will have opportunities to study families in the community, as well as in ambulatory care and hospital settings.

MENTAL HEALTH NURSING

You will learn the basic concepts of mental health, mental illness, and the role of the nurse in caring for clients with mental health needs. You will put into practice the concepts of nursing process, therapeutic communication, and legal/ethical/ professional standards of care as they influence mental health nursing practices.

You will develop skills in differentiating between various mental disorders in terms of symptoms, nursing diagnoses, treatment modalities. You will also develop skills in the formulation of intervention strategies. You will have the opportunity to develop skills in assessment and intervention for clients experiencing abuse, grief, or psychotic manifestations of medical illness.

EVIDENCE-BASED NURSING CARE

Also known as nursing research, evidence-based nursing efforts look critically at the rationale for nursing interventions. You begin your own exploration by defining the problem, determining the study purpose, choosing a data selection instrument, and planning for data analysis. You will need to understand the importance of protection of human rights in research. You will be given practice in the reading of research reports for applicability to nursing practices.

COMMUNITY HEALTH NURSING

Also known as public health nursing, you will explore the nurse's role in promoting and preserving the health of the population as a whole. You will learn about epidemiological standards of community health nursing practice, political processes, environmental health, and health care delivery systems.

NURSING ROLES/LEADERSHIP

You will have the opportunity to develop as a leader, as a designer/manager/coordinator of health care, and as a member of the nursing profession. You will learn methods

KAPLAN)

to ensure professional growth and development in communication, critical-thinking, and problem-solving skills. You will discuss current issues in heath care and in the nursing profession and learn how the health care team coordinates multidisciplinary care

THERAPEUTIC COMMUNICATION

Therapeutic communication involves listening to and understanding the patient. It emphasizes clarification of needs and treatments, and gaining insight. Therapeutic communication uses both verbal and nonverbal cues to form a working relationship with both patients and peers. Basic counseling techniques depend on this skill. Therapeutic responses include:

Response	Goal/Purpose
Using silence	Allows the patient time to think and reflect; conveys acceptance. Allows the patient the opportunity to take the lead in the dialogue.
Using general leads or broad opening	Encourages the patient to talk. Indicates your interest in the patient's welfare. Allows the patient the opportunity to choose a topic for discussion.
Clarification	Encourages recall and details of a particular experience. Promotes sharing of feelings. Seeks explanations; pinpoints specifics.
Reflecting	Paraphrases what the patient has said. Can add explicit information about feelings.

INFECTION PREVENTION AND CONTROL

You will learn the advantages of using sterile techniques in clinical settings and hand-washing in all environments. This will allow you to prevent the transmission of illness and disease, especially nosocomial infections (those acquired and transmitted within the health care facility).

PATIENT AND FAMILY EDUCATION

You will learn how to use both oral and written communication to convey your message to patients. You will also have access to the wealth of support materials available online and in print. While you are gaining this knowledge to help others, you will become more knowledgeable about how to better care for yourself. Make sure you practice what you preach!

Illness and Injury Prevention

You will learn the basic elements of a healthy lifestyle, along with the fundamental principles of wellness education, nutrition, exercise, and stress management so that you can teach others.

Response to Illness and Injury and Medical Interventions

You will learn how to make patients partners in their care, by helping them understand their situation. You will learn what self-care techniques will help the patient at home, and you will be shown how to involve care-givers in the healing process.

PAIN ASSESSMENT AND MANAGEMENT

Pain is sometimes called the "fifth vital sign," meaning that when you assess your patient's status, pain assessment should be a routine component. You will learn to assess pain using the acronym PAINED:

P   Place (location) and time

A   Amount (severity) evaluated using a numerical scale (0 = no pain, 10 = the worst pain imaginable)

I   Intensifiers (what makes the pain worse?)

N   Nullifiers (what makes the pain better?)

E   Effects on the activities of daily living (ADLs), sleep, concentration, relationships, mood, enjoyment of life

D   Descriptors (what does the pain feel like?)

To assess pain in young individuals from age 3 to adulthood, you might use the Wong-Baker FACES model. If you wanted to assess special populations like infants to seven-year-olds, developmentally delayed persons, and nonverbal adults, you would use the information from the FLACC table.

FLACC SCALE (FACE, LEGS, ACTIVITY, CRY, CONSOLABILITY)

	0	1	2
Face	No particular expression or smile	Occasional grimace or frown; withdrawn, disinterested	Frequent to constant frown, clenched jaw, quivering chin
Legs	Normal position or relaxed	Uneasy, restless, tense	Kicking, or legs drawn up
Activity	Lying quietly; normal position; moves easily	Squirming, shifting back/forth, tense	Arched, rigid, or jerking
Cry	No cry (awake or asleep)	Moans or whimpers; occasional complaint	Crying steadily; screams or sobs; frequent complaints
Consolability	Content, relaxed	Reassured by occasional touching, hugging, or talking to; distractible	Difficult to console or comfort

The **FLACC** is a behavior pain assessment scale for use in nonverbal patients unable to provide reports of pain. Instructions:

1. Rate patient in each of the five measurement categories
2. Add together
3. Document total pain score

DEATH AND DYING

You will learn about the grief cycles described by Elizabeth Kubler-Ross in her famous 1969 book, *On Death and Dying*.[1] She found that a person goes through the following stages when they realize they have a terminal illness or if they are mourning someone who has died:

1. *Stability*. This is the initial state before the bad news is known.
2. *Denial*. The individual has no response to the news, behaving as if it never happened.
3. *Anger*. The explosion of emotion, asking "Why me?" Blaming others is common.
4. *Bargaining*. Searching for ways to avoid the inevitable consequences of the event. Bargaining depends on an unfounded hope that the bad news is reversible.
5. *Depression*. The individual understands the bad news and becomes unbearably sad.
6. *Acceptance*. The person is ready and actively involved in moving on to the next stage of life, no matter how short. They will put their lives in order and help other people accept the loss.

NCLEX PREPARATION

To prepare you for the NCLEX exam, your instructor will review all major content from your nursing courses to reinforce and complement the knowledge you gained during school. You will assess the strengths and weaknesses of your nursing knowledge using diagnostic tools, and you will formulate a plan to address weak areas. You will learn about time management, goal-setting, and test-taking skills.

Now that you have reviewed the major nursing concepts, you are ready to move on to some helpful information about getting a job.

---

1   Elizabeth Kubler-Ross. *On Death and Dying* (New York, Macmillan 1969).

PART FIVE

Getting a Job

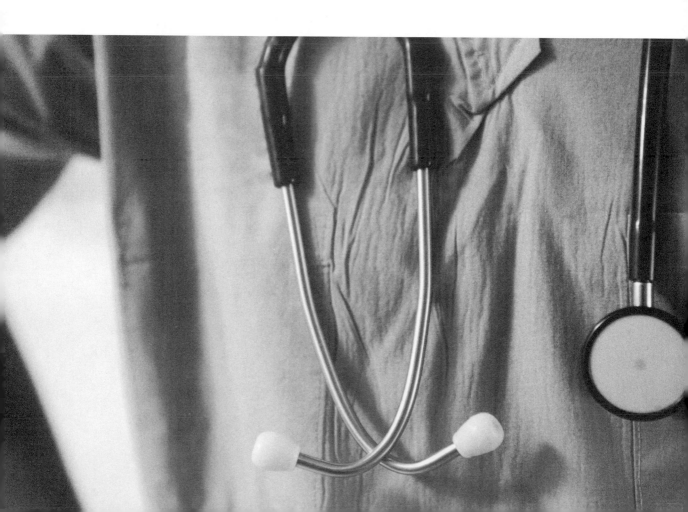

CHAPTER 14

Job-Hunting Resources

Sooner than you might think, you'll be ready to find your first professional nursing position. Getting your first job as a licensed nurse is a process of discovery that typically takes a little bit of luck, a fair share of patience, and a lot of initiative. Along the way, you're likely to meet lots of interesting people, learn many new things, and discover as much about yourself as you will about the nursing profession.

Because so many different types of nurses are needed in so many different kinds of health care settings, you'll find a myriad of job openings and a myriad of job hunting resources. While it may seem overwhelming at first, remember that this is a good thing; you are lucky to have so many different avenues to pursue. In this chapter, you will learn how to be clear about your goals and desired outcomes, and to be systematic in your approach. With these lessons learned, you should be able to find the entry-level position you desire.

KNOW WHAT YOU WANT—AND DON'T WANT

Though it may seem like hunting for a nursing job is so far away you shouldn't even think about it yet, this is a good time to start daydreaming about your ideal future position. Where do you see yourself working? In what setting? Performing what tasks, and with what kind of patients?

You might already have a general idea of the clinical, administrative, or entrepreneurial area in nursing where you'd like to start working. That could eventually lead to you becoming a specialist with considerable expertise in that field. Sometimes you can even identify the rungs on that career ladder early on.

If you don't have a clear picture, consider a position that offers a variety of job duties. As a generalist, you'd have the opportunity to exercise many of your skills. You might find that you enjoy the diversity and remain a generalist throughout your career. Or, you might shift into a specialty after you've discovered which particular field you most enjoy.

Based on your clinical rotations and any other work experience you have while in school, you'll have some idea of what to expect from various health care settings. But it's important to remember that not all hospitals (nor all clinics or nursing homes) are alike. Each hospital—and each department within a hospital—has its own personality, as does each clinic or nursing home. While the setting will determine the type of duties you'll perform and the kinds of patients you'll treat, the personality of a workplace depends in large part on the person in charge. So while you might imagine yourself in a hospital neonatal ward, for example, you might equally enjoy working in a private practice with a pediatrician whose work you respect and company you enjoy.

Job Profile Worksheet

To get a good idea of your ideal job profile, answer the following questions as accurately as you can.

1. What is your ideal job setting? Rank your top three choices.

   ☐ Hospital (if so, which department or unit?)
   ☐ Doctor's office or clinic (if so, what kind of doctor or clinic?)
   ☐ Nursing home
   ☐ Public health agency
   ☐ School (if so, what level?)
   ☐ Home
   ☐ Occupational health/industrial nurse
   ☐ Travel nurse

2. Would you like to work in an urban, suburban, or rural area?

3. How far are you willing to travel to get to work?

4. Would you like to work on a cohesive team, or do you prefer to function as a solo player?

5. What kind of pace do you prefer: hurried, steady, or slow and thoughtful? Why?

6. Do you want to get to know the people you give care to? Do you want them to get to know you? Why or why not?

7. What type of patient do you want to care for? Do you want to work mostly with children, the elderly, the terminally ill? Or do you want to care for patients of every type? Why?

8. Do you want to work with patients who have the same type of illness, or do you prefer to work with patients with a wide range of ailments? If the former, what type of illness? Why?

9. What percentage of your time do you want to spend providing clinical care versus performing administrative duties?

10. Do you want to participate in or conduct research?

11. Do you want to be responsible for helping to build a business?

12. Do you want a permanent position in the same location? A temporary or per diem job? A travel nursing position?

13. What kind of support would you like to have if you wish to continue your education?

14. What are your minimum salary requirements?

DEVELOPING YOUR JOB-HUNTING STRATEGY

Chances are the right job isn't just going to fall into your lap—you're going to have to go out and look for it. A carefully planned and systematic job search is your best bet for finding exactly what you're looking for.

General Strategies for Success

First, keep in mind these general strategies for job-hunting success:

- Keep it manageable. Start small and branch out as you search.
- Keep a job hunting to-do list with specific goals to achieve each week.
- Make several contacts each day. Even if you've just sent a dozen résumés, keep networking and talking to prospective contacts.
- Don't just sit and surf the Internet all day. Make sure you take specific actions that will lead to your landing a job.
- Remember the importance of documentation. Have a clear system for organizing your job hunt: a folder for job leads, a folder for résumés and cover letters, and a folder for follow-up. Keep track of where you have been and who has been helpful.
- Follow every potential lead—or at least keep it in a file. Follow-up is everything.
- Think of every contact as a potential job offer. You never know—a friend of a friend's cousin's neighbor just might lead you to your dream position.
- Be flexible. You might benefit from analyzing opportunities "outside the box."
- Stay positive. Focus on the things you're learning and the great people you're meeting while you wait for the right opportunity.

The Three Ps

To maximize your resources and time, create an individualized plan that focuses on the three Ps: first on *People*, then *Places*, and lastly *Pointers*. If you approach your job search using all three Ps, you'll be amazed at how one prospect leads to another. Here is more about how each P can help you.

People: The Power of Networking

While you may be tempted to start your job search with the Sunday classifieds or an Internet search engine, the best job-hunting strategy is still the old-fashioned art of networking. Networking opens you up to countless opportunities to exchange ideas, learn information, and, of course, find the kind of job you're looking for.

By networking, you can learn about:

- Currently available or soon-to-be-available positions
- Good (or bad) places to work with specific reasons why they're good (or bad)
- What kind of working conditions to expect—the realities of routines and crises
- Actual duties of a job, especially as compared to official job descriptions
- Upsides of a particular job
- Downsides of a specific job

So don't keep your job search a secret. Be ready to engage other people in your search. If necessary, practice telling your friends you are looking for a nursing job—that will make it easier to speak to strangers and acquaintances about your job search. Be receptive to all input; everyone is a potential job contact.

Whom to Talk to

People are your most effective resource, and the nursing community can be your best bet. Let all of the following know that you are looking for a nursing position and what kind of position you're looking for. Don't be shy about it; after all, you're not asking them for a job. You're simply letting them know that you are available.

Network with the following people in your nursing community:

- Working or retired nurses in your neighborhood
- The nurse supporting your personal physician
- Nurse recruiters
- Family members of nurses
- Your nursing instructors

- Your fellow students
- Members of your professional nursing organizations
- Fellow conference or workshop attendees
- Nursing school counselors

Outside the nursing community, tell everyone you know that you are looking for a job: relatives, neighbors, and friends; other parents at sporting events, PTA meetings, and other school or club activities; people at your place of worship or your social or volunteer organizations; your heath care providers; job hunting networks and support organizations; and your nursing school support group members.

What to Say: Crafting an Effective Elevator Speech

As you begin talking to people and making new contacts, it's important to be able to talk about your employment goals and qualifications effectively. What do you say to someone when you're networking? How do you introduce yourself and convey your goals? The answer lies in a formula called an *elevator speech*.

An elevator speech is essentially a carefully thought-out sales pitch. The idea is to "sell yourself" in the time it would take to ride a few floors in an elevator with a prospective employer.

Your elevator speech should answer the following questions:

- *Who* are you? Introduce yourself.
- *What* position are you in? State what you do and what you want to do.
- *What* do you have to offer? How can you fulfill the employer's needs?
- *What* sets you apart from the competition? What special skills, training, experience, or vision distinguishes you from others seeking the same position? Be as specific as possible.
- *What* action do you want to take? Get a name and number, schedule an interview, leave a résumé?

Here's how it looks in a fill-in-the-blank format:

Hello, my name is _____. I [will be graduating from/have just graduated from] _____ with a degree in _____. I'm looking for _____. I [describe special skills, specific qualifications, etc.] _____. Do you know of any positions/May I _____ [state action]?

An elevator speech should always come across as warm, enthusiastic, and sincere. The key is good writing and *practice*. The more you practice, the more natural and conversational your speech will feel. Be sure to maintain eye contact whenever giving your speech face to face. Watch for signs of interest or boredom and adjust your speech accordingly.

Of course, if you're giving your elevator speech to a prospective employer, be sure to research the organization first. Know the needs of that organization and make sure your elevator speech conveys how you can successfully meet those needs.

> KISS your elevator speech: Keep It Simple and Sincere. Eliminate any unnecessary jargon. Be concise and precise.

Places: Where to Look

Once you've started networking, it's time to get up and go—to places where job resources are readily available. These places include:

- Hospitals, clinics, and other medical/health care facilities. (Don't forget the magnet hospital designation—see Chapter 5.) Some places post current openings on bulletin boards that are accessible to the public.
- Medically related companies
- General job fairs
- Health care job fairs
- Professional organization meetings
- Nursing/medical conferences and conventions
- Continuing education events
- Public health events
- Human resource offices
- Area chambers of commerce

Be sure to dress professionally and bring copies of your résumé when you visit these locations. You never know who you might meet, and a drop-in just to see if there's an opening on a job board could turn into an interview.

Pointers: Extending Your Search

Pointers are resources that point you in other directions to broaden the scope of your job search. They may lack the flavor that comes with person-to-person contact, but they extend your range and alert you to a great variety and number of job opportunities that you may otherwise not have discovered.

The best pointer by far is the Internet. Other pointers include:

- Professional journals and specialty publications (free ones supported by advertising often have great listings)
- Local-focus magazines and other publications, which feature local openings
- Newspapers (look at advertisements, health-related articles, and classifieds)
- Telephone directories (find area hospitals, clinics, doctor offices, etc.)
- Local television news and health-related programs
- Nursing organizations

Internet Job-Hunting Resources

There's no doubt that the Internet is an amazing resource, especially for job seekers. Within minutes, you can find dozens of job opportunities as close as your hometown and as far as the other side of the globe.

Most nursing employment Web sites offer many of the same services, including résumé posting, job searches, and information on the different types of nursing positions available. Below are some of the best Web sites for a nursing job search. These sites are easy to use and offer a wide variety of services that can make hunting for a nursing position easier and more effective. They all include résumé posting and job search features. Below are their Web site names, URLs and a description of their distinguishing features or services.

- nursing jobs.org (*www.nursingjobs.org*). This extensive and comprehensive job search site offers the ability to set job alerts that inform you via e-mail when a job fitting your specifications is available. Founded by a nurse with over twenty years of professional experience.
- Absolutely Health Care!(*www.absolutelyhealthcare.com*). This site has a salary wizard feature that allows you as an RN or an LPN/LVN/CNA to find average job salaries based on job type and location. Includes a video about the site on its home page.
- Nurse Recruiter.com (*www.nurse-recruiter.com*). This site has received over 100 awards for quality of information, ease of use, creativity, and design. Their motto is "For nurses, by nurses."

- nurseoptions.com (*www.nurseoptions.com*). This site provides links to sites that help new nurses create effective résumés and cover letters.
- Nurses123 (*www.nurses123.com*). This site helps you research the health care facilities where you might be interested in applying. Has a toll-free phone number for further contact.
- Nursetown.com (*www.nursetown.com*). This site offers a question-and-answer forum that allows visitors to post questions and get feedback from nurses about a variety of nursing topics. Has a wide-ranging list of link to professional articles.
- AWHONN Nursing Career Center (*www.awhonn.org/nc/career.htmc*). This site, part of the Association of Women's Health, Obstetrician, and Neonatal Nurses organization, offers practical career advice, including the top ten things to do when negotiating a salary.

Nursing Organizations

There are many local and national nursing organizations that can help new nurses with job hunting and placement. A simple Internet search for "nursing organizations" will link you to hundreds of them. You'll probably want to join several organizations first as a student and later as a licensed nurse. For now, though, you don't have to be a member to take advantage of the job preparation and search resources many of these organizations offer.

Here's a brief look at what a few of the generalized nursing organizations have to offer in addition to help with job hunting and placement:

- The Academy of Medical-Surgical Nursing (AMSN) (*www.medsurgnurse.org*, 866-877-AMSN). The AMSN Web site offers a new online career center, as well as links to discussion boards, volunteer organizations, study resources, and shopping for nursing needs.
- The American Nurses' Association (ANA) (*www.nursingworld.org*, 800-274-4ANA). The ANA is a nurse advocacy organization that consistently fights for the rights of nurses and helps to maintain a high level of care from the nurses that it sponsors. This is also the organization that provides post-graduate certification through the American Nurses' Credentialing Center (ANCC), America's leading credentialing organization. The online Nursing Career Center is a great place to start a search.

- The National Student Nurses' Association (NSNA) (*www.nsna.org*, 718-210-0705). This organization is wonderful for new nurses because it offers career counseling, educational resources, and a live chat room where nurses and students can interact.
- The National League for Nursing (NLN) (*www.nln.org*, 1-800-669-1656). This organization is dedicated to the professional development of all its members. To that end, the NLN hosts a long list of workshops, conferences, and seminars that are available throughout the United States. For those that are unable to travel, some workshops can be attended online.

Now that you've reviewed job-hunting strategies and resources, it's time to get that résumé together and prepare for your interview.

CHAPTER 15

Making Your Résumé, Cover Letter, and Application Work for You

Getting through nursing school and obtaining your license both stand to prove that you are capable of dedicated and accurate work. However, there's one more step you need to take to further prove this. You must create and execute a flawless résumé, cover letter, and interview. In this chapter you will learn how to write a cover letter and résumé tailored exactly to the job you want, as well as how to avoid common mistakes when writing cover letters and résumés, or when filling out applications.

MOVING FROM READING ABOUT A JOB TO INTERVIEWING FOR IT

The purpose of writing an effective résumé and cover letter is to communicate effectively with a potential employer about your relevant skills and strengths. The potential employer could be a nurse recruiter or even the person who will become your supervisor. The potential employer could start with a phone screening or schedule you for an in-person interview.

The bottom line is that from the start you must give them a compelling reason to choose you as the first contact above all other applicants. To achieve this, you must make a good impression during what will most likely be a cursory inspection of a very limited amount of information about you. If you are successful in making a strong, positive first impression, potential interviewers will be telling themselves "I must interview that nurse who used to be an accountant," or whatever your previous career was.

Because nursing is a second career for you, have confidence in the fact that this sets you apart from greener applicants. You have had some measure of vocational success and you are ready to build on that foundation. Better yet, you made it though nursing school as a more mature and well-rounded person.

If you still have access to your original résumés from your last career hiring quest, review them with an eye toward identifying some cross-over experience. If necessary, you can reread Chapter 6 to get up to speed on your transferable skills. Don't take the easy way out and just update your old résumés; remember, you are marketing a new and improved version of your former self—a nurse.

Customize Your Résumé and Cover Letter

You will not be successful if you use a boilerplate approach, writing just one résumé and using it to apply for all jobs. This approach may seem efficient, but remember that you want to make a strong impression the very first time your résumé is read by a potential employer. So, each time you apply for a job, you need to create *customized* documents that make a solid connection in the mind of the potential employer between your particular knowledge, skills, and abilities and those needed for this *specific* nursing job.

THE BUILDING BLOCKS OF YOUR RÉSUMÉ

Although potential employers usually read your cover letter before your résumé, a useful approach is to write the résumé first. Think of writing your résumé as building a house; you must have the foundation, walls, and roof in place before you move in. Then you can add the finishing touch, your cover letter, which highlights the most important features of your house. The cover letter accents your résumé, making it attractive so that a potential employer will want to read about the details of your employment history and relevant skills.

Your Contact Information

Although you want to impress potential employers enough to earn an interview, you must first realize that prospective employers need to be able to easily contact you to schedule that interview, so include:

- Your full name (often the middle initial is added to give a more professional image)
- Full street address
- Home telephone number (clearly label it as your home phone)
- Cell telephone number (optional, but usually included)
- E-mail address (if you are currently working, consider setting up a personal e-mail account.)
- Web address, if you have a Web site that markets the entire range of your nursing skills. If not, consider adding this to your portfolio.

Objective

You can place an objective at the top of your résumé. Just make sure that the specific job that you are applying for fits within that description. Your objective should state where you hope to go in your career and the ways in which you want to grow. That statement can take the following form: "Obtain a home health care nursing position with an opportunity to teach self-care concepts."

Success Is Spelled R-E-S-U-M-E

Here are seven elements to include in your résumé.

R: Results of Your Previous Employment

Highlight all your past accomplishments, either nursing-related (being a nursing assistant), or entirely outside the health care field. Your work might have made a significant difference in the outcome of a program or a project. Don't be modest. You need to take credit for your efforts. Don't forget to include shared accomplishments when you contributed to a team effort.

If you can use numbers to explain the scope of the project or the impressive size of the outcome, your potential employer is more likely to be impressed. If you can state it in terms of dollars saved, that's even better. If you can describe how your achievements affected people's lives in positive ways, that's the best.

E: Education and Expertise

List all degrees and diplomas for programs, curriculums, and certifications you completed after high school, and the name of each educational institution. Don't forget to include *all* forms of education, including any apprenticeships or internships, special training and clinical experiences, seminars, or special school projects. You want prospective employers to know your level of nursing education, so be specific about your licensure (e.g. LPN/LVN or RN) and your further education, such as the masters or doctorate level.

S: Skills

List all technical equipment skills gained before, during, and after your nursing school experience. Perhaps you had an opportunity to participate in an advanced clinical curriculum and were trained to operate complex equipment, such as dialysis machines. Or, if in your previous career you had knowledge of how to operate, or better yet fix, particular kinds of equipment, make sure to point this out.

Be specific about your computer skills. Don't stretch the truth about your familiarity, but list both general software (MS Office, Outlook, Adobe Dreamweaver) and specialized applications, such as medical practice management software.

For your résumé, you should also pick three skills or character traits that best represent you as a nurse and write a statement about each. Make sure to highlight skills or traits that your potential employer is looking for. Here is an example:

Experienced as both a team leader and a team player

Effective communicator with proven skills in patient education

Strong ability to multitask and to perform under pressure

U: Unpaid Experiences

These are experiences you had as a volunteer. They can be nursing-related, such as service work you did over-and-above your nursing school education—tutoring children in the pediatric unit on your own time is an example. Or they could be when you helped out as a community health fair worker, Red Cross disaster-recovery nurse, or free clinic volunteer nurse. Depending on the job, you might talk about volunteering in a classroom or library or performing some other civic service.

M: Media

Include all your creative endeavors: Web sites you designed or maintained for yourself or your group or organization, newsletters, press releases for charity events, poster and oral presentations at conferences and workshops, or professional publications about nursing or science.

E: Extras

List all your unique qualifications that do not fit into other categories. One example could be your ability to speak, write, and read in a language other than English. Another could be awards that have recognized your outstanding contributions. You can also list memberships in professional organizations, including state and national groups—general (e.g., California Nurses Association, American Nurses Association), specialty-focused (e.g., Emergency Nurses Association, the Oncology Nursing Society, the Intravenous Nurses Society, and the American Psychiatric Nurses Association), or academic and nursing honor societies (e.g., Phi Kappa Phi, Sigma Theta Tau). If you have volunteered as an officer or chairperson, or if you've headed a professional event such as a conference, be sure to include that as well.

BE SPECIFIC ABOUT YOUR QUALITIES AND ACHIEVEMENTS

As you write your qualifications, remember that, when your résumé and cover letter are read, there are standard questions the interviewer is going to ask. This person will want to know what your past history shows about your current individual character traits. To be sure you cover each of these in your résumé. You can check off the items beneath each question below as you prepare.

Are you adaptable and flexible?

☐ In a previous job setting, did you successfully move from one role to another within the same organization?

Are you reliable?

☐ Does your work history show that others could count on your strong performance and quality work?

☐ Were the evaluations of your efforts positive?

Are you people-oriented?

☐ Did you successfully work with customers, clients, teams? If applicable, include the diversity of people who you worked with or for.

Are you sensitive, perceptive, and compassionate?

☐ Did you make a difference in how other people were able to adapt to life changes?

Are you logical and analytical?

☐ Did you use data or facts to create a clear course of action? Your résumé should include numbers when describing quantifiable outcomes of your previous work.

Are you deadline-oriented?

☐ Did you successfully meet tight or naturally recurring time limits for projects or programs?

Are you inquisitive?

☐ By going back to nursing school, you show a commitment to lifelong learning. If you've taken continuing education classes and/or attended conferences and workshops, make sure to mention these also.

Are you thoughtful and organized?

☐ The information on your résumé about each previous job should give a clear picture of its "who, what, when, and where" characteristics.

Are you goal-oriented?

☐ Your job history should show a jagged course of short working episodes at a succession of employers.

Are you accurate and detail-oriented?

☐ Any typo will be a disaster here, so have another person proofread your documents before submitting them.

Are you team-oriented?

☐ In your prior jobs, could you function as both a team leader and a team player rather than always acting as a solo performer?

Are you an effective communicator?

☐ Did prior jobs include written and oral presentations? You can also list publications or relevant educational material that you developed, including student assignments.

Are you a person who can take initiative?

☐ Do you have leadership skills?

☐ Are the words *initiated, started, founded,* or *led* in your listing of your previous jobs? If not, can you add them?

AVOID COMMON RÉSUMÉ MISTAKES

Do not include the following *personal* information:

- Your age or date of birth
- Your marital status
- Names of your spouse, partner, or children
- Your ethnic group
- Your religious affiliation
- Your height or weight
- Your health status or disabilities
- Your hobbies, unless they pertain to the specific job you are interested in

Do not include the following *employment* information:

- Salaries of previous jobs
- Supervisors' names
- Reasons for leaving previous positions
- Professional references

Do not use these *style formats*:

- Putting the title "Résumé" at the top of your résumé.
- Using colored or patterned paper. White or off-white, 20-pound bond paper is standard.
- Adding "References available upon request" in the résumé or cover letter. The employer knows that you will have to supply them when they ask for them.
- Making your résumé longer than two pages. You should have a solid reason for making it that long. You do not want to smother a potential employer with details. If you have a long job history because you have "been there, done that," make sure to edit your résumé so it only includes more current experience.

COVER LETTER BASICS

Your cover letter should present a summary of what you want and who you are. Open with a brief statement that includes the exact title of the job for which you are applying, and then state who you are (your accomplishments, expertise, and experience).

Limit your cover letter to less than one page. Remember its function is to make the potential interviewer want to know more.

Here is a sample cover letter template:

Dear (title, name):

I am applying for your _____ position posted on the _____ Web site.

My skills and experience give me the capabilities needed to _____ _____.

I am interested in this position because _____.

I have attached my résumé for your review.

Thank you for considering me for the _____ position. I look forward to hearing from you.

Sincerely,

Name

(Signature)

REVIEWING YOUR DOCUMENTS

When you have completed your résumé and cover letter, read through them at least once slowly and out loud. You are looking for portions that need more detail and explanation, mistakes and typos, omitted information, and verbose passages.

When you're finished, put them out of sight for a while—at least overnight. This is one situation where you truly need to sleep on it. This period of rest gives you a chance to review the documents objectively, almost as if someone else wrote them. After your break, read your résumé and cover letter once more as though you were a busy nursing recruiter or hiring manager who has to quickly decide whether to include your materials in a "possibilities" pile. In your alternate persona, ask yourself, "Are they brief, clear, and to the point?" and "Would I hire this person?"

If you have family members, friends, or colleagues who are willing to review your first drafts, their feedback will be a great benefit. Another set of eyes can discover grammar, syntax, typographical, and spelling errors. Their objectivity can also identify your weak or incomplete areas. They might also suggest important points you overlooked, such as an experience or talent that you take for granted but that should be included. To select the best person to review your résumé, choose someone who knows your talents and experience and cares enough to be honest with you. Ask your reviewer to respond to the question, "Would you want to hire this person?" as though he or she were the interviewer.

Have your résumé easily available to share at all times. Have it handy during your regular daily activities, at professional meetings, even social activities—any place you might encounter people who can help you get the job you want. This might mean having copies in your car or in your bag. You never know when you might encounter an employment possibility, or someone who can connect you to a great job.

APPLICATION SAVVY

Job applications look so simple to the untrained eye. The formal job application has many sections to fill out, whether online or on paper. If you fill it out on your computer or with a typewriter, you won't give a potential employer reason to review your handwriting and neatness. But most often, it is on paper, which can show them proof of how careful you are about documentation. So treat the application as you would a showcase of your style. If you can type it, questions of legibility will not come up. If you cannot type it (usually due to the form's format), then print the information if your handwriting is less-than-Palmer-perfect.

Some employers send or give you their application before they even schedule an interview, and you have lots of time to fill it out and contemplate your information. In other cases, you might be asked to fill out an application when you arrive for an interview, or immediately afterward. If they don't already have an application from you, always be prepared to fill it out onsite and leave it with them.

Ten Tips for a Tip-Top Application

1. In most cases, you can use a copy of your résumé as a guide to fill out the application. However, you should also have notes that include the following information:
   - Your supervisor's name and contact information for each position.
   - Exact start and stop dates for formerly held positions. These may or may not also appear on your résumé.
   - Your beginning and ending salary for each position. Be sure to have it calculated in a number of ways: per hour, per week, per month, per year.
   - The addresses and phone numbers of organizations at which you formerly worked.
   - Other jobs not listed on your résumé. You may be asked to disclose information for all previous employers on the application.

2. Always use a good, well-functioning, black or blue pen. This is no time for pencils or pens with red or green ink.
3. Take your time filling out the application form; remember, this is an opportunity for you to make a good impression as a professional.
4. Double check what each item asks for before completing it.

5. Write clearly and neatly. Remember, a potential employer is going to evaluate your writing for quality and effectiveness.

6. Be prepared with names and contact information for at least three *recent* professional references. Beforehand, ask your references how they want to be contacted. Some people object to a sudden, unexpected call from your potential employer.

7. Don't include any information not asked for. Unless the form specifically directs you to attach further information, do not attach other documents to it.

8. Ask questions if you don't understand an item. If you are completing the form at home, you can usually call the Human Resources department. If you are at the interview site, ask the support staff or the interviewer. It is better to ask than give inappropriate information. You always want to give proof that you are an effective communicator.

9. As you did with your résumé and cover letter, always look over your completed application at least twice to check for errors and omissions. One suggestion is to start with the last item and then go upward to the beginning for at least one review.

10. If mailing your completed application, type and include a short, signed letter. Be sure to identify the position for which you are applying both by name and ID number. If you have a direct contact, address the envelope to that person.

Now, it's time to get ready for your job interview.

CHAPTER 16

Succeeding in Your Job Interview

Don't believe people who tell you they know how you can "sail though an interview with flying colors." That approach assumes the unreasonable expectation that the job seeker takes complete control of the interview. This, however, rarely describes the reality of the situation. Instead, your role in the job interview is only half of it. Both you and the interviewer will take responsibility to steer the dialogue so that their questions and yours are answered. They want to know "Should we hire this person?" and you want to be assured that you want to work for them:

- At this workplace
- With this group (colleagues and supervisor)
- For this salary (and perks)
- With these growth opportunities

In this chapter, you will learn how to prepare for your interview, from planning your transportation, selecting your outfit, and preparing your responses to some commonly asked interview questions. You will also learn the best tips for following up with potential employers after your interview is over.

CONGRATULATIONS, YOU GOT THE INTERVIEW!

Congratulations, a potential employer wants to interview you. Now you need to prepare for a positive and worthwhile interview experience. Every interview gets you closer to your new career as a nurse, and thorough planning and preparation are critical to your success in landing a job.

Just as each nursing job is different, so is each interview. Therefore, you need to customize how you prepare and participate in each interview you go on. Making sure to perform at your best is the key factor in completing a successful, worthwhile interview.

As you embark on nursing interviews, expect to be rewarded by the experience in one way or another. This could include:

- Getting the job
- Learning more about what you need or don't need in your work life
- Learning more about what you want or don't want in your work life, and how your "wish list" is different than your "needs list"

Even if you don't get the job, you may have made a useful contact, or you might have a "whew, I'm glad I don't work there" sense of relief.

YOUR INTERVIEW STRATEGY

You found an interesting and appealing nursing job you might want, and now you're scheduled for an interview, which means you've climbed one step closer to your new career as a nurse. Now, prepare to move even closer with a successful interview.

Before developing your interview strategy, take a moment to acknowledge your accomplishment: You created a résumé and cover letter that caught the attention and interest of the employer. And, if you've already completed an application, you've also impressed upon the screening person that you are qualified for the job.

Now it's time to build your interview strategy. Here are a few tips for making the most of your interview experience and putting your best foot forward:

- Present yourself as a self-assured, capable person during the interview.
- Make sure to bring copies of your résumé and cover letter. Having a printed list of references can also be handy.

- Bring additional "props," such as patient education materials you developed or the professional journal articles you authored. Even if they're not discussed during the interview, just having them can boost your confidence.
- Treat *everyone* you speak to—on the telephone, via e-mail, or in person—with courtesy and respect; you never know who will be asked for their opinion about the impression you made.
- Remember that you are a mature, responsible adult who has valuable experience, expertise, and education to offer a nursing employer. If the interview session does not result in a job offer, perhaps your best fit is elsewhere.

With these strategies and objectives in mind, you are in good shape to present your best self to a potential employer, learn more about the employer and the job, and communicate the qualifications, abilities, and wealth of experience you have to offer.

WHAT A JOB INTERVIEW IS

Although many people think of a job interview as a test for which they must perform, this is only one part of the interview experience, and focusing exclusively on this aspect doesn't do justice to the overall experience of interviewing for a new job. An interview is as much an opportunity for you to investigate a new environment as it is an opportunity for a company to learn more about you. Here are some useful ways to think of a job interview that focus on how the experience helps you.

As an Energizing Growth Experience

Bring a positive mind-set to job interviews. Before, during, and after the event, keep your thoughts and actions positive. Also remember that an interview is an opportunity to further discover yourself as a person and a professional. The anxiety you might experience can actually stimulate insightful thinking. If you are a note-taker, you might want to record your thoughts before and after the interview. If you don't tend to take notes, ask a family member or a close friend to serve as a pre- and post-interview sounding board.

As a Mutual Exchange of Information between You and a Potential Employer

Keep in mind that this two-way sharing and interactive experience enables you and the employer to discover whether you want to begin a new working relationship. Not only do you have the opportunity to present yourself to the employer as an attractive job candidate, the employer wants to show you that this environment is a place you want to work.

As an Opportunity to Promote Yourself

The interview is your chance to introduce and market yourself to a new and interested audience. You have prepared to express your strengths and weaknesses, which are addressed in some of the most commonly asked interview questions. During the interview, you will see how your answers are received. Does the interviewer seem interested? Does he or she ask you further questions?

As an Experimental Learning Experience

Every interview enables you to discover what works and what doesn't in these essentially unpredictable situations. Even if you aren't selected for the job or it isn't right for you at this time, you have learned something about yourself and the employer. As with any experiment, when you change the variables, you can expect a different outcome.

WHAT A JOB INTERVIEW ISN'T

It's normal to feel nervous before an interview; it's an unknown situation and you often can't predict exactly how it will play out. However, if you've taken the necessary steps to prepare, you are more than likely to have a worthwhile and, perhaps, enjoyable experience. Here are some things to remember when you begin to feel nervous about your interview.

It Isn't Something to Dread

You shouldn't approach it with an "I have to get this done and over with so I can go on with my life" attitude.

Don't look at it as the worst part of getting a new job. Rather, consider it a unique event in a very interesting process—one with great potential for you as a new nurse. If you are going to thrive in your new position, you will have to make sure you find the right place to be.

It Isn't an Inquisition or Interrogation

Potential employers rarely ask you to defend yourself, so resist being defensive. If you sense that the interviewer is trying to put you on the defensive, respond with inquisitiveness instead of defensiveness. You can ask specific, clarifying questions instead of reacting. You also have at least one career behind you, and you have the ability to stay detached and keep a level head in anxiety-producing situations.

Come prepared with some questions to ask the interviewer. Wait to ask them until after the interviewer has finished the formal part of the interview. That will allow you to judge whether or not your questions are still relevant. Balance your effort to look interested with the need to appear flexible. Some unasked questions can be answered later by surfing through the employer's Web site or reading brochures that you picked up at the interview site.

It Isn't a Lifetime or Legal Commitment

You don't have to accept the job during the interview, even in the rare instance that an interviewer asks you to do so. Your only commitment is to engage in a mutually beneficial dialogue and discovery process.

If asked to make a binding decision during the interview, respond with a statement like "I'll consider everything we've discussed and get back to you."

It Isn't an Opportunity to Vent Your Feelings

Don't bring *anything* negative into the interview process—not your current worries, nor your frustrations. Don't criticize yourself, the local or national economy, the employer's competition, or your previous employers or colleagues.

In addition to your choice of topics for discussion, your facial expression and posture can broadcast an image that either supports or detracts from your employability. One useful technique is to go to a restroom right before the interview and look in the mirror. Stand up straight—smile at the reflection of an excited person. Research has shown that the very act of smiling can release natural substances in your body to make you *feel* happier and more relaxed.

WHAT TO DO BEFORE THE INTERVIEW

Before going to a job interview, there are a few steps you should take to make sure you're as prepared as possible. Not only will this help you make the best first impression that you can, but it will also help you feel calm, collected, and confident during the interview process.

Plan Your Route to the Interview

Plan how you are going to get to and park at the interview location. Get a detailed map of the area, in case traffic is unexpectedly gridlocked or diverted, and take a dry-run trip. Also take into account more chronic situations that can cause transportation crises: rush hour or road and building construction. If you are arriving by public transportation, leave yourself extra time in case of any unexpected travel delays.

Polish Yourself

- Polish your appearance and pay attention to your well being by eating and sleeping well before the interview. Schedule time for exercise and recreational activities.
- On the day of the interview, take time for yourself; don't plan any stressful activities, like going to the dentist, immediately prior to the interview.
- Make sure your hair contributes to your professional image. Get a haircut the week before, if you need one.

You should decide what to wear the night before. Dress business professional, even if you know the staff wears business casual clothing. Have an interview outfit and a back-up ready to go in your closet. Keep your clothes and shoes simple and flattering—nothing flashy or outlandish. Don't forget your reading glasses if you use them.

Review Your Résumé

Before you arrive for your interview, take some time to review the talking points you want to share with the interviewer. Here are a few pointers to help you feel fully prepared and confident when you arrive:

- You should be able to recite the highlights of your résumé without looking at it.
- If you have a personal Web site, update it if necessary.
- Consider what you have accomplished in previous jobs or school settings that makes you qualified for this nursing job. It doesn't have to be nursing experience, but an experience that nurses can appreciate and relate to.
- Review your education—your degrees, certifications, professional organization memberships—and how it prepared you for *this specific* job.

Arrive Early

Be sure to arrive at least 10 to 15 minutes early. This will give you time to settle yourself and prepare for a successful experience. If meditation or deep breathing helps you relax, this is the time to use those techniques. If you need to distract yourself in the minutes before the interview, bring one small item to read, something that you can hold and tuck away easily.

Bring a notepad and pen to take brief notes during the interview, such as a reminder to later ask a specific question. Keep your notes as succinct as possible so you can make the best use of them later.

COMMON INTERVIEW QUESTIONS YOU MIGHT BE ASKED

Interviewers often ask some fairly standard questions. Here are a few examples of questions you should be prepared to answer at each interview you go on:

1. *Can you tell me about yourself? What is your philosophy of nursing? Why did you become a nurse? What didn't you like about your previous career? Why do you want this job? What do you expect to contribute?*
2. *What are your strengths?* Plan to use action verbs to describe them, such as *led, organized, planned*. Review the characteristics that recruiters/interviewers are looking for, identify several that apply to you, and plan to include them in your response.
3. *What are your weaknesses?* Be ready to turn them around to show how, once you have identified them, you have worked to improve yourself or change the pattern. With proper planning, you won't sabotage yourself. You can say "I tend to get emotionally involved," if you follow-up with "I am learning how to become more objective. I find it helps me give better patient care."

4. *How did your previous nonnursing work experience prepare you for this nursing job?* Remember those transferable skills and be ready to describe them.

5. *Have you faced working with a difficult person? Have you had to work through an ethically challenging nursing situation?* The anecdote you share should be brief so the interviewer does not get lost in details but recognizes that you have coping skills and solid values.

6. *What do you want to be doing in your nursing career five years from now?* The starting point of your answer should be the job you're interviewing for. Your answer should have three characteristics: enthusiasm, a vision, and a reason for satisfaction. An example: "I really love working with _____ patients, I can see myself in the future even better helping them by _____. That is because I find a sense of accomplishment when I _____."

7. Prepare to have an firm answer such as "I don't wish to comment" when asked illegal questions about your age, family status, religion, national origin, financial status, children, health status, criminal record, and previous employers' nondisclosable information. You should not feel intimidated into responding to those questions.

Common Interview Questions You Should Ask

You should also prepare your own list of key questions to ask the interviewer. The basic six are:

1. What is the organization of the nursing staff?
2. What are the responsibilities and duties of the job?
3. What is the time commitment—does it involve off-shift work or rotating work shifts?
4. What are the informal training and formal educational opportunities?
5. How does this department fit into the overall organization?

The six basic questions to ask a potential co-worker interviewer are:

1. How long have you worked here?
2. What is your day like?
3. Who do you report to?
4. What do you like best about your job?
5. What challenges you the most?
6. What technology do you use?

MAKING A GREAT IMPRESSION DURING YOUR INTERVIEW

During the interview, there are several things you can do to maintain focus and keep up your confidence. Below are some suggestions for how to conduct yourself during the interview that help you make the best impression you can:

- Turn all your electronic devices off. Better yet, don't bring them unless they contain information the interviewer might ask for (e.g., a PDA).
- Roll with the punches. As an example of "grace under pressure," when one candidate arrived for an interview, she tripped over a hidden phone cord in the waiting room. Getting up, she quickly chuckled and said "I wasn't expecting that." Everyone relaxed after that.
- Smile and focus on being calm. Introduce yourself with your full name. Shake hands with the interviewer, look the interviewer in the eye, and create the impression that you are glad to meet him or her. Say, "I'm glad to meet you" and mean it.
- Keep eye contact so your interviewer knows you are staying focused.
- Sit straight and maintain a posture that shows you are attentive and interested
- Be honest—remember, you don't have to exaggerate to get the job. Your qualifications give you enough credibility.
- Feel free to take a moment to pause and think before you answer questions or make comments. You can say, "That's a good question…" to give you time.
- Actively listen and give brief acknowledgements; you don't have to comment about everything you hear.
- Don't be reluctant to say the word I ("I led a group" or "I explored the possibilities" or "I was responsible for…."
- Postpone asking what's-in-it-for-me questions about salary, benefits, or promotions until the end of the interview. After that, restate the follow-up actions you and the interviewer have agreed to. Ask "What's the next step?" or "When can I expect a decision?" Thank the interviewer and say that you enjoyed talking with him or her. If the interview experience tells you that you want the job, tell the interviewer, "I look forward to hearing from you."

Qualities and factors nursing recruiters/interviewers are looking for:

- Enthusiasm
- Interest
- Motivation
- Responsiveness
- Preparedness
- Honesty
- Teamwork attitude
- Experience that transfers to this nursing job
- Professional commitment
- Communication skills (written and verbal)
- Critical-thinking skills
- Leadership qualities
- Maturity
- Evidence of previous success
- Confidence
- A sense of commitment to previous employers

WHEN THE INTERVIEW IS OVER

Make sure you leave with everything you brought to the interview, unless you agreed to loan samples of your work or other appropriate items. Be clear about how you are going to get these items back if they are originals.

Smile and thank the people who directed or assisted you during the interview process. Leave promptly and with courtesy toward everyone you meet on your way out.

Do a post-interview rehash with a family member or close friend:

- Consider your successes during the interview.
- Accept the things that didn't go well.
- Relax and enjoy your accomplishment.

FOLLOWING UP AFTER YOUR INTERVIEW

After the interview, you can continue to build yourself up in the eyes of your potential employer and solidify the strong first impression you made by taking the following steps:

- If you think it's appropriate, send a thank you e-mail message or letter to the interviewer. Be specific about what continues to interest you about that position.
- If you want the job, prepare to answer a request for another interview. If you feel that the job isn't right for you after the interview, prepare to respond by saying that this job wouldn't be a good fit for you right now.
- Regardless of whether or not you want the job, and especially if you are undecided, write a list of questions about the job and the employer that still intrigue you. You might not be in a position to get the answers this time, but you have an idea of what facts would constitute a more complete employment picture. You are ready for a follow-up or for a new interview.
- Be responsive to further requests from the employer or interviewer. Promptly submit or send any requested items, such as a completed application or professional references.
- Contact your references and let them know the potential employer might contact them. Clarify what that means to you and review your qualifications so they will be easily able to recall them when contacted.
- Don't count on this job and wait to be hired; keep networking and continue to look for your best-fit second-career nursing job.

Congratulations! You have now learned a great deal about everything from getting into nursing school, all the way to acing your job interviews. Remember, changing your career is a process, so you should pace yourself and keep focused on your ultimate goal—a new career in nursing. At each step in the process, you should also go back and review the relevant chapters in this book. If you would like to learn even more, turn to the appendixes that follow. There you will find a comprehensive list of nursing associations by state and a broad selection of nursing journals to which you may want to subscribe. Finally, in Appendix C, you will find stories from people just like you—real stories of people who started a brand-new career in nursing. Good luck!

Nursing Associations by State and Canadian Nurses Associations

Alabama

Alabama State Nurses Association
  (*alabamanurses.org*)
Board of Nursing
RSA Plaza, Suite 250
770 Washington Avenue
Montgomery, AL 36104
Mailing address: PO Box 303900
Montgomery AL 36130-3900
Phone: 334-242-4060 or 800-656-5318
Fax: 334-242-4360
abn@abn.state.al.us
abn.state.al.us

Alaska

Alaska Nurses Association (*aknurse.org*)
Alaska Nurse Practitioner Association
  (*alaskanp.org*)
Board of Nursing
550 West 7th Avenue, Suite 1500
Anchorage, AK 99501
Phone: 907-269-8196
Fax: 907-269-8196
license@commerce.state.ak.us
dced.state.ak.us/occ/pnur.htm

American Samoa

American Samoa Health Service Regulatory
  Board
LBJ Tropical Medical Center
Pago Pago, AS 96799
Phone: 684-633-1222
Fax: 684-633-1869

Arizona

Arizona Nurses Association (*aznurse.org*)

Board of Nursing

4747 North 7th Street, Suite 200

Phoenix, AZ 85014-3653

Phone: 602-889-5150

Fax: 602-889-5155

azboardofnursing.org, on the home page, Imposter Alert of individuals who claimed licensure

Arkansas

Arkansas Nurses Association (*arna.org*)

Arkansas Licensed Practical Nurses' Association (*arkansaslpna.org*)

State Board of Nursing

University Tower Building

1123 South University, Suite 800

Little Rock, AR 72204-1619

Phone: 501-686-2700

Fax: 501-686-2714

arsbn.org

California

ANA/California (*anacalifornia.org*)

Board of Registered Nursing

1625 North Market Boulevard, Suite N-217

Sacramento, CA 95834-1924

Mailing address: PO Box 944210

Sacramento, CA 94244-2100

Phone: 916-322-3350

Fax: 916-574-8637

rn.ca.gov

Board of Vocational Nursing and Psychiatric Technicians

2535 Capital Oaks Drive, Suite 205

Sacramento, CA 95833-0545

Phone: 916-263-7800

Fax: 916-263-7859

bvnpt.ca.gov

Colorado

Colorado Nurses Association (*nurses-co.org*)

Colorado Center for Nursing Excellence (*coloradonursingcenter.org*) Dedicated to ensuring adequate numbers of highly qualified nurses, focusing on education, recruitment, and retention

Colorado Federation of Nursing Organizations (*coloradonursing.org*) Coalition of thirty state, regional, and local nursing organizations

c/o VA Hospital

5015 E. 17th Avenue

Denver, CO 80220

Phone 303-377-5780

Judith.burke@med.va.gov

Board of Nursing

1560 Broadway, Suite 880

Denver, CO 80202

Phone: 303-894-2430

Fax: 303-894-2821

dora.state.co.us/nursing

Connecticut

Connecticut Nurses Association (*ctnurses.org*)
Board of Examiners for Nursing
Department of Public Health
RN Licensure
410 Capitol Avenue, MS# 13PHO
Hartford, CT 06134-0308
Phone: 860-509-7648
Fax: 860-509-509-75553
dph.state.ct.us, then click Programs and Services,
then go to Nursing, Board of Examiners

Delaware

Delaware Nurses Association (*denurses.org*)
Division of Professional Regulation
Board of Nursing
861 Silver Lake Boulevard
Cannon Building, Suite 203
Dover, DE 19904-2467
Phone: 302-744-4516
Fax: 302-739-2711
*professionallicensing.state.de.us/boards/nursing/
index.shtml*

District of Columbia

District of Columbia Nurses Association, Inc.
(*dcna.org*)
Board of Nursing
Department of Health
717 14th Street, NW, Suite 600
Washington, DC 20005
Phone: 877-672-2174
Fax: 202-727-8471
hpla.doh.dc.gov/hpla/site/default.asp

Florida

Florida Nurses Association (*floridanurse.org*)
Board of Nursing
4052 Bald Cypress Way, BIN C02
Tallahassee, FL 32399-3252
Phone: 850-245-4125
Fax: 850-245-4172
doh.state.fl.us/PHNursing/index.html

Georgia

Georgia Nurses Association (*georgianurses.org*)
Board of Nursing
237 Coliseum Drive
Macon, GA 31217-3858
Phone: 478-207-1640
Fax: 478-207-1660
sos.state.ga.us/plb/rn

Board of Licensed Practical Nurses
237 Coliseum Drive
Macon, GA 31217-3858
Phone: 478-207-1640
Fax: 478-207-1660
sos.state.ga.us/plb/lpn/

Guam

Board of Nurse Examiners
651 Legacy Square Commercial Complex
South Route 10, Suite 9
Mangilao, GU 96913
Mailing address: PO Box 2816
Hagatna, GU 96932

Hawaii

Hawaii Nurses Association (*hawaiinurses.org*)
Board of Nursing
King Kalakaua Building
335 Merchant Street, 3rd Floor
Honolulu, HI 96813
Phone: 808-586-3000
Fax: 808-586-2689
hawaii.gov.dcca/areas/pvl/boards/nursing/

Idaho

Idaho Nurses Association
(*nursingworld.org/snas/id/*)
Board of Nursing
280 North 8th Street, Suite 210
PO Box 83720
Boise, ID 83720-0061
Phone: 208-334-3110
Fax: 208-334-3262
www2.state.id.us/ibn/ibn

Illinois

Illinois Nurses Association (*illinoisnurses.com*)
Department of Professional Regulation
320 W. Washington Street, 3rd Floor
Springfield, IL 62786
Phone: 217-782-8556
Fax: 217-782-7645
dpr.state.il.us/WHO/nurs.asp

Indiana

Indiana State Nurses Association
(*indiananurses.org*)
State Board of Nursing
Professional Licensing Agency
402 West Washington Street, Room W072
Indianapolis, IN 46204
Phone: 317-234-2043
Fax: 317-233-4236
state.in.us/hpb/boards/isbn

Iowa

Iowa Nurses Association (*iowanurses.org*)
Board of Nursing
Riverpoint Business Park
400 SW 8th Street, Suite B
Des Moines, IA 50309-4685
Phone: 515-281-3255
Fax: 515-281-4825
state.ia.us/government/nursing

Kansas

Kansas State Nurses Association
(*nursingworld.org/snas/ks/*)
State Board of Nursing
Landon State Office Building
900 SW Jackson, Suite 1051
Topeka, KS 66612-1230
Phone: 785-296-4929
Fax: 785-296-3929
ksbn.org

Kentucky

Kentucky Nurses Association
    (*kentucky-nurses.org*)
Board of Nursing
312 Whittington Parkway, Suite 300
Louisville, KY 40222-5172
Phone: 502-429-3300
Fax: 502-429-3311
kbn.ky.gov

Louisiana

Louisiana State Nurses Association (*lsna.org*)
Board of Nursing
3510 North Causeway Boulevard, Suite 601
Metairie, LA 70002
Phone: 504-838-5332
Fax: 504-838-5349
lsbn.state.la.us
Temporary address: 5207 Essen Lane, Suite 6
Baton Rouge, LA 70809
Phone: 225-763-3570 or 225-763-3577
Fax: 225 763-3580

Board of Practical Nurse Examiners
3510 North Causeway Boulevard, Suite 505
Metairie, LA 70002
Phone: 504-838-5332
Fax: 504-838-5349
lsbpne.com

Maine

ANA-MAINE (*anamaine.org*)
Board of Nursing
161 Capitol Street
Augusta, ME 04333
Mailing address: 158 State House Station
Augusta, ME 04333
Phone: 207-287-1133
Fax: 207-287-1149
maine.gov/boardofnursing

Maryland

Maryland Nurses Association (*marylandrn.org*)
Board of Nursing
4140 Patterson Avenue
Baltimore, MD 21215-2254
Phone: 410-585-1900
Fax: 410-358-3530
mbon.org

Massachusetts

Massachusetts Association of Registered Nurses
    (*maronline.org*)
Massachusetts Association of Public Health
    Nurses: (*maphn.org*)
Board of Registration in Nursing
Commonwealth of Massachusetts
239 Causeway Street, Second Floor
Boston, MA 02114
Phone: 617-973-0800 or 800 414-0168
Fax: 617-973-0984
mass.gov/dpl/boards/rn

Michigan

Michigan Nurses Association (*minurses.org*)

Michigan Licensed Practical Nurses Association
(*mlpna.org*)

Bureau of Health Professions

Michigan Department of Community Health

Board of Nursing

Ottawa Towers North

611 West Ottawa, 1st Floor

Lansing, MI 48933

Phone: 517-335-0918

Fax: 517-373-2179

michigan.gov/healthlicense

Minnesota

Minnesota Nurses Association (*mnnurses.org*)

Board of Nursing

2829 University Avenue, SE #500

Minneapolis, MN 55414-3253

Phone: 612-617-2270

Fax: 612-617-2190

nursingboard.state.mn.us

Mississippi

Mississippi Nurses Association (*msnurses.org*)

Board of Nursing

1935 Lakeland Drive, Suite B

Jackson, MS 39216-5014

Phone: 601-987-4188

Fax: 601-364-2352

msbn.state.ms.us

Missouri

Missouri Nurses Association (*missourinurses.org*)

Board of Nursing

3605 Missouri Boulevard

PO Box 656

Jefferson City, MO 65102-0656

Phone: 573-751-0681

Fax: 573-751-0075

pr.mo.gov/nursing.asp

Montana

Montana Nurses Association (*mtnurses.org*)

Department of Labor and Industry

Board of Nursing

301 South Park, Room 430

PO Box 200513

Helena, MT 59620-0513

Phone: 406-841-2340

Fax: 406-841-2305

app.discoveringmontana.com/cgi-bin/bsdrnw.cgi

Nebraska

Nebraska Nurses Association
(*nursingworld.org/cmas/ne/*)

Department of HHS Regulation and Licensure

Nursing and Nursing Support Section

301 Centennial Mall South, 3rd Floor

Lincoln, NE 68509-4986

Phone: 402-471-4376

Fax: 402-471-1066

hhs.state.ne.us/crl/nursing/Rn-Lpn/rn-lpn.htm

Nevada

Nevada Nurses Association (*nvnurses.org*)
Board of Nursing
5011 Meadowood Mall, #201
Reno, NV 89502-6547
Phone: 775-688-2620
Fax: 775-688-2628
nursingboard.state.nv.us

New Hampshire

New Hampshire Nurses Association
   (*nhnurses.org*)
Board of Nursing
21 South Fruit Street, Suite 16
Concord, NH 03301-2431
Phone: 603-271-2323
Fax: 603-271-6605
state.nh.us/nursing

New Jersey

New Jersey State Nurses Association (*njsna.org*)
Board of Nursing
PO Box 45010
124 Halsey Street, 6th Floor
Newark, NJ 07101
Phone: 973-504-6586
Fax: 973-648-3481
state.nj.us/lps/ca/medical/nursing.htm

New Mexico

New Mexico Nurses Association
   (*nursingworld.org/snas/nm/*)
Board of Nursing
6301 Indian School NE, Suite 710
Albuquerque, NM 87110
Phone: 505-841-8340
Fax: 505-841-8347
state.nm.us/clients/nursing

New York

New York State Nurses Association (*nysna.org*)
Board of Nursing
NYS Education Department
Office of the Professions
Division of Professional Licensing Services,
   Nurse Unit
89 Washington Avenue
2nd Floor West Wing
Albany, NY 12234-1000
Phone: 518-474-3817, ext. 280
Fax: 518-474-3706
nysed.gov/nurse.htm

North Carolina

North Carolina Nurses Association (*ncnurses.org*)
North Carolina Emergency Nurses Association
Board of Nursing
3724 National Drive, Suite 201
Raleigh, NC 27602-2129
Phone: 919-782-3211
Fax: 919-781-9461
ncbon.com

North Dakota

Board of Nursing
919 South 7th Street, Suite 504
Bismarck, ND 58504-5881
Phone: 701-328-9778
Fax: 701-328-9785
ndbon.org

Northern Mariana Islands

Commonwealth Board of Nurse Examiners
PO Box 501458
Saipan, MP 96950
Phone: 670 664-4812
Fax: 614 664-4813

Ohio

Ohio Nurses Association (*ohnurses.org*)
Board of Nursing
17 South High Street, Suite 400
Columbus, OH 43215-7410
Phone: 614-466-3947
Fax: 614-466-0388
www5.state.oh.us/nur

Oklahoma

Oklahoma Nurses Association (*oknurses.com*)
Board of Nursing
2915 North Classen Boulevard, Suite 524
Oklahoma City, OK 73106
Phone: 405-962-1800
Fax: 405-962-1821
youroklahoma.com/nursing

Oregon

Oregon Nurses Association (*oregonrn.org*)
Board of Nursing
800 NE Oregon Street, Box 25, Suite 465
Portland,OR 97232-2162
Phone: 971-673-0685
Fax: 971-673-0684
osbn.state.or.us

Pennsylvania

Pennsylvania State Nurses Association (*psna.org*)
Board of Nursing
PO Box 2649
Harrisburg, PA 17105-2649
Phone: 717-783-7142
Fax: 717-783-0822
dos.state.pa.us/bpoa/site/default.asp

Puerto Rico

Commonwealth of Puerto Rico
Board of Nurse Examiners Nurse
 (*www.nurse.org/pr-index.shtml*)
800 Roberto H. Todd Avenue
Room 202, Stop 18
Santurce, PR 00908

Rhode Island

Rhode Island State Nurses Association (*risnarn.org*)
Board of Nurse Registration and Nursing Education
105 Cannon Building
Three Capitol Hill
Providence, RI 02908
Phone: 401-222-5700
Fax: 401-222-3352
Health.ri.org/hsr/professions/#N

South Carolina

South Carolina Nurses Association (*scnurses.org*)
Board of Nursing
119 Centerview Drive, Suite 202
Columbia, SC 29210
Phone: 803-896-4550
Fax: 803-896-4525
llr.state.sc.us/pol/nursing

South Dakota

South Dakota Nurses Association (*sdnursesassociation.org*)
Board of Nursing
4305 S. Louise Avenue, Suite 201
Sioux Falls, SD 57106-3115
Phone: 605-362-2760
Fax: 605-362-2768
state.sd.us/doh/nursing

Tennessee

Tennessee Nurses Association (*tnaonline.org*)
Board of Nursing
425 Fifth Avenue North
Cordell Hull Building, 1st Floor
Nashville, TN 37247-1010
Phone: 615-532-5166
Fax: 615-741-7899
www2.state.tn.us/health/Boards/Nursing

Texas

Texas Nurses Association (*texasnurses.org*)
Board of Nurse Examiners
333 Guadalupe, Suite 3-460
Austin, TX 78701
Phone: 512-305-7400
Fax: 512-305-7401
bne.state.tx.us

Utah

Utah Nurses Association (*utahnurses.org*)
Board of Nursing
Division of Occupational and Professional Licensing
160 East 300 South
Salt Lake City, UT 84114-6628
Phone: 801-530-6628
Fax: 801-530-6511
commerce.utah.gov/opl/licensing/nurse.html

Vermont

Vermont State Nurses Association (*vsna-inc.org*)
Board of Nursing
Office of the Secretary of State
81 River Street
Montpelier, VT 05609-1106
Phone: 802-828-2396
Fax: 802-828-2484
vtprofessionals.org/nurses

Virgin Islands

Board of Nurse Licensure (*vibnl.org*)
Veterans Drive Station
St. Thomas, VI 00803
Phone: 340-776-7397
Fax: 340-777-4003

Virginia

Virginia Nurses Association (*virginianurses.com*)
Board of Nursing
6603 West Broad Street, 5th Floor
Richmond, VA 23230-1712
Phone: 804-662-9909
Fax: 804-662-9512
dhp.state.va.us/nursing

Washington

Washington State Nurses Association (*wsna.org*)
Nursing Care Quality Assurance Commission
Department of Health
HPQA #6
310 Israel Road SE
Tumwater, WA 98501-7864
Phone: 360-236-4700
Fax: 360-236-4738
doh.wa.gov/licensing.htm#N

West Virginia

West Virginia Nurses Association (*wvnurses.org*)
Board of Examiners for Registered Professional
    Nurses
101 Dee Drive
Charleston, WV 25311-1620
Phone: 304-558-3596
Fax: 304-558-3666
lpnboard.state.wv.us

Board of Examiners for Licensed Practical Nurses
101 Dee Drive
Charleston, WV 25311-1620
Phone: 304-558-3572
Fax: 304-558-4367
wvrnboard.com

Wisconsin

Wisconsin Nurses Association
    (*wisconsinnurses.org*)
Bureau of Health Service Professions—RN
Department of Regulation and Licensing
1400 East Washington Avenue, RM 173
Madison, WI 53708-8935
Phone: 608-266-0145
Fax: 608-261-7083
drl.wi.gov/prof/rn/def.htm

Wyoming

Wyoming Nurses Association (*wyonurse.org*)
Board of Nursing
2020 Carey Avenue, Suite 110
Cheyenne, WY 82002
Phone: 307-777-7601
Fax: 307-777-3519
nursing.state.wy.us

Canada

Canada Nurses Association (*cna-nurses.ca/cna*)
Cerification Program
50 Driveway
Ottowa, ON, Canada K2P 1E2
Phone: 613-237-2133 or 800-361-8404
Fax: 613-237-3520
certification@cna-aiic.ca

Alberta

College and Association of Registered Nurses of
    Alberta
11620 - 168 Street
Edmonton AB T5M 4A6
Tel: (780) 451-0043
Fax: (780) 452-3276
E-mail: carna@nurses.ab.ca

British Columbia

College of Registered Nurses of British Columbia
2855 Arbutus Street
Vancouver BC V6J 3Y8
Tel: (604) 736-7331
Fax: (604) 738-2272
E-mail: info@crnbc.ca

Manitoba

College of Registered Nurses of Manitoba
890 Pembina Hwy
Winnipeg MB R3M 2M8
Tel: (204) 774-3477
Fax: (204) 775-6052
E-mail: info@crnm.mb.ca

New Brunswick

Nurses Association of New Brunswick
165 Regent Street
Fredericton NB E3B 7B4
Tel/Tél. : (506) 458-8731
Fax/Télécopieur : (506) 459-2838
E-mail/Courriel : nanb@nanb.nb.ca

Newfoundland And Labrador

Association Of Registered Nurses Of
    Newfoundland And Labrador
55 Military Rd
St. John's NL A1C 2C5
Tel: (709) 753-6040
Fax: (709) 753-4940
E-mail: info@arnnl.nf.ca

Northwest Territories

Registered Nurses Association of the
Northwest Territories and Nunavut
Box 2757
Yellowknife NT X1A 2R1
Tel: (867) 873-2745
Fax: (867) 873-2336
E-mail: nwtrna@theedge.ca

Nova Scotia

College of Registered Nurses of Nova Scotia
Suite 600, Barrington Tower
1894 Barrington St.
Halifax NS B3J 2A8
Tel: (902) 491-9744
Fax: (902) 491-9510
E-mail: info@crnns.ca

Ontario

College of Nurses of Ontario
101 Davenport Road
Toronto ON M5R 3P1
Tel/Tél. : 1-800-387-5526 / (416) 928-0900
Fax/Télécopieur : (416) 928-6507
E-mail/Courriel : cno@cnomail.org

Prince Edward Island

Association of Registered Nurses of Prince
   Edward Island
53 Grafton Street
Charlottetown PE C1A 1K8
Tel: (902) 368-3764
Fax: (902) 628-1430
E-mail: anpei@pei.aibn.com

Québec

Ordre des infirmières et infirmiers du Québec
4200, boul. Dorchester Ouest
Montréal QC H3Z 1V4
Tel/Tél. : (514) 935-2501 / 1-800-363-6048
Fax/Télécopieur : (514) 935-1799
E-mail/Courriel : inf@oiiq.org

Saskatchewan

Saskatchewan Registered Nurses' Association
2066 Retallack Street
Regina SK S4T 7X5
Tel: 1-800-667-9945 / (306) 359-4200
Fax: (306) 525-0849
E-mail: info@srna.org

Yukon

Yukon Registered Nurses Association
204 - 4133 - 4th Avenue
Whitehorse YT Y1A 1H8
Tel: (867) 667-4062
Fax: (867) 668-5123
E-mail: yrna@yknet.ca

Nursing Journals

AACN Clinical Issues: Advanced Practice in Acute and Critical Care (www.lww.com)

Accident and Emergency Nursing (journals.elsevierhealth.com)

Advances in Nursing Science (www.lww.com)

Advances in Skin and Wound Care: The Journal for Prevention and Healing (www.lww.com)

American Journal of Infection Control
(www.apic.org/Content/NavigationMenu/Publications/AJIC/AJIC.htm)

American Journal of Nursing (AJN) (www.lww.com)

AORN Journal (aorn.org)

Applied Nursing Research (journals.elsevierhealth.com)

Archives of Psychiatric Nursing (journals.elsevierhealth.com)

AWHONN Lifelines (Association of Women's Health, Obstetric, and Neonatal Nurses)
(awhonnlifelines.awhonn.org)

Cancer Nursing: An International Journal for Cancer Care (www.lww.com)

Cancer Nursing Practice (www.nursing-standard.co.uk)

CIN: Computers, Informatics, Nursing (www.lww.com)

Clinical Effectiveness in Nursing (journals.elsevierhealth.com)

Clinical Nurse Specialist: The Journal for Advanced Nursing Practice (www.lww.com)

Clinical Journal of Oncology Nursing (www.ons.org)

Clinical Nursing Research (www.sagepub.com)

Complementary Therapies in Nursing and Midwifery (journals.elsevierhealth.com)

Critical Care Medicine (www.lww.com)

Critical Care Nursing Clinics of North America (journals.elsevierhealth.com)

Critical Care Nursing Quarterly (www.lww.com)

Dermatology Nursing (dnanurse.org)

Dimensions of Critical Care Nursing (www.lww.com)

Emergency Nurse (www.nursing-standard.co.uk)

Evidence Based Nursing (www.nursing-standard.co.uk)

Gastrointestinal Nursing (www.nursing-standard.co.uk)

Geriatric Nursing (journals.elsevierhealth.com)

Heart and Lung: The Journal of Critical Care (journals.elsevierhealth.com)

Holistic Nursing Practice (www.lww.com)

Home Health Care Management & Practice (www.sagepub.com)

Home Healthcare Nurse: The Journal for the Home Care and Hospice Professional (www.lww.com)

Image—the Journal of Nursing Scholarship from Sigma Theta Tau International Honor Society of Nursing (www.nursingsociety.org)

Intensive and Critical Care Nursing (journals.elsevierhealth.com)

International Journal of Nursing Studies (journals.elsevierhealth.com)

International Journal of Trauma Nursing (journals.elsevierhealth.com)

JANAC: Journal of the Association of Nurses in AIDS Care (www.sagepub.com)

JOGNN: Journal of Obstetric, Gynecologic, and Neonatal Nursing (www.sagepub.com)

JONA (Journal of Nursing Administration) Healthcare Law, Ethics, and Regulation (www.lww.com)

Journal for Nurses in Staff Development (JNSD) Opportunities, Partnerships, and Outcomes for Today's Healthcare Educators (www.lww.com)

Journal of Advanced Nursing (www.journalofadvancednursing.com)

Journal of Clinical Nursing (blackwellppublishing.com)

Journal of Emergency Nursing (journals.elsevierhealth.com)

Journal of Family Nursing (www.sagepub.com)

Journal of Holistic Nursing (www.sagepub.com)

Journal of Hospice and Palliative Nursing: The Official Journal of the Hospice and Palliative Nursing Association (www.lww.com)

Journal of Infusion Nursing (www.lww.com)

Journal of Midwifery and Women's Health (journals.elsevierhealth.com)

Journal of Neuroscience Nursing (www.aann.org)

Journal of Nursing Care Quality (www.lww.com)

Journal of Nursing Scholarship (journalofnursingscholarship.org)

Journal of Orthopaedic Nursing (journals.elsevierhealth.com)

Journal of Pediatric Nursing (journals.elsevierhealth.com)

Journal of Pediatric Oncology Nursing (www.sagepub.com)

Journal of PeriAnesthesia Nursing (journals.elsevierhealth.com)

Journal of Perinatal and Neonatal Nursing (www.lww.com)

Journal of Professional Nursing (journals.elsevierhealth.com)

Journal of the American Psychiatric Nurses Association (journals.elsevierhealth.com)

Journal of Transcultural Nursing: A Forum for Cultural Competence in Health Care (www.sagepub.com)

Journal of Vascular Nursing (journals.elsevierhealth.com)

Journal of WOCN: Wound, Ostomy, and Continence Nursing (journals.elsevierhealth.com)

Learning Disability Practice (www.nursing-standard.co.uk)

Lippincott's Case Management (www.lww.com)

MCN, American Journal of Maternal Child Nursing (www.lww.com)

Mental Health Practice (www.nursing-standard.co.uk)

Nephrology Nursing Journal (nephrologynursing.net)

Newborn and Infant Nursing Reviews (journals.elsevierhealth.com)

Nursing Education in Practice (journals.elsevierhealth.com)

Nursing Education Today (journals.elsevierhealth.com)

Nurse Educator (www.lww.com)

Nurse Leader (journals.elsevierhealth.com)

Nursing (www.lww.com)

Nursing Administration Quarterly (www.lww.com)

Nursing Clinics of North America (journals.elsevierhealth.com)

Nursing Economic$, The Journal for Health Care Leaders (www.ajj.com)

Nursing Management (www.lww.com)

Nursing Outlook (journals.elsevierhealth.com)

Nursing Research (www.lww.com)

Nursing Science Quarterly (www.sagepub.com)

Nutrition Today (www.lww.com)

Oncology Nursing Forum (www.ons.org)

Oncology Times (www.lww.com)

Orthopaedic Nursing (www.lww.com)

Outcomes Management for Nursing Practice (www.lww.com)

Pain Management Nursing (journals.elsevierhealth.com)

Pediatric Nursing (www.pediatricnursing.net)

Policy, Politics, & Nursing Practice (www.sagepub.com)

Quality Management in Heath Care (www.lww.com)

Reflections on Nursing Leadership (www.nursingsociety.org)

Research in Nursing and Health (www.wileyeurope.com)

RN (www.rnweb.com)

Seminars in Oncology Nursing (journals.elsevierhealth.com)

The Journal of Cardiovascular Nursing (www.lww.com)

The Journal of Nursing Administration (JONA) (www.lww.com)

The Nurse Practitioner: The American Journal of Primary Health Care (www.lww.com)

Western Journal of Nursing Research (www.sagepub.com)

Worldviews on Evidence-Based Nursing (www.nursingsociety.org)

Real Stories from Career Changers

THE RN ROUTE

By Cathryn Domrose

December 6, 2001

Source: copyright 2006. Nursing Spectrum Nurse Wire (*www.nursingspectrum.com*). All rights reserved. Used with permission.

With the promise of meaningful work, job security, and new opportunities, second-career nurses bring maturity, commitment, and life experience to the workplace.

When Heather Kaz was a child, she made IVs out of twigs for her dolls. As a five-year-old, she helped her grandmother, a World War II nurse, take care of her ailing grandfather. As far as she could remember, nursing had been an important part of her life. So it seemed natural that when she was 18 and enrolled in the University of Wyoming, she would choose nursing as her major. Then the doubts set in.

Her family told her she was too bright, too promising for nursing. She couldn't imagine herself changing bedpans and following orders from a doctor. She changed her major to premed, graduated with a bachelor's degree in biology in 1996 and took entrance exams before she realized she did not want to go to medical school.

Instead, she took a job as manager of a cancer surveillance program. As part of her work, she traveled the state, teaching people about cancer prevention. She was good at the research, but working with people excited her more.

"You become alive with these people," her director told her. "You need to rethink where you're going." Kaz considered pursuing a master's degree in public health. "What's wrong with going back and being a nurse?" her director asked. "You're meant for it."

Across the country, people in fields from engineering to psychology, English to computer technology, are taking another look—sometimes a first look—at a career in nursing. For some, like Kaz—now enrolled in an accelerated bachelor's degree in nursing program at the University of Northern Colorado—it's a journey back to their heart's desire.

Some say that after years of just making money, they want to do meaningful work. Others feel trapped in limited professions or have lost their jobs in a sliding economy and see new opportunities in nursing.

To attract and keep their interest, many nursing schools have established accelerated bachelor's degree programs for students who already have a degree in another field. These programs allow students to earn a BSN in 16 to 20 months, rather than completing a traditional four-year program. Some hospitals sponsor students through these programs and pay tuition in exchange for work after they graduate.

Hospital administrators say second-career nursing students make terrific nurses. They are mature, broadly educated, and know how to conduct themselves in the workplace.

But the life experience that makes them great nurses also often leads them to expect more from their careers and their employers than they might as graduates fresh out of school, say health care consultants, nursing school professors, and the students themselves.

The American Association of Colleges of Nursing does not have enrollment figures specifically for the accelerated programs at its member schools. But Robert Rosseter, spokesman for the association, said the number of accelerated programs has increased from 60 in 1995 to 72 last year, with 11 schools planning to add accelerated programs.

The Duke University School of Nursing in Durham, North Carolina, plans to offer an accelerated BSN program next year—its only baccalaureate program—as a direct response to the nursing shortage, said Mary Champagne, PhD, RN, FAAN, the school's dean. So far, the school has had 200 inquiries about the program, she said.

"Young people today go into college and many of them take liberal arts or basic science courses. They're not committed to a career, and until recently, nursing hasn't been an option for them," Champagne said. "This is a real, untapped pool that we might bring into nursing and help ease the severe nursing shortage that this country is going to face."

Perceptions Change

Champagne is referring to people such as Holly Cousins, who works as a secretary for Nursing Student Services at South Dakota State University. Cousins said she has always been interested in health care, but never considered nursing until she began working at the university.

"One concern was going in and having doctors order me around and I'm too much of an independent person to like that very much," Cousins said.

Cousins has a degree in English. She taught for three years before deciding it wasn't for her. She admires the skill and dedication of nurses she has met in her present job. Her original perception of nursing has changed, and she plans to apply for the new accelerated program that the SDSU College of Nursing plans to offer next year.

"You kind of grow up and realize that things change in life," she said. "Nursing just fits into my life right now."

Most students in accelerated programs have degrees in psychology or biology, say nursing school deans and accelerated program directors. But they also report enrolling students with degrees in English, theater, music, art, engineering, business, marketing, philosophy, and sociology.

Many say they've always wanted to be nurses but were dissuaded by family members or their own belief that nursing somehow wasn't "good enough," said nursing school deans and directors of accelerated programs.

Others say they want to go into nursing because they feel dissatisfied with their careers. One student in the accelerated program at the Research College of Nursing in Kansas City, MO, is an accountant in his 30s who discovered he was much happier volunteering at a local children's hospital, said Nancy DeBasio, PhD, RN, the school's dean.

He sees nursing as a profession that not only gives him the satisfaction of helping people, but also has more variety and opportunities for growth than his old job, she said.

As the economy changes and workers in other fields are laid off, and as the image of nursing changes, nursing school and hospital administrators believe the field will attract more people. Recruiters for nursing schools are going to job fairs for retrenched tech workers, talking with personnel departments of troubled telecommunications companies, and thinking of ways to approach the airline industry to see if laid-off flight attendants would consider a nursing career.

Deans at many nursing schools with accelerated programs report increased enrollments, often at rates higher than for traditional programs. The Research College of Nursing expects enrollment in the accelerated program to double from 30 students to about 60 in 2002, DeBasio said. The 11-year-old accelerated program at the University of Wisconsin–Milwaukee School of Nursing doubled its enrollment in September, from 24 to 48 students.

Second-career nursing students say they like accelerated programs because they don't have to revisit the university scene they left behind and they can enter the workforce quickly. In addition to a long list of prerequisite courses, mostly human sciences and psychology, most programs last three semesters and require 18 to 20 hours of coursework and another three to five hours of clinicals per week.

"You have to be absolutely committed," said Geralyn Meyer, PhD, RN, coordinator of the accelerated option at Saint Louis University School of Nursing, the oldest accelerated nursing program in the country. "But if they can do it in a year, they know they'll be out there doing what they want to do, and that makes the program attractive."

When the school began its program in 1971, some hospital nurses and administrators questioned whether schools could turn out good nurses in a year, Meyer said. Now, hospitals across the country are clamoring for graduates from accelerated programs.

In some places, such as Creighton University School of Nursing in Omaha, Nebraska, health care organizations pay tuition for some accelerated students, who often are not eligible for government financial aid because they already have a degree. In exchange for tuition, students agree to work for the hospital after they graduate.

Poudre Valley Hospital in Fort Collins, Colorado, sponsors the accelerated program at the University of Northern Colorado. The hospital pays faculty from the university, as well as full tuition for the nine students in the program. Poudre Valley, a magnet hospital known for its commitment to nurses, had already offered scholarships to the university's four-year program, said Margo Karsten, MSN, RN, chief operating officer at the hospital.

"We were trying to think creatively about how to throw the net out a little farther and get people interested in nursing," she said. In exchange for fees and tuition, the students have contracted to work for four years at the hospital after graduation.

They Catch On Quickly

Unlike many traditional students fresh out of high school, second-career students have good study habits and are more interested in earning their degrees than in hanging out with friends and learning the ropes of campus life, deans and instructors say.

"They catch on quickly," said Sister Carol Purzycki, PhD, RN, coordinator of the accelerated BSN program at Mount St. Mary's College in Los Angeles. "They're very motivated. They're adult learners."

Many have researched the field and have talked to or shadowed nurses, said Connie Miller, MSN, RN, chair of the accelerated program at Creighton.

Although about 80 percent of the students in the University of Wisconsin–Milwaukee accelerated nursing program work in hospitals after they graduate, most plan to continue their education and go into a specific field of nursing such as family nurse practitioner or community health, said Susan Dean-Baar, PhD, RN, FAAN, associate dean of the school of nursing.

Tracy Hulbert, 31, a student in the UW–Milwaukee accelerated program, has traveled around the world, worked four years as a consultant in Japan, speaks Spanish and Japanese, and has bachelor's degrees in Spanish and psychology. After earning her BSN, she plans to pursue a dual master's degree in public health and family nurse practitioner. Her dream, she said, is to work in the World Health Organization, perhaps with developing countries in Southeast Asia.

Professors and administrators do not usually intimidate second-career students, who tend to see them as peers. For example, Dean-Baar said her nursing students meet twice a year with the president of a large local health care system that works with the school. In the spring, he meets with traditional four-year students; in the fall with the accelerated group. The traditional students have little to say and the president does most of the talking, she said.

But the accelerated students ask about everything from what the health care system is doing for nurses, to how it serves the community, to the inner workings of its finances.

Perhaps because of their study habits, maturity, and commitment, second-career students usually pass the boards without much trouble, deans and instructors say. Some accelerated classes report regular 100 percent pass rates, while others are consistently in the high 90s.

Professional, Responsible

The same qualities that make them excellent students, plus their work experience, make many second-career graduates favorites with hospital supervisors and coworkers.

"I find that the accelerated students are much more professional, responsible individuals," said Shelly Spencer, MSN, RN, nurse manager of trauma and general surgery at Saint Louis University Hospital. "You find that they are more mature in looking at patient care and patient needs. They are outcome-focused. Their accountability is much greater than that of traditional students."

Spencer hired four graduates of the university's accelerated program last year. One graduate, who previously worked in business and management, already has worked as a charge nurse many times, Spencer said. Her business experience has helped her organize and delegate responsibilities to peers and nursing assistants.

Because they know what's out there, second-career nurses often expect something back from their employers, Meyer said.

"These are individuals who are going to ask the tough economic questions," Dean-Baar said. "They're going to want to be paid for what they're worth."

Many second-career nurses do not see their careers ending in the hospital at the bedside, said Tim Porter-O'Grady, PhD, RN, FAAN, a professor at Emory University in Atlanta and the head of Tim Porter-O'Grady Associates Inc., a consulting firm that works with health care organizations in crisis.

They want to go to graduate school, work as nurse practitioners or nurse midwives, become nurse anesthetists, go into public health or community education.

Hospitals that want to attract and keep top second-career students need to offer good pay and benefits, flexible schedules, autonomy, and respect for nurses and strong leadership, he said. They need to show they are committed to patient care. They need to have a reputation for recognizing what nurses do and what they need to do it.

In return, he said, health care organizations can expect more from these nurses and trust their decisions. Instead of becoming frustrated by problems in health care and leaving the field, "they're more likely to stay and change things," Porter-O'Grady said.

Realizing Their Dream

Even mid-career nurses who set out to work at the bedside may find themselves swept into roles they'd never imagined.

John Shier, RN, a graduate of the University of Wisconsin–Milwaukee accelerated program, chose nursing as a third career, after caring for a dying friend.

He has a doctorate in philosophy and taught at the University of Wisconsin–Madison for 14 years, then served as an executive for two large nonprofit organizations for 18 years.

After graduating from the nursing program in the mid-1990s, he worked as a hospice nurse and on a cardiac unit at Bellin Health in Green Bay, Wisconsin. Seeing so many advanced cases of heart disease made him wonder what he could do to get people to take care of themselves before it was too late.

Using his philosophy, teaching, business, and nursing experience, he developed a program called "Live Long and Die Healthy" that is used by corporations and two nationwide trucking firms. He promotes healthful lifestyles as coordinator of the hospital's corporate health and wellness program. And he continues his hospice work. "That's why I went into nursing," he said.

As for Kaz, her images of bedpans are long gone. "I didn't realize the scope of nursing, how many things you can do with a nursing degree," she said.

But for now, she can't wait to do the work she believes she was born to do. "I just want to be with the people, the kids, the babies," she said. "I like the fact that I'm going to be a staff nurse and finally realize my dream."

CAREER SUCCESS STORY: INTERVIEW WITH JOHN DEEX, RN, BSN, NP, COHNS

Q: *What was your original profession and when did you get your RN degree?*

A: I was an arborist for ten years, and I became an RN when I was 32 years old.

Q: *What prompted you to change to nursing?*

A: I went to Foothill Community College and took a battery of personality and occupational-interest tests. They showed that I was best suited for (1) a military officer, (2) a doctor, (3) a nurse. Of the three, I choose nursing.

Q: *What school did you go to?*

A: I went to Foothill for a year and a half, paying for it myself, working full time as a night auditor at a hotel. Then I went to the University of San Francisco for three years, working full time as a bouncer in a bar. I received an equal opportunity education grant from the state of California, since I was a minority (a white male) in the School of Nursing. The grant covered tuition and books, but no living expenses.

Q: *What was it like going back to school?*

A: I loved it. It opened up a whole new world for me. But it was very stressful on my family. Nursing is a unique profession—you can't go to school at night. Due to the clinical rotations, you have to be there in the daytime. It's a real sacrifice. You're not making money and you're not getting a lot of sleep.

Q: *Any tips for others?*

A: You have to make sure that you have all the components of your life in order, the emotional, the physical, and the socio-economic.

Q: *What nursing jobs have you held?*

A: I first worked in a step-down unit. Three years later I became an occupational health manager. After several years, I wanted to get back to patient care. It took me two and a half years full-time at the University of California in San Francisco to become a nurse practitioner (NP).

Q: *How did you use your NP credential?*

A: I became the Director of Employee Health and Safety, supervising a staff of six. But recently I went back to the bedside as a staff nurse. I like the gratification of seeing my impact as a nurse immediately. I have never been happier!

U.S. House of Representatives Honor Nurses

On April 4, 2006, the House approved Texas Congresswoman Eddie Bernice Johnson's legislation, House Resolution 245, supporting the goals and ideals of National Nurses Week by a voice vote. Here is the statement she made that day on the House floor:

> "Mr. Speaker, I rise in support of this resolution supporting the goals and ideals of National Nurses Week, and I am indebted to my colleague from California for her scholarly presentation.
>
> I started my career as a nurse and worked for more than 15 years as a psychiatric nurse, and it helps me here. I was the chief psychiatric nurse at the VA Hospital, Day Treatment Center, as well as the Day Hospital in Dallas, Texas.
>
> Next week, May 6-12, is National Nurses Week; and it is fitting for this body to honor the millions of nurses in America.
>
> Nurses are usually very, very dedicated individuals. In my personal experience, nurses tend to be intelligent, detail oriented. They tend to be ready to act at the spur of the moment, and with knowledge.
>
> Their work touches all aspects of patient care, whether it is in the emergency room, in the operating room, in the doctor's office, at the neighborhood clinic, in the schools, and battlefields. Nurses stand at the forefront of many lines of our health care system, and they must make life and death decisions, often with little advance notice, and they have frequent hands-on contact with the patient.

For these reasons, a caring attitude and compassionate heart are required for the hard work nurses do. In my years as a nurse, I have seen miracles and I have seen tragedies. At the VA, I worked with soldiers fresh from battle, as well as men and women who fought bravely years before. It was an honor to serve America's veterans, each one on his or her individual path to recovery of good health.

Nurses Week is really appropriate, because there hardly is anyone alive who will be born and finish life without contact with a nurse.

We have a severe shortage right now; and I would hope that we would be more open to attempting to get more nurses, American-educated nurses, so that we will not lose the care that the nurses give. They work very hard for their patients. The American public needs to know that Congress recognizes nurses for the great work they do.

I thank the leadership for its support of this bill. I would like to especially thank the two other Members of Congress who also are nurses (*Rep. Lois Capps, RN, of California and Rep. Carolyn McCarthy of New York*) for their collaboration and united stance in support of issues important to nurses. Both of them have been more active since than I have in nursing. But it is an old saying, once a nurse, always a nurse.

I commend this legislation to my colleagues and urge their support."

109th Congress, 2D Session **H. RES. 245**

Supporting the goals and ideals of National Nurses Week

IN THE HOUSE OF REPRESENTATIVES
April 27, 2005

RESOLUTION

Supporting the goals and ideals of National Nurses Week

Whereas since 2003, National Nurses Week is celebrated annually from May 6, also known as National Nurses Day, through May 12, the birthday of Florence Nightengale, the founder of modern nursing;

Whereas National Nurses Week is the time each year when the importance of nursing in health care can be demonstrated;

Whereas well-trained health professionals are the cornerstone of the Nation's complex health system;

Whereas registered nurses ("RNs") represent the largest single component of the health care profession, with an estimated 2.7 million RNs in the United States;

Whereas nurses historically have provided hands-on patient care at the bedside, and will continue to do so;

Whereas nurses have a mandate to serve those in need, and to try to ease the suffering of those in pain;

Whereas nurses also are deeply involved in health education, research, business and public policy;

Whereas nurses bear the primary responsibility for the care and well-being of hospital patients;

Whereas unfortunately, too few nurses are caring for too many patients in our Nation's hospitals;

Whereas according to a report from the Department of Health and Human Services, the United States currently has a nurse shortage of nearly 150,000 RNs and will have a shortage of more than 800,000 RNs by the year 2020;

Whereas cutting-edge technologies are useless without a staff of trained professionals to implement them; and

Whereas nurses are the unsung heroines and heroes of the medical profession: Now, therefore, be it

Resolved, That the House of Representatives—

    (1)   recognizes the important contributions of nurses to the health care system of the United States

    (2)   supports the goals and ideals of National Nurses Week, as founded by the American Nurses Association, and

    (3)   encourages the people of the United States to observe National Nurses Week with appropriate recognition, ceremonies, activities, and programs to demonstrate the importance of nurses to the every-day lives of patients.

Top Ranked Nursing Graduate Schools

US News & World Report ranks America's Best Graduate Schools. It last ranked these higher education facilities in Nursing in 2003. A rank of 5.0 is the highest rank.

Master's in Nursing

1. University of Washington — 4.7
2. University of California—San Francisco — 4.6
3. University of Michigan—Ann Arbor — 4.5
   University of Pennsylvania — 4.5

Nursing Service Administration

1. University of Iowa
2. University of Pennsylvania
3. University of Washington
   University of North Carolina—Chapel Hill

Family Nurse Practitioner

1. University of California—San Francisco
2. University of Washington
3. University of Pennsylvania

Adult Nurse Practitioner

1. University of Pennsylvania
2. University of Washington
3. University of California—San Francisco

Pediatric Nurse Practitioner

1. University of Colorado Health Sciences Center
2. University of Pennsylvania
3. University of Washington

Gerontological/Geriatric Nurse Practitioner

1. University of Pennsylvania
2. University of Iowa
3. New York University
4. Oregon Health and Sciences University

Adult/Medical-Surgical Clinical Nurse Specialist

1. University of Washington
2. University of California—San Francisco
3. University of Pennsylvania

Community/Public Health Clinical Nurse Specialist

1. University of Washington
2. Johns Hopkins University, Maryland
3. University of North Carolina—Chapel Hill (School of Public Health)

Psychiatric/Mental Health Clinical Nurse Specialist

1. University of Washington
2. University of Pennsylvania
3. University of California—San Francisco

Nurse Anesthetist

1.	Virginia Commonwealth University	4.0
2.	US Army Graduate Program in Anesthesia Nursing (TX)	3.8
3.	Navy Nurse Corps (MD)	3.7
4.	Rush University (IL)	3.7

Nurse Midwife

1.	Oregon Health and Science University	4.3
2.	University of Pennsylvania	4.3
3.	University of Illinois—Chicago	4.2
4.	University of Michigan—Ann Arbor	4.2
5.	University of Minnesota—Twin Cities	4.2
6.	University of New Mexico	4.2

("America's Best Graduate Schools 2007," US News and World Report, accessed at *www.usnews.com/usnews/edu/grad/rankings/hea/ brief/nmp_brief.php* on October 29, 2006)

NATIONAL INSTITUTES OF HEALTH (NIH) RESEARCH GRANTS, TOTAL AWARDS

1. University of California—San Francisco
2. University of Washington
3. University of Illinois—Chicago
4. University of North Carolina—Chapel Hill
5. University of Pennsylvania

NIH Total Dollars Awarded for Training Nurses

1. University of Washington
2. University of Michigan
3. University of North Carolina—Chapel Hill
4. University of Pennsylvania
5. Johns Hopkins University

(Jelise Balon, "Guide to Nursing School Ratings," NursingSchools.com accessed at *www.nursingschools .com/articles/ranking.html* on October 29, 2006

Index

KAPLAN

KAPLAN